CATABUNGA!

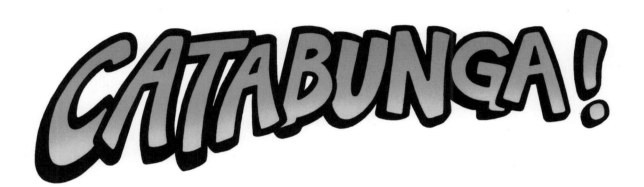

Other *Get Fuzzy* Books

The Dog Is Not a Toy (House Rule #4)

Fuzzy Logic: Get Fuzzy 2

The Get Fuzzy Experience: Are You Bucksperienced

I Would Have Bought You a Cat, But . . .

Blueprint for Disaster

Say Cheesy

Scrum Bums

I'm Ready for My Movie Contract

Take Our Cat, Please!

Ignorance, Thy Name Is Bucky

Dumbheart

Masters of the Nonsenseverse

Survival of the Filthiest

The Birth of Canis

The Fuzzy Bunch

You Can't Fight Crazy

Clean Up on Aisle Stupid

Treasuries

Groovitude: A Get Fuzzy Treasury

Bucky Katt's Big Book of Fun

Loserpalooza

The Potpourrific Great Big Grab Bag of Get Fuzzy

Treasury of the Lost Litter Box

The Stinking

Jerktastic Park

I'm Gluten Furious

CATABUNGA!

a **GET FUZZY** collection
by darby conley

Andrews McMeel
PUBLISHING®

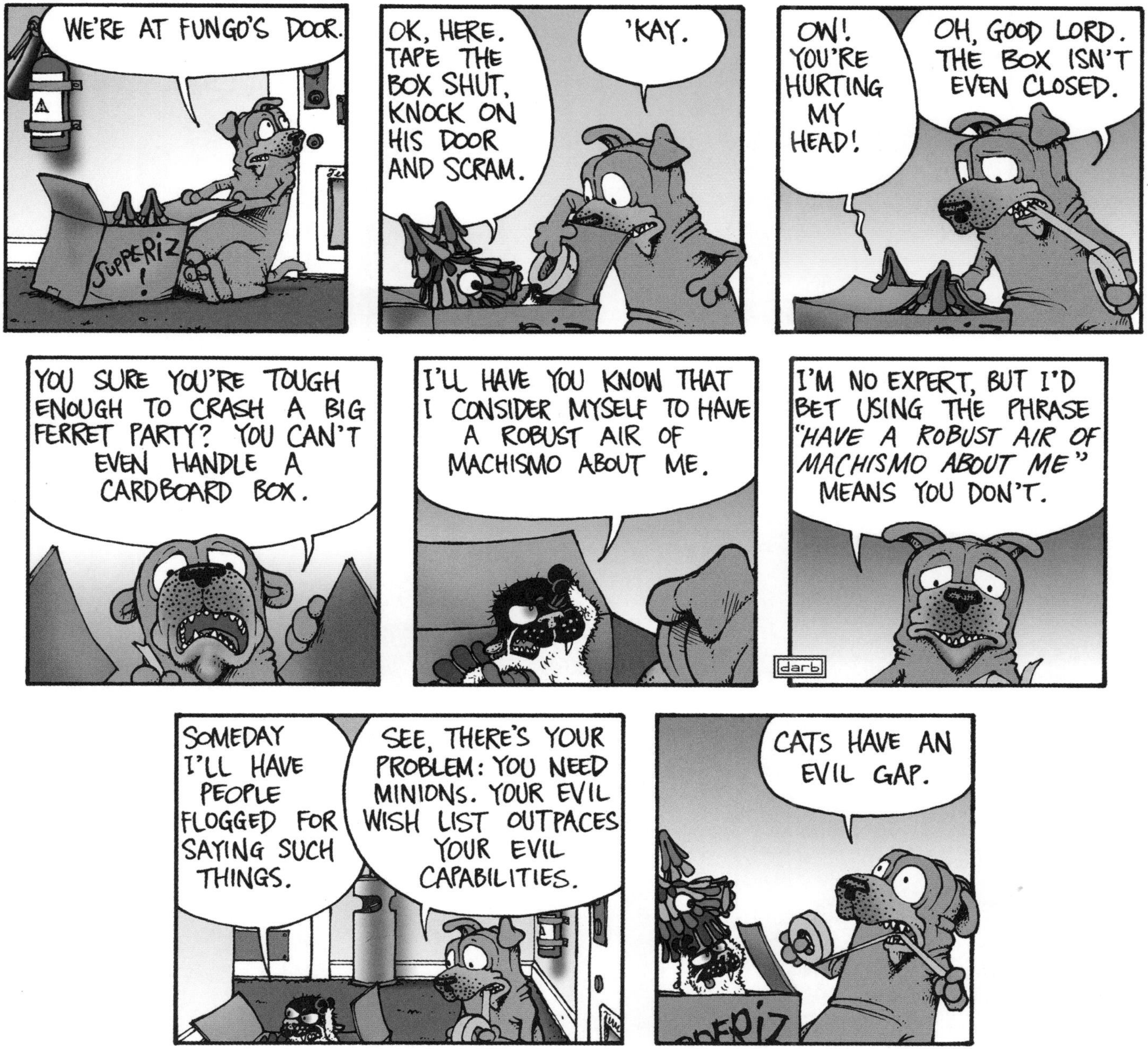
WE'RE AT FUNGO'S DOOR.
SUPPERIZ !
OK, HERE. TAPE THE BOX SHUT, KNOCK ON HIS DOOR AND SCRAM.
'KAY.
OW! YOU'RE HURTING MY HEAD!
OH, GOOD LORD. THE BOX ISN'T EVEN CLOSED.
YOU SURE YOU'RE TOUGH ENOUGH TO CRASH A BIG FERRET PARTY? YOU CAN'T EVEN HANDLE A CARDBOARD BOX.
I'LL HAVE YOU KNOW THAT I CONSIDER MYSELF TO HAVE A ROBUST AIR OF MACHISMO ABOUT ME.
I'M NO EXPERT, BUT I'D BET USING THE PHRASE "*HAVE A ROBUST AIR OF MACHISMO ABOUT ME*" MEANS YOU DON'T.
darb
SOMEDAY I'LL HAVE PEOPLE FLOGGED FOR SAYING SUCH THINGS.
SEE, THERE'S YOUR PROBLEM: YOU NEED MINIONS. YOUR EVIL WISH LIST OUTPACES YOUR EVIL CAPABILITIES.
CATS HAVE AN EVIL GAP.

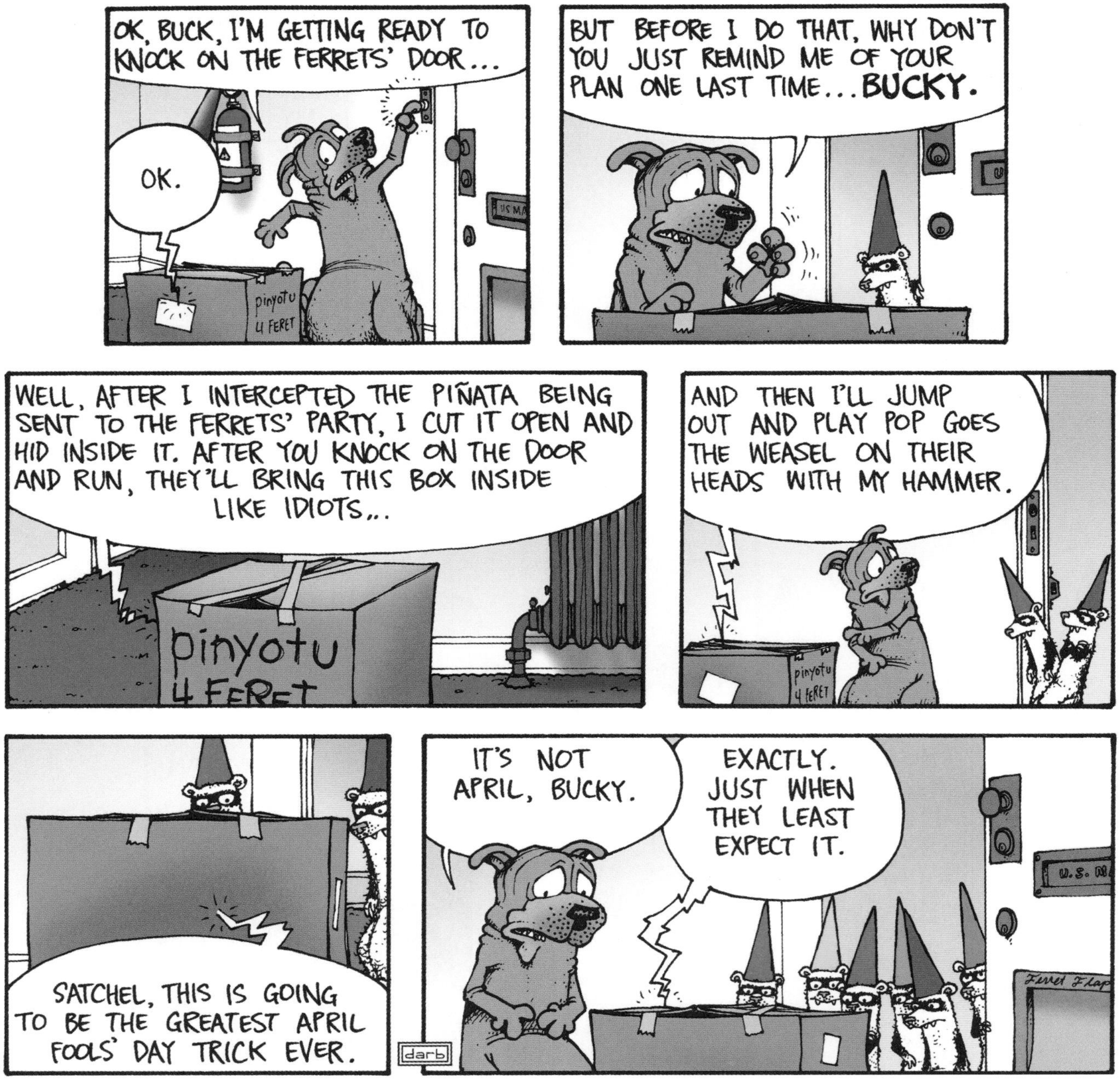
OK, BUCK, I'M GETTING READY TO KNOCK ON THE FERRETS' DOOR...
OK.
BUT BEFORE I DO THAT, WHY DON'T YOU JUST REMIND ME OF YOUR PLAN ONE LAST TIME... **BUCKY.**
WELL, AFTER I INTERCEPTED THE PIÑATA BEING SENT TO THE FERRETS' PARTY, I CUT IT OPEN AND HID INSIDE IT. AFTER YOU KNOCK ON THE DOOR AND RUN, THEY'LL BRING THIS BOX INSIDE LIKE IDIOTS...
pinyotu 4 FERET
AND THEN I'LL JUMP OUT AND PLAY POP GOES THE WEASEL ON THEIR HEADS WITH MY HAMMER.
SATCHEL, THIS IS GOING TO BE THE GREATEST APRIL FOOLS' DAY TRICK EVER.
darb
IT'S NOT APRIL, BUCKY.
EXACTLY. JUST WHEN THEY LEAST EXPECT IT.

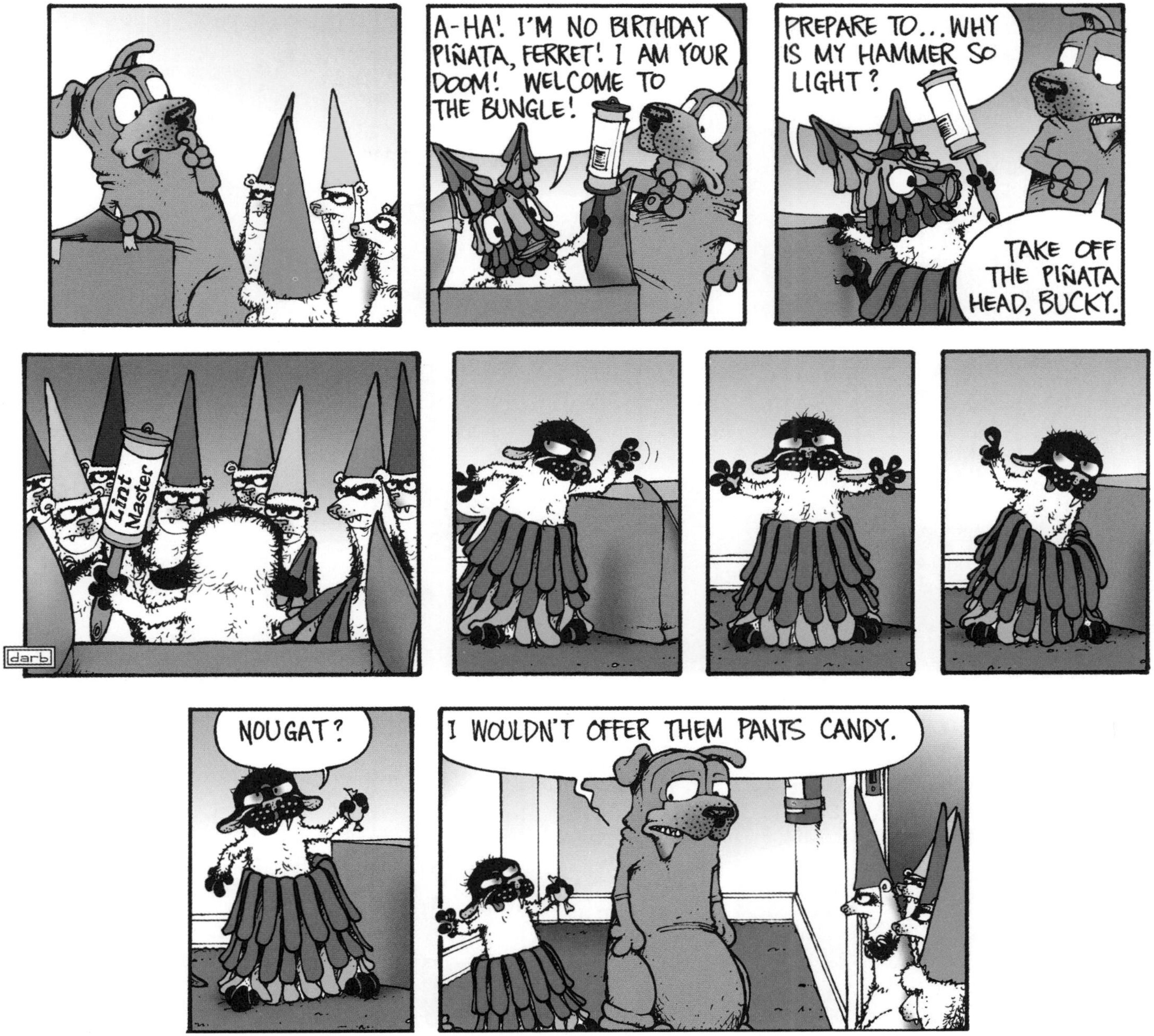
A-HA! I'M NO BIRTHDAY PIÑATA, FERRET! I AM YOUR DOOM! WELCOME TO THE BUNGLE!
PREPARE TO...WHY IS MY HAMMER SO LIGHT?
TAKE OFF THE PIÑATA HEAD, BUCKY.
Lint Master
darb
NOUGAT?
I WOULDN'T OFFER THEM PANTS CANDY.

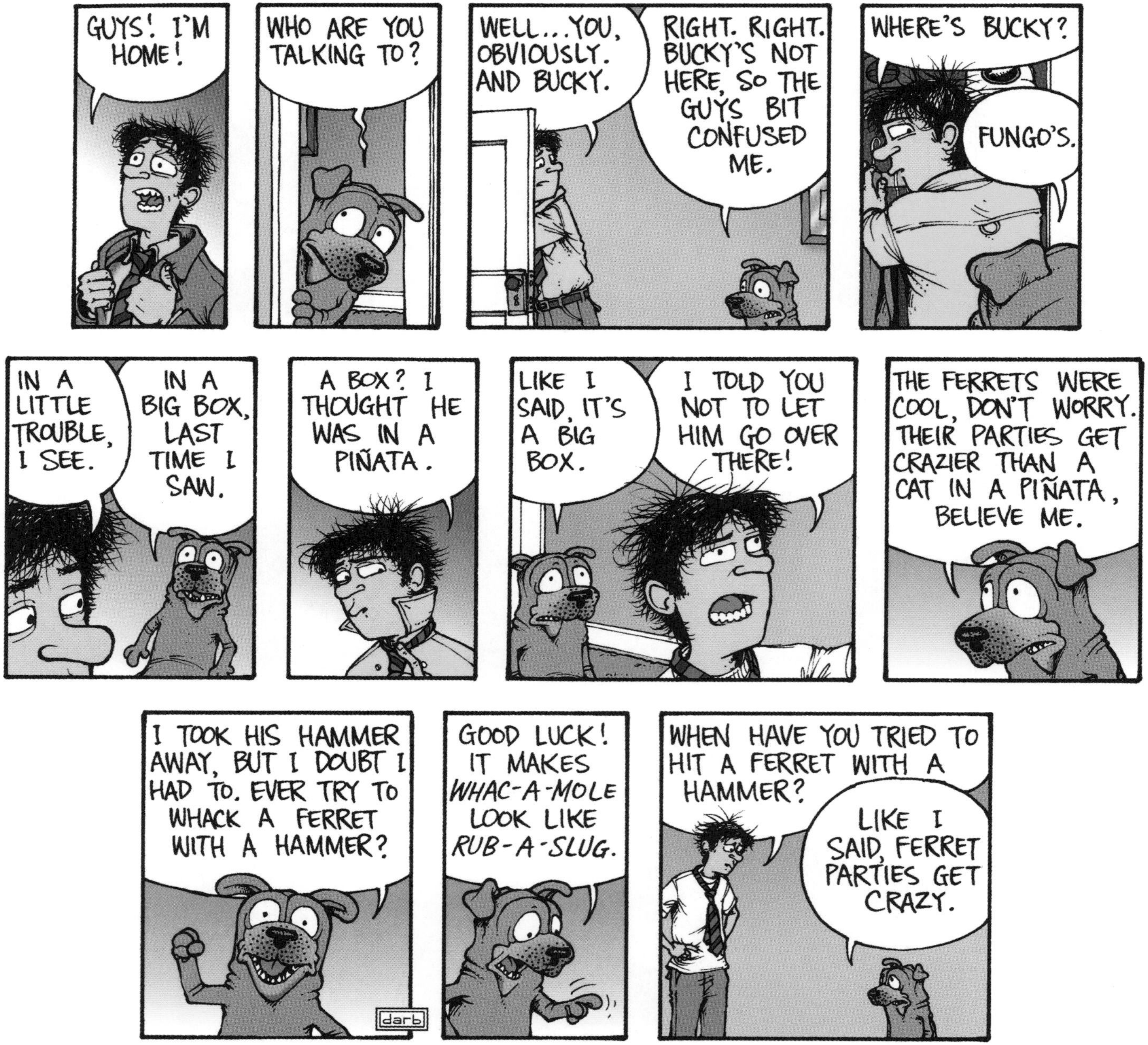
GUYS! I'M HOME!
WHO ARE YOU TALKING TO?
WELL... YOU, OBVIOUSLY. AND BUCKY.
RIGHT. RIGHT. BUCKY'S NOT HERE, SO THE GUYS BIT CONFUSED ME.
WHERE'S BUCKY?
FUNGO'S.
IN A LITTLE TROUBLE, I SEE.
IN A BIG BOX, LAST TIME I SAW.
A BOX? I THOUGHT HE WAS IN A PIÑATA.
LIKE I SAID, IT'S A BIG BOX.
I TOLD YOU NOT TO LET HIM GO OVER THERE!
THE FERRETS WERE COOL, DON'T WORRY. THEIR PARTIES GET CRAZIER THAN A CAT IN A PIÑATA, BELIEVE ME.
I TOOK HIS HAMMER AWAY, BUT I DOUBT I HAD TO. EVER TRY TO WHACK A FERRET WITH A HAMMER?
darb
GOOD LUCK! IT MAKES *WHAC-A-MOLE* LOOK LIKE *RUB-A-SLUG*.
WHEN HAVE YOU TRIED TO HIT A FERRET WITH A HAMMER?
LIKE I SAID, FERRET PARTIES GET CRAZY.

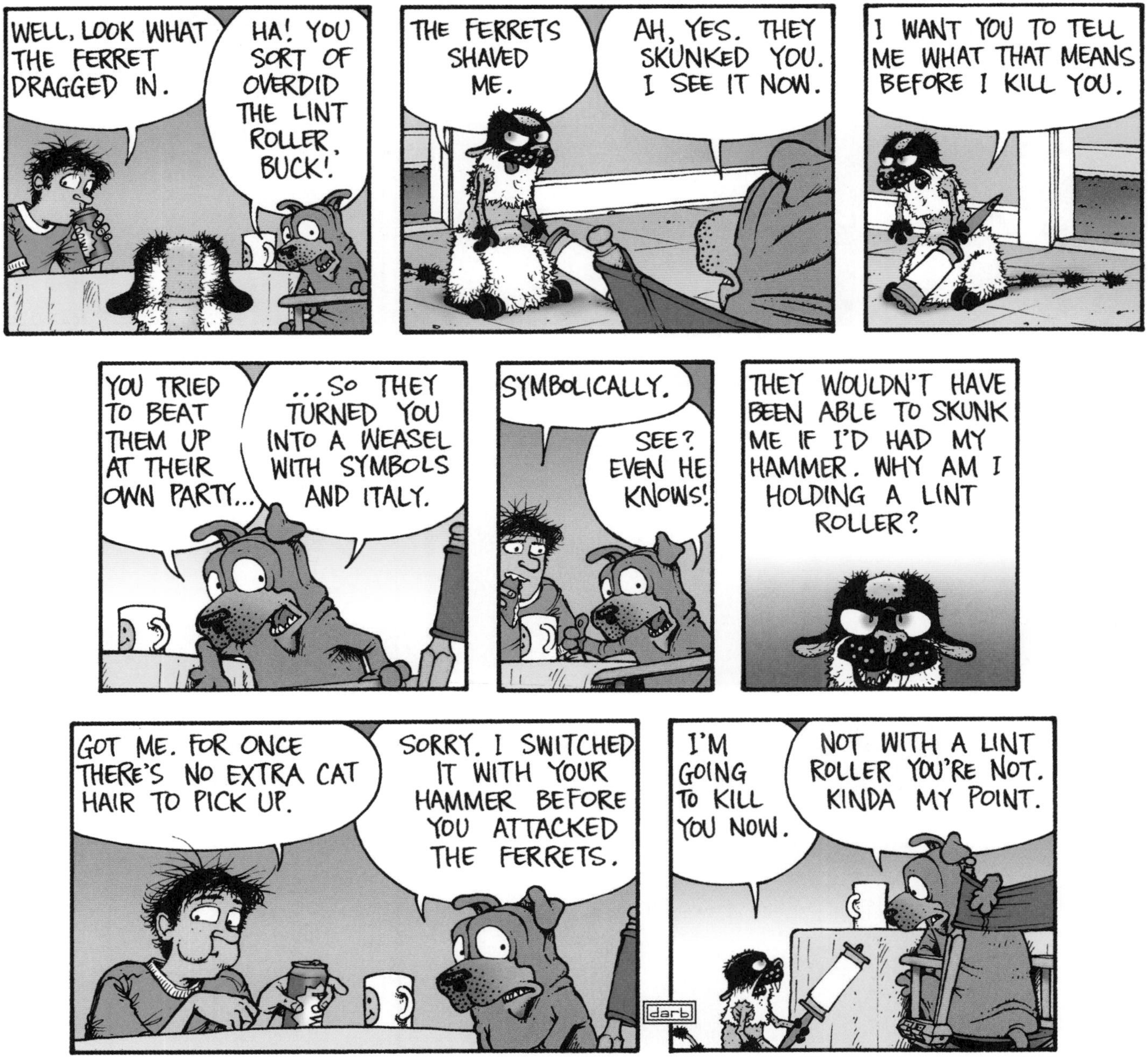
WELL, LOOK WHAT THE FERRET DRAGGED IN.
HA! YOU SORT OF OVERDID THE LINT ROLLER, BUCK!
THE FERRETS SHAVED ME.
AH, YES. THEY SKUNKED YOU. I SEE IT NOW.
I WANT YOU TO TELL ME WHAT THAT MEANS BEFORE I KILL YOU.
YOU TRIED TO BEAT THEM UP AT THEIR OWN PARTY...
...SO THEY TURNED YOU INTO A WEASEL WITH SYMBOLS AND ITALY.
SYMBOLICALLY.
SEE? EVEN HE KNOWS!
THEY WOULDN'T HAVE BEEN ABLE TO SKUNK ME IF I'D HAD MY HAMMER. WHY AM I HOLDING A LINT ROLLER?
GOT ME. FOR ONCE THERE'S NO EXTRA CAT HAIR TO PICK UP.
SORRY. I SWITCHED IT WITH YOUR HAMMER BEFORE YOU ATTACKED THE FERRETS.
darb
I'M GOING TO KILL YOU NOW.
NOT WITH A LINT ROLLER YOU'RE NOT. KINDA MY POINT.

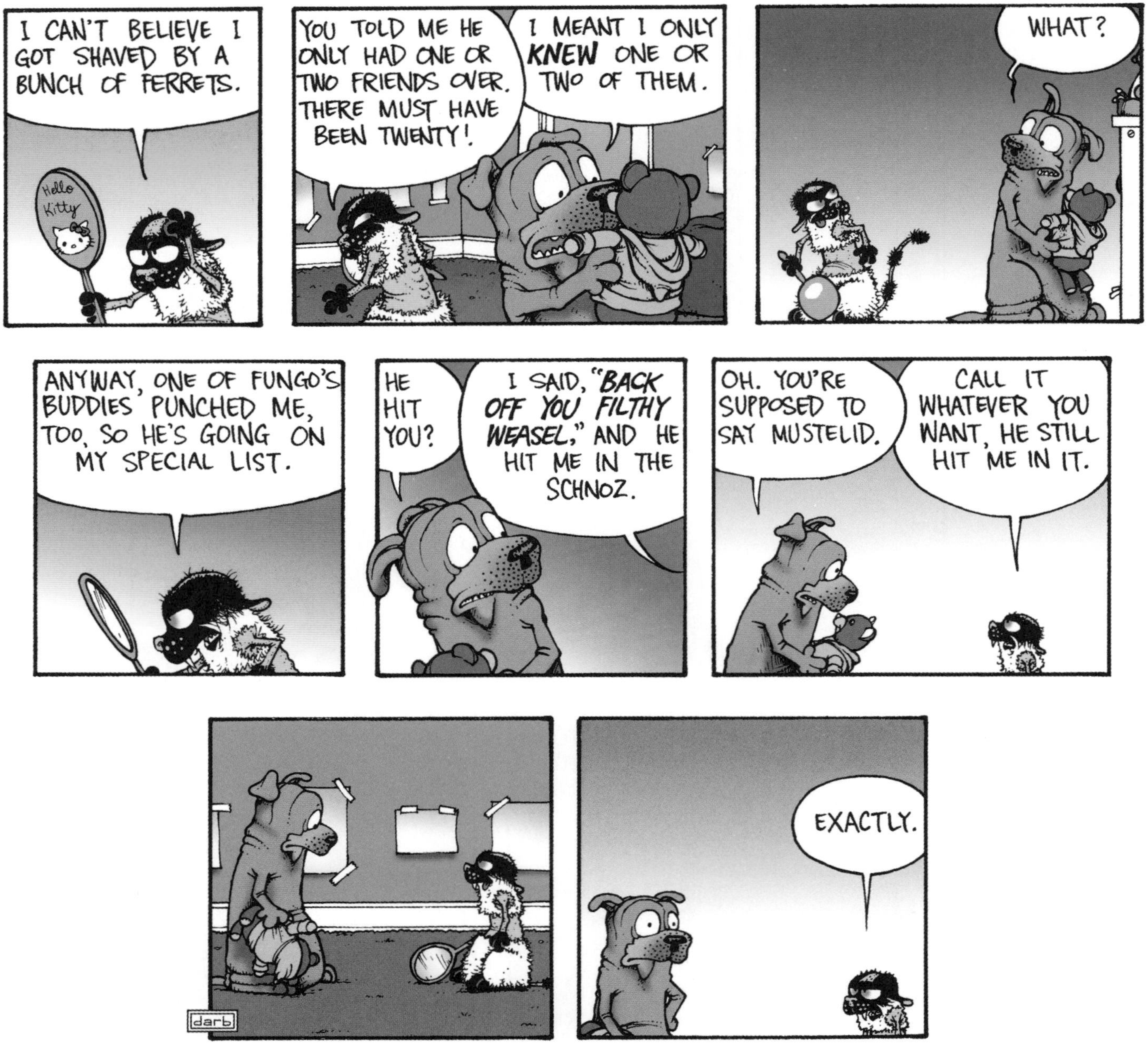
I CAN'T BELIEVE I GOT SHAVED BY A BUNCH OF FERRETS.
Hello Kitty
YOU TOLD ME HE ONLY HAD ONE OR TWO FRIENDS OVER. THERE MUST HAVE BEEN TWENTY!
I MEANT I ONLY **KNEW** ONE OR TWO OF THEM.
WHAT?
ANYWAY, ONE OF FUNGO'S BUDDIES PUNCHED ME, TOO, SO HE'S GOING ON MY SPECIAL LIST.
HE HIT YOU?
I SAID, "*BACK OFF YOU FILTHY WEASEL,*" AND HE HIT ME IN THE SCHNOZ.
OH. YOU'RE SUPPOSED TO SAY MUSTELID.
CALL IT WHATEVER YOU WANT, HE STILL HIT ME IN IT.
darb
EXACTLY.

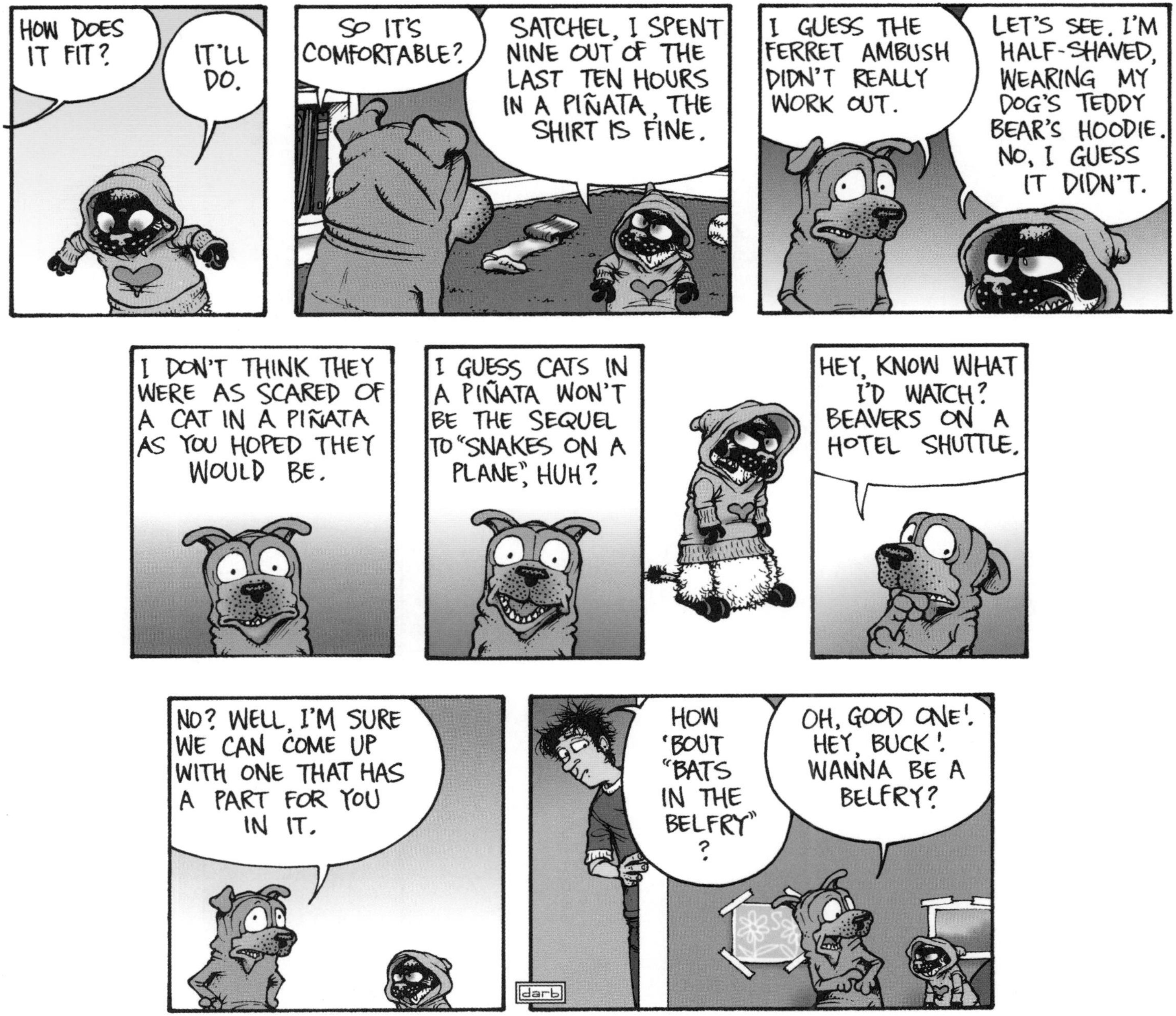

HOW DOES IT FIT?
IT'LL DO.
SO IT'S COMFORTABLE?
SATCHEL, I SPENT NINE OUT OF THE LAST TEN HOURS IN A PIÑATA, THE SHIRT IS FINE.
I GUESS THE FERRET AMBUSH DIDN'T REALLY WORK OUT.
LET'S SEE. I'M HALF-SHAVED, WEARING MY DOG'S TEDDY BEAR'S HOODIE. NO, I GUESS IT DIDN'T.
I DON'T THINK THEY WERE AS SCARED OF A CAT IN A PIÑATA AS YOU HOPED THEY WOULD BE.
I GUESS CATS IN A PIÑATA WON'T BE THE SEQUEL TO "SNAKES ON A PLANE", HUH?
HEY, KNOW WHAT I'D WATCH? BEAVERS ON A HOTEL SHUTTLE.
NO? WELL, I'M SURE WE CAN COME UP WITH ONE THAT HAS A PART FOR YOU IN IT.
HOW 'BOUT "BATS IN THE BELFRY"?
OH, GOOD ONE! HEY, BUCK! WANNA BE A BELFRY?
darb

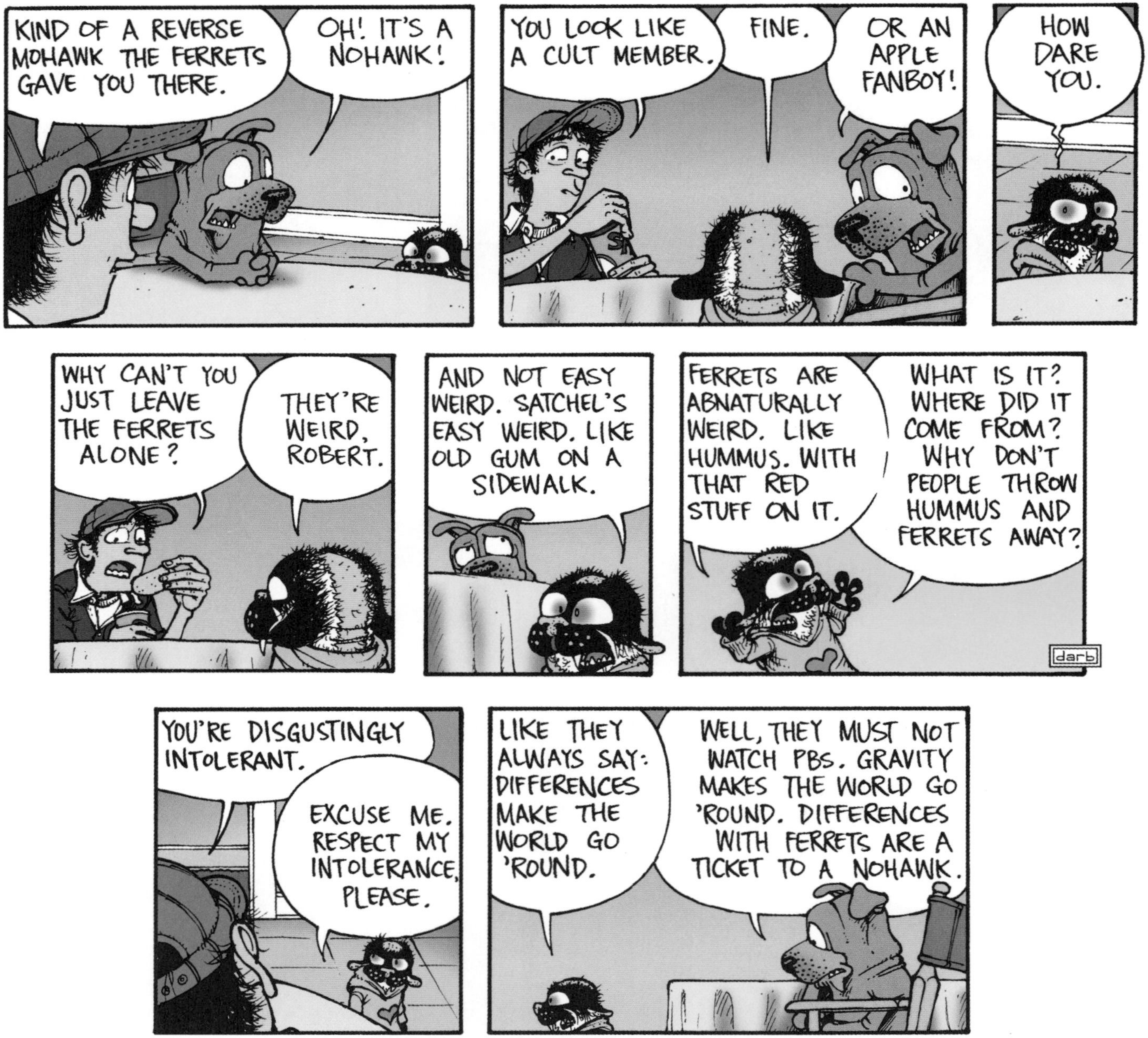
KIND OF A REVERSE MOHAWK THE FERRETS GAVE YOU THERE.
OH! IT'S A NOHAWK!
YOU LOOK LIKE A CULT MEMBER.
FINE.
OR AN APPLE FANBOY!
HOW DARE YOU.
WHY CAN'T YOU JUST LEAVE THE FERRETS ALONE?
THEY'RE WEIRD, ROBERT.
AND NOT EASY WEIRD. SATCHEL'S EASY WEIRD. LIKE OLD GUM ON A SIDEWALK.
FERRETS ARE ABNATURALLY WEIRD. LIKE HUMMUS. WITH THAT RED STUFF ON IT.
WHAT IS IT? WHERE DID IT COME FROM? WHY DON'T PEOPLE THROW HUMMUS AND FERRETS AWAY?
darb
YOU'RE DISGUSTINGLY INTOLERANT.
EXCUSE ME. RESPECT MY INTOLERANCE, PLEASE.
LIKE THEY ALWAYS SAY: DIFFERENCES MAKE THE WORLD GO 'ROUND.
WELL, THEY MUST NOT WATCH PBS. GRAVITY MAKES THE WORLD GO 'ROUND. DIFFERENCES WITH FERRETS ARE A TICKET TO A NOHAWK.

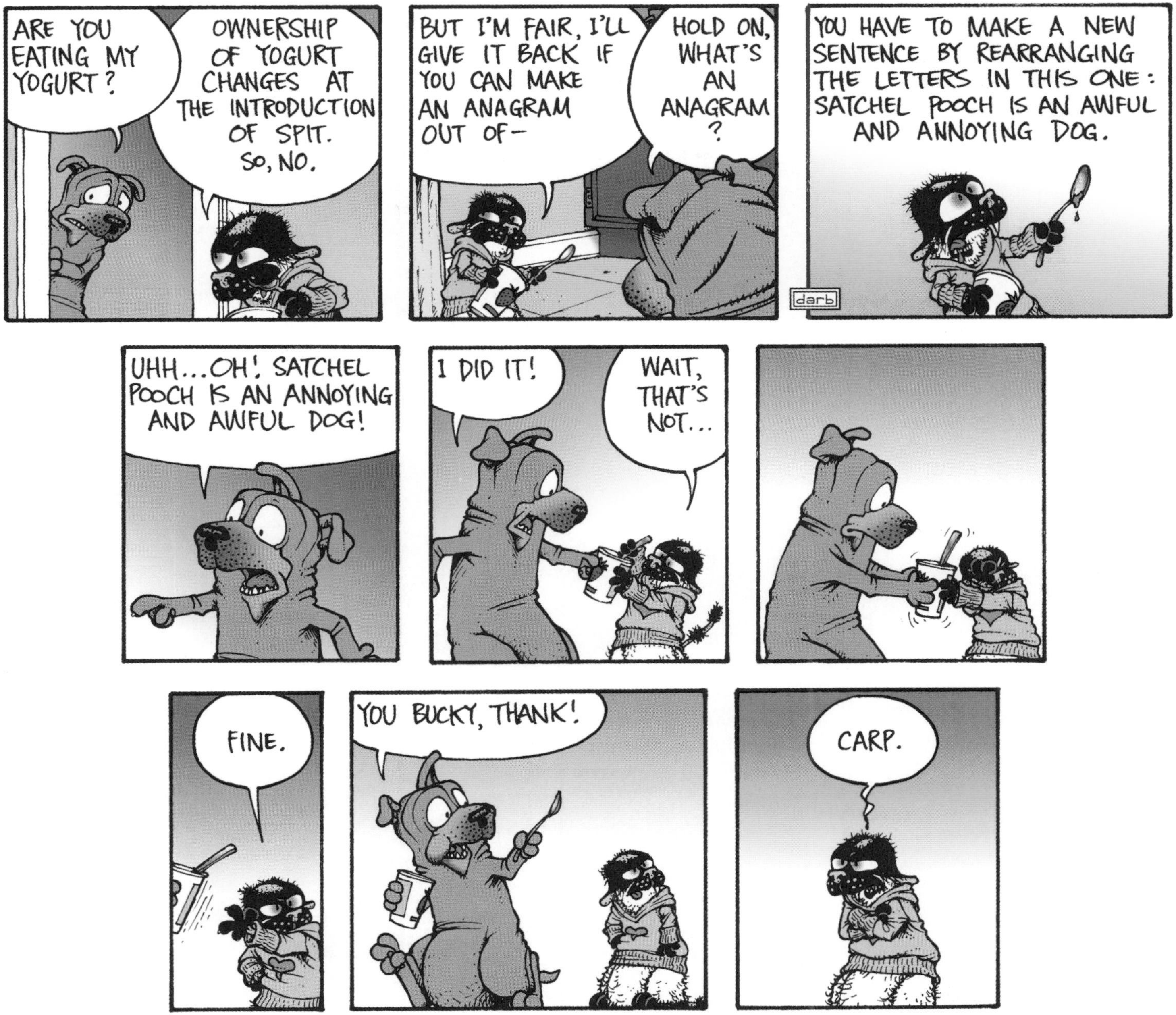
ARE YOU EATING MY YOGURT?
OWNERSHIP OF YOGURT CHANGES AT THE INTRODUCTION OF SPIT. SO, NO.
BUT I'M FAIR, I'LL GIVE IT BACK IF YOU CAN MAKE AN ANAGRAM OUT OF–
HOLD ON, WHAT'S AN ANAGRAM?
YOU HAVE TO MAKE A NEW SENTENCE BY REARRANGING THE LETTERS IN THIS ONE: SATCHEL POOCH IS AN AWFUL AND ANNOYING DOG.
darb
UHH...OH! SATCHEL POOCH IS AN ANNOYING AND AWFUL DOG!
I DID IT!
WAIT, THAT'S NOT...
FINE.
YOU BUCKY, THANK!
CARP.

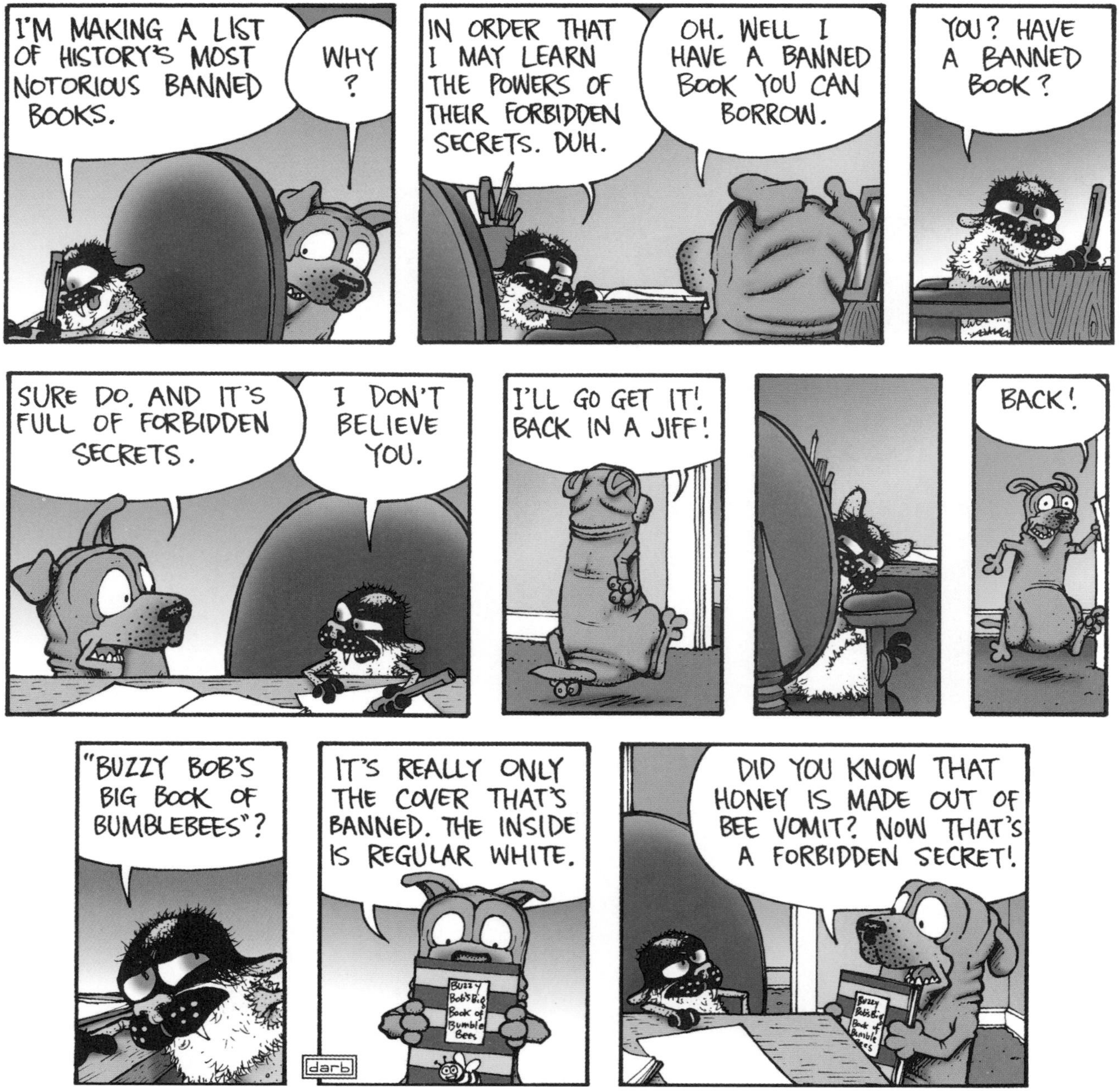
I'M MAKING A LIST OF HISTORY'S MOST NOTORIOUS BANNED BOOKS.
WHY?
IN ORDER THAT I MAY LEARN THE POWERS OF THEIR FORBIDDEN SECRETS. DUH.
OH. WELL I HAVE A BANNED BOOK YOU CAN BORROW.
YOU? HAVE A BANNED BOOK?
SURE DO. AND IT'S FULL OF FORBIDDEN SECRETS.
I DON'T BELIEVE YOU.
I'LL GO GET IT! BACK IN A JIFF!
BACK!
"BUZZY BOB'S BIG BOOK OF BUMBLEBEES"?
IT'S REALLY ONLY THE COVER THAT'S BANNED. THE INSIDE IS REGULAR WHITE.
darb
DID YOU KNOW THAT HONEY IS MADE OUT OF BEE VOMIT? NOW THAT'S A FORBIDDEN SECRET!

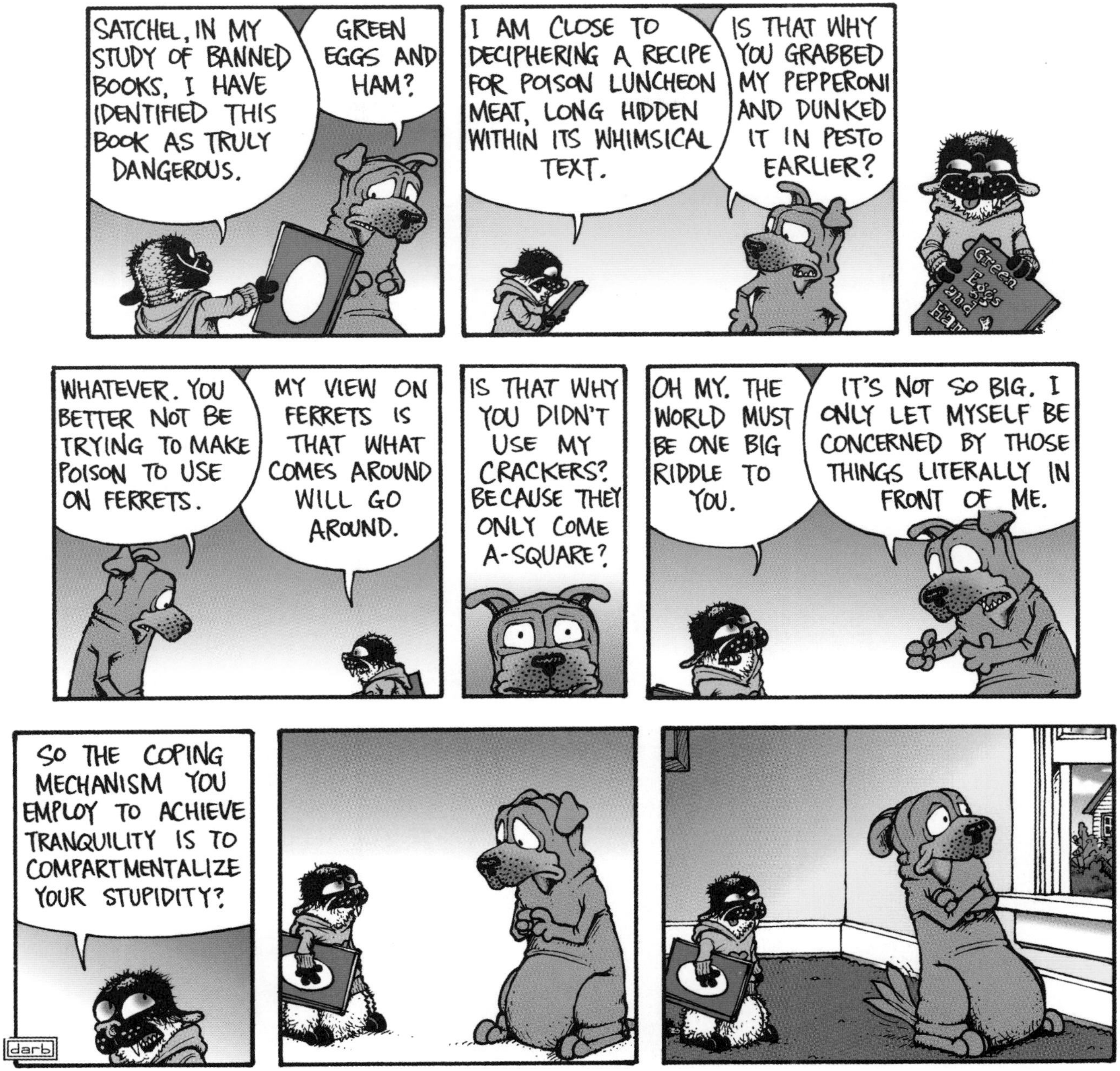
SATCHEL, IN MY STUDY OF BANNED BOOKS, I HAVE IDENTIFIED THIS BOOK AS TRULY DANGEROUS.
GREEN EGGS AND HAM?
I AM CLOSE TO DECIPHERING A RECIPE FOR POISON LUNCHEON MEAT, LONG HIDDEN WITHIN ITS WHIMSICAL TEXT.
IS THAT WHY YOU GRABBED MY PEPPERONI AND DUNKED IT IN PESTO EARLIER?
Green Eggs and Ham
WHATEVER. YOU BETTER NOT BE TRYING TO MAKE POISON TO USE ON FERRETS.
MY VIEW ON FERRETS IS THAT WHAT COMES AROUND WILL GO AROUND.
IS THAT WHY YOU DIDN'T USE MY CRACKERS? BECAUSE THEY ONLY COME A-SQUARE?
OH MY. THE WORLD MUST BE ONE BIG RIDDLE TO YOU.
IT'S NOT SO BIG. I ONLY LET MYSELF BE CONCERNED BY THOSE THINGS LITERALLY IN FRONT OF ME.
SO THE COPING MECHANISM YOU EMPLOY TO ACHIEVE TRANQUILITY IS TO COMPARTMENTALIZE YOUR STUPIDITY?
darb

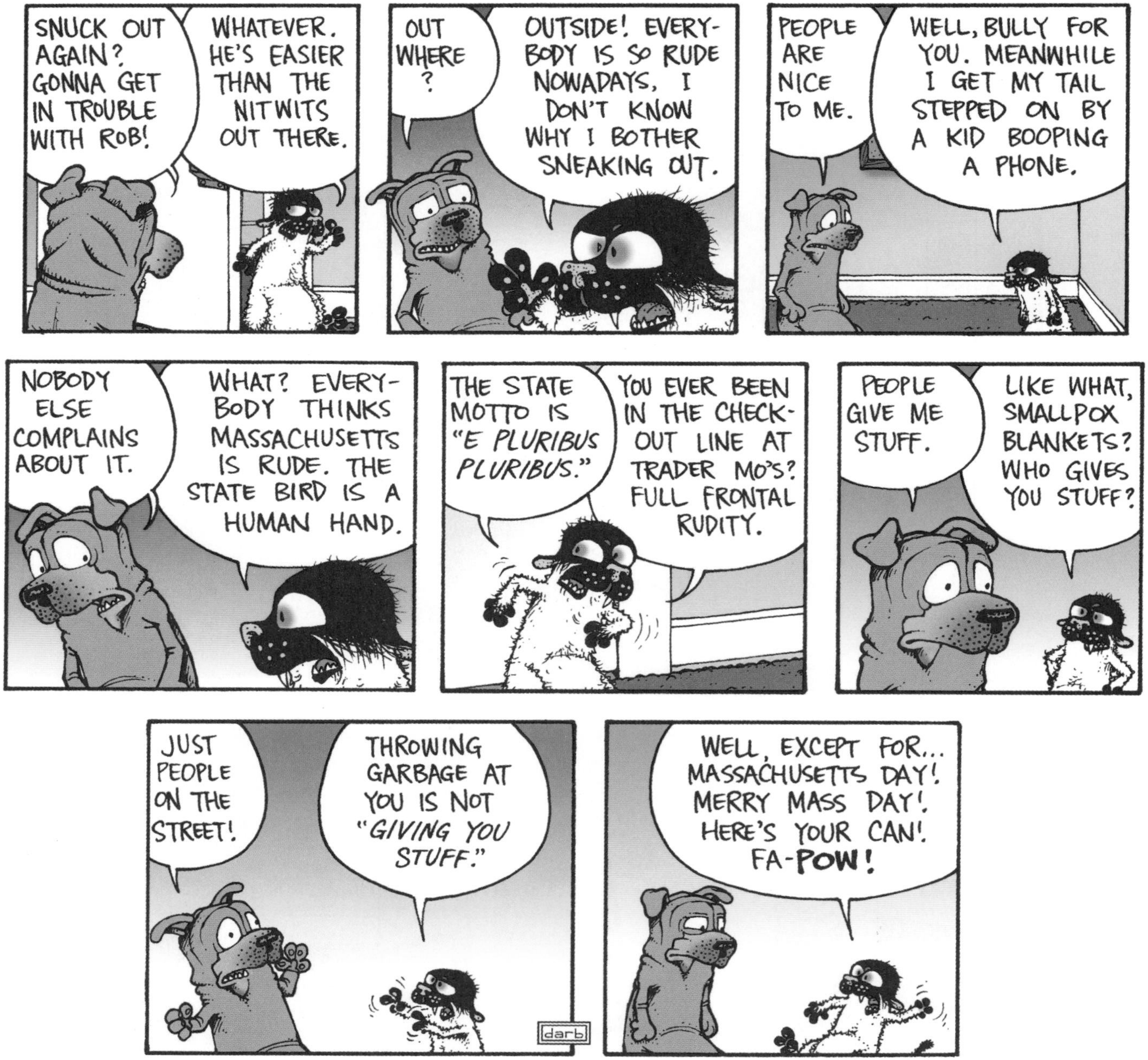
SNUCK OUT AGAIN? GONNA GET IN TROUBLE WITH ROB!
WHATEVER. HE'S EASIER THAN THE NITWITS OUT THERE.
OUT WHERE?
OUTSIDE! EVERYBODY IS SO RUDE NOWADAYS, I DON'T KNOW WHY I BOTHER SNEAKING OUT.
PEOPLE ARE NICE TO ME.
WELL, BULLY FOR YOU. MEANWHILE I GET MY TAIL STEPPED ON BY A KID BOOPING A PHONE.
NOBODY ELSE COMPLAINS ABOUT IT.
WHAT? EVERYBODY THINKS MASSACHUSETTS IS RUDE. THE STATE BIRD IS A HUMAN HAND.
THE STATE MOTTO IS "*E PLURIBUS PLURIBUS*."
YOU EVER BEEN IN THE CHECK-OUT LINE AT TRADER MO'S? FULL FRONTAL RUDITY.
PEOPLE GIVE ME STUFF.
LIKE WHAT, SMALLPOX BLANKETS? WHO GIVES YOU STUFF?
JUST PEOPLE ON THE STREET!
THROWING GARBAGE AT YOU IS NOT "*GIVING YOU STUFF.*"
darb
WELL, EXCEPT FOR... MASSACHUSETTS DAY! MERRY MASS DAY! HERE'S YOUR CAN! FA-**POW**!

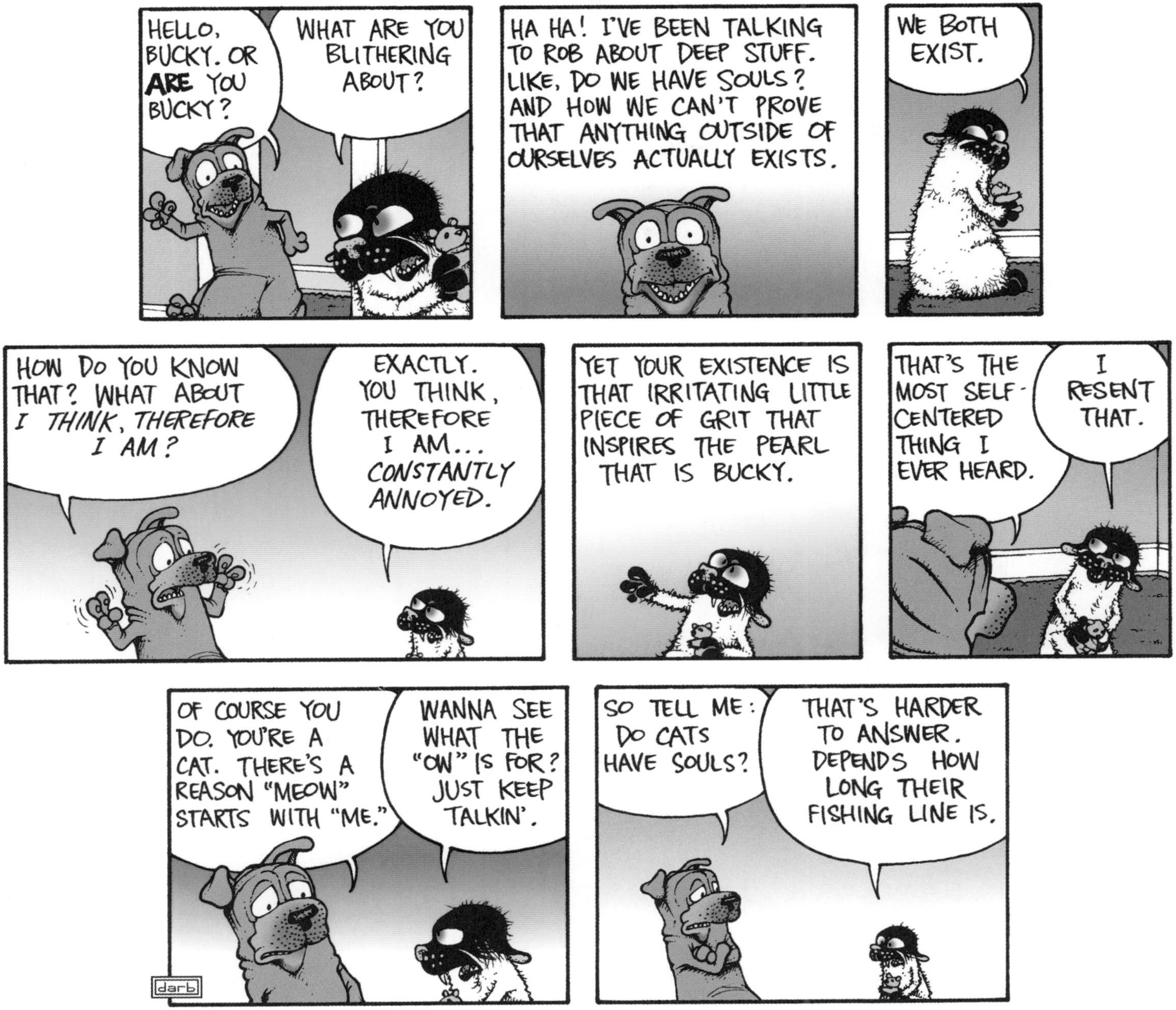
HELLO, BUCKY. OR **ARE** YOU BUCKY?
WHAT ARE YOU BLITHERING ABOUT?
HA HA! I'VE BEEN TALKING TO ROB ABOUT DEEP STUFF. LIKE, DO WE HAVE SOULS? AND HOW WE CAN'T PROVE THAT ANYTHING OUTSIDE OF OURSELVES ACTUALLY EXISTS.
WE BOTH EXIST.
HOW DO YOU KNOW THAT? WHAT ABOUT *I THINK, THEREFORE I AM?*
EXACTLY. YOU THINK, THEREFORE I AM... *CONSTANTLY ANNOYED.*
YET YOUR EXISTENCE IS THAT IRRITATING LITTLE PIECE OF GRIT THAT INSPIRES THE PEARL THAT IS BUCKY.
THAT'S THE MOST SELF-CENTERED THING I EVER HEARD.
I RESENT THAT.
OF COURSE YOU DO. YOU'RE A CAT. THERE'S A REASON "MEOW" STARTS WITH "ME."
WANNA SEE WHAT THE "OW" IS FOR? JUST KEEP TALKIN'.
darb
SO TELL ME: DO CATS HAVE SOULS?
THAT'S HARDER TO ANSWER. DEPENDS HOW LONG THEIR FISHING LINE IS.

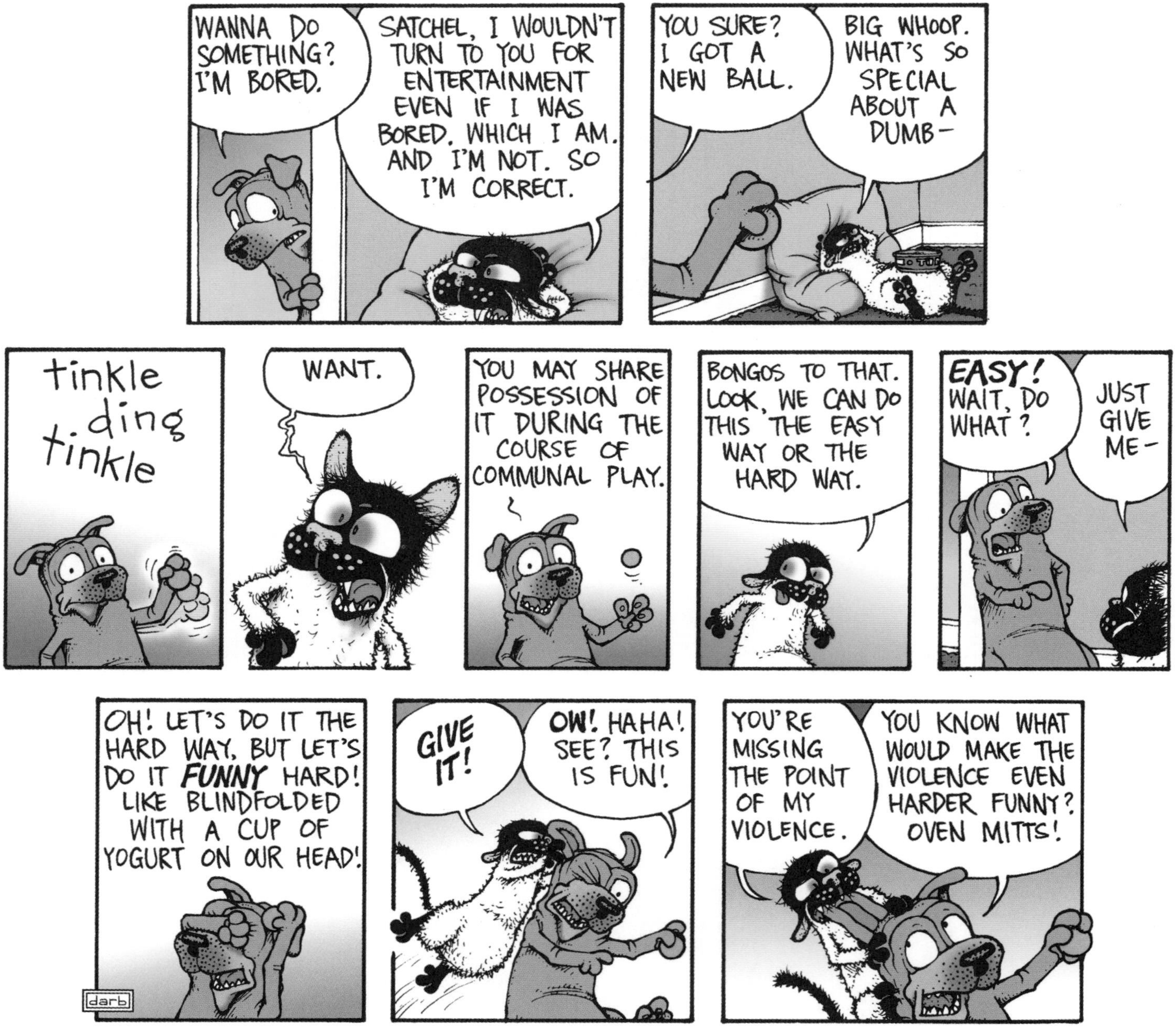
WANNA DO SOMETHING? I'M BORED.
SATCHEL, I WOULDN'T TURN TO YOU FOR ENTERTAINMENT EVEN IF I WAS BORED. WHICH I AM. AND I'M NOT. SO I'M CORRECT.
YOU SURE? I GOT A NEW BALL.
BIG WHOOP. WHAT'S SO SPECIAL ABOUT A DUMB-
tinkle ding tinkle
WANT.
YOU MAY SHARE POSSESSION OF IT DURING THE COURSE OF COMMUNAL PLAY.
BONGOS TO THAT. LOOK, WE CAN DO THIS THE EASY WAY OR THE HARD WAY.
EASY! WAIT, DO WHAT?
JUST GIVE ME-
OH! LET'S DO IT THE HARD WAY, BUT LET'S DO IT FUNNY HARD! LIKE BLINDFOLDED WITH A CUP OF YOGURT ON OUR HEAD!
darb
GIVE IT!
OW! HAHA! SEE? THIS IS FUN!
YOU'RE MISSING THE POINT OF MY VIOLENCE.
YOU KNOW WHAT WOULD MAKE THE VIOLENCE EVEN HARDER FUNNY? OVEN MITTS!

WHAT WAS THAT POP? WHY DID THE LIGHTS DIM?

THE TOASTER'S BAGEL SETTING CAN'T HANDLE LOX. SURELY THAT'S FALSE ADVERTISING.

YOU HAVE TO TELL ROB *YOU* BROKE THE TOASTER! I'M STILL ON APPLIANCE BAN!

AS I DIDN'T PUT A FISH IN IT, AND I HAVE MY OWN FREE WILL...NO.

I'LL GIVE YOU TWO DOLLARS...

APPARENTLY YOU HAVE *CHEAP* WILL.

YEAH. AND TWO BUCKS.

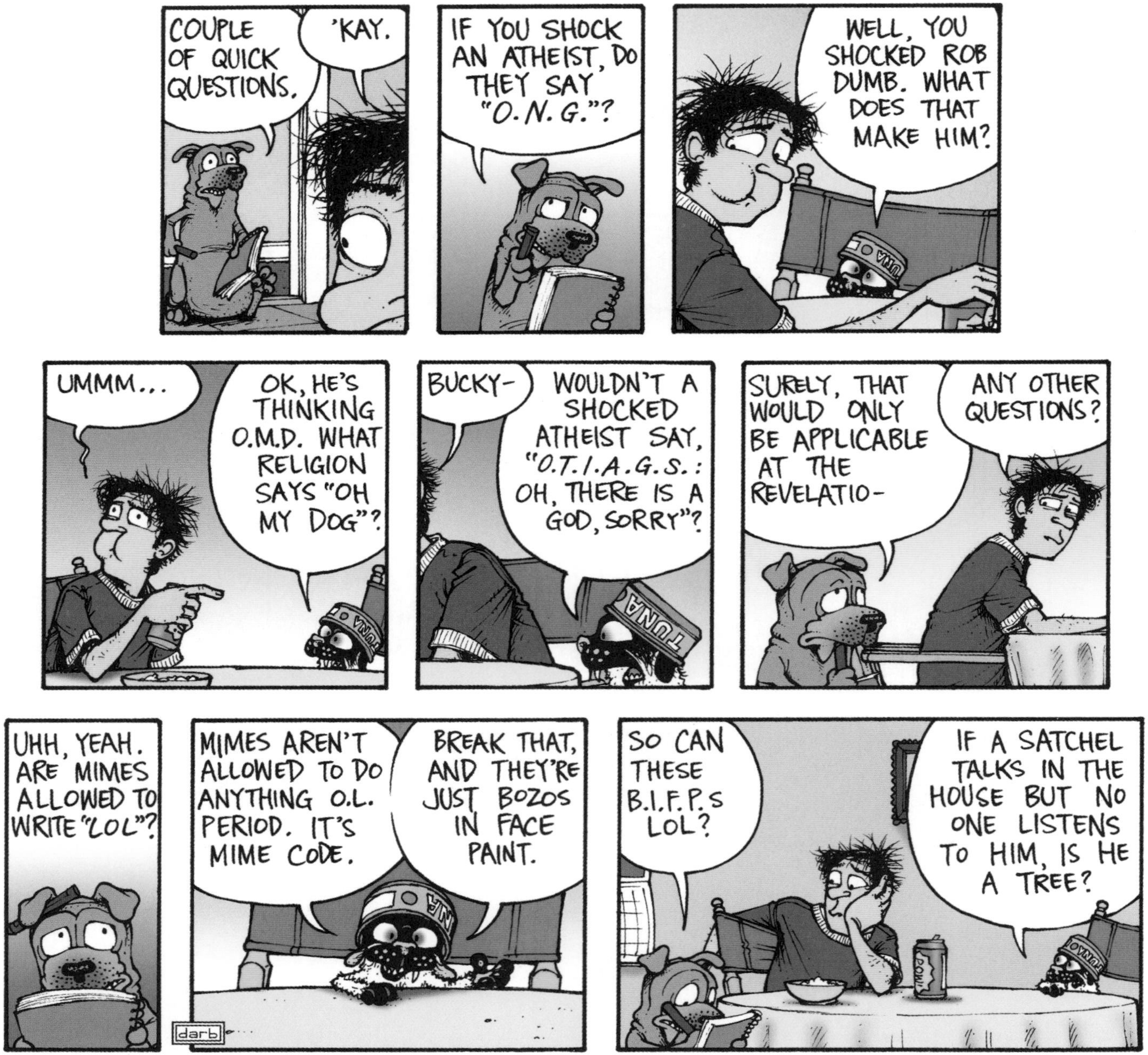
COUPLE OF QUICK QUESTIONS.
'KAY.
IF YOU SHOCK AN ATHEIST, DO THEY SAY "O.N.G."?
WELL, YOU SHOCKED ROB DUMB. WHAT DOES THAT MAKE HIM?
UMMM...
OK, HE'S THINKING O.M.D. WHAT RELIGION SAYS "OH MY DOG"?
BUCKY-
WOULDN'T A SHOCKED ATHEIST SAY, "O.T.I.A.G.S.: OH, THERE IS A GOD, SORRY"?
SURELY, THAT WOULD ONLY BE APPLICABLE AT THE REVELATIO-
ANY OTHER QUESTIONS?
UHH, YEAH. ARE MIMES ALLOWED TO WRITE "LOL"?
MIMES AREN'T ALLOWED TO DO ANYTHING O.L. PERIOD. IT'S MIME CODE.
BREAK THAT, AND THEY'RE JUST BOZOS IN FACE PAINT.
darb
SO CAN THESE B.I.F.P.s LOL?
IF A SATCHEL TALKS IN THE HOUSE BUT NO ONE LISTENS TO HIM, IS HE A TREE?

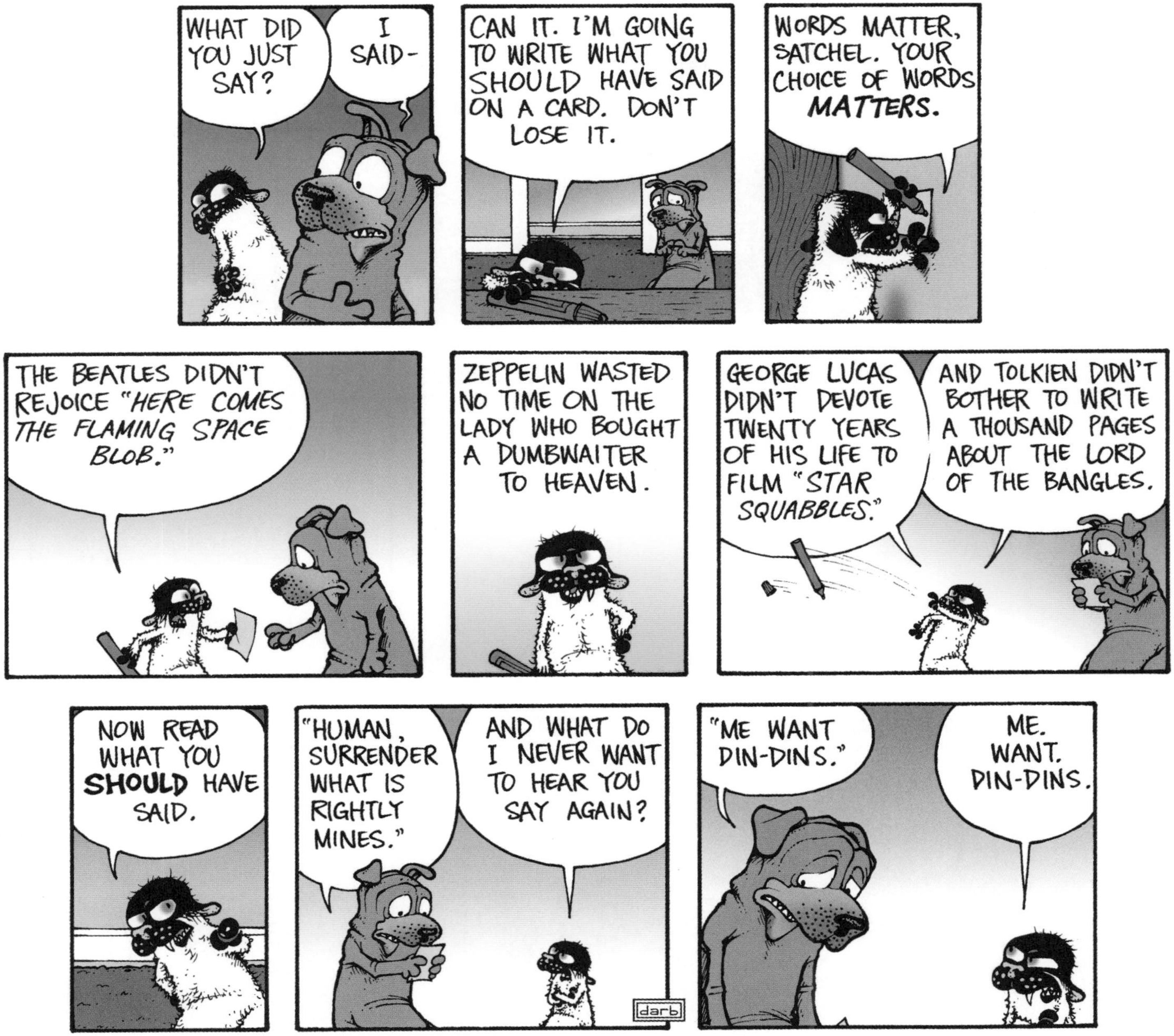
WHAT DID YOU JUST SAY?
I SAID-
CAN IT. I'M GOING TO WRITE WHAT YOU SHOULD HAVE SAID ON A CARD. DON'T LOSE IT.
WORDS MATTER, SATCHEL. YOUR CHOICE OF WORDS MATTERS.
THE BEATLES DIDN'T REJOICE "HERE COMES THE FLAMING SPACE BLOB."
ZEPPELIN WASTED NO TIME ON THE LADY WHO BOUGHT A DUMBWAITER TO HEAVEN.
GEORGE LUCAS DIDN'T DEVOTE TWENTY YEARS OF HIS LIFE TO FILM "STAR SQUABBLES."
AND TOLKIEN DIDN'T BOTHER TO WRITE A THOUSAND PAGES ABOUT THE LORD OF THE BANGLES.
NOW READ WHAT YOU SHOULD HAVE SAID.
"HUMAN, SURRENDER WHAT IS RIGHTLY MINES."
AND WHAT DO I NEVER WANT TO HEAR YOU SAY AGAIN?
darb
"ME WANT DIN-DINS."
ME. WANT. DIN-DINS.

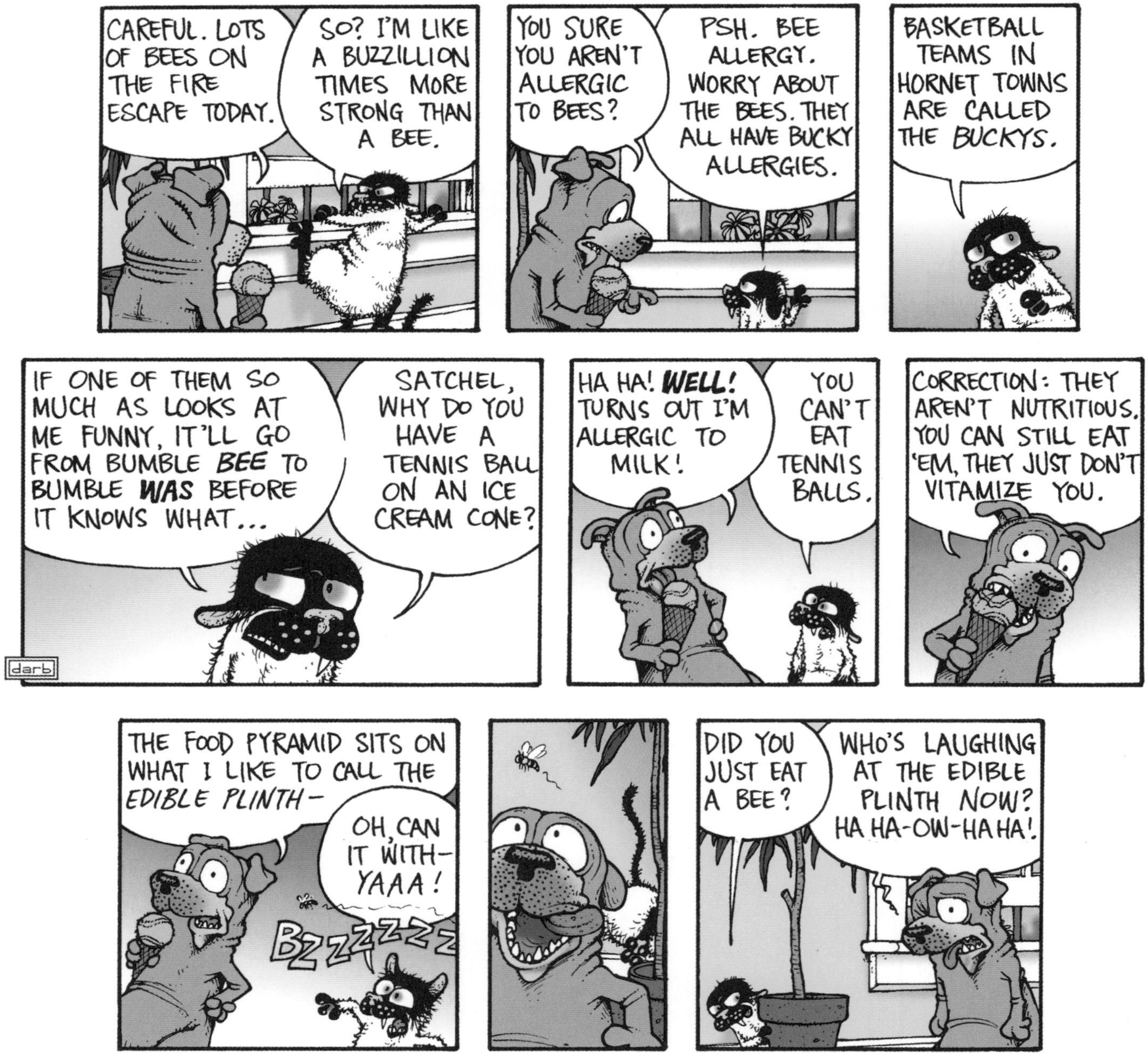
CAREFUL. LOTS OF BEES ON THE FIRE ESCAPE TODAY.
SO? I'M LIKE A BUZZILLION TIMES MORE STRONG THAN A BEE.
YOU SURE YOU AREN'T ALLERGIC TO BEES?
PSH. BEE ALLERGY. WORRY ABOUT THE BEES. THEY ALL HAVE BUCKY ALLERGIES.
BASKETBALL TEAMS IN HORNET TOWNS ARE CALLED THE BUCKYS.
IF ONE OF THEM SO MUCH AS LOOKS AT ME FUNNY, IT'LL GO FROM BUMBLE BEE TO BUMBLE WAS BEFORE IT KNOWS WHAT...
SATCHEL, WHY DO YOU HAVE A TENNIS BALL ON AN ICE CREAM CONE?
darb
HA HA! WELL! TURNS OUT I'M ALLERGIC TO MILK!
YOU CAN'T EAT TENNIS BALLS.
CORRECTION: THEY AREN'T NUTRITIOUS. YOU CAN STILL EAT 'EM, THEY JUST DON'T VITAMIZE YOU.
THE FOOD PYRAMID SITS ON WHAT I LIKE TO CALL THE EDIBLE PLINTH-
OH, CAN IT WITH-YAAA!
BZZZZZZ
DID YOU JUST EAT A BEE?
WHO'S LAUGHING AT THE EDIBLE PLINTH NOW? HA HA-OW-HA HA!

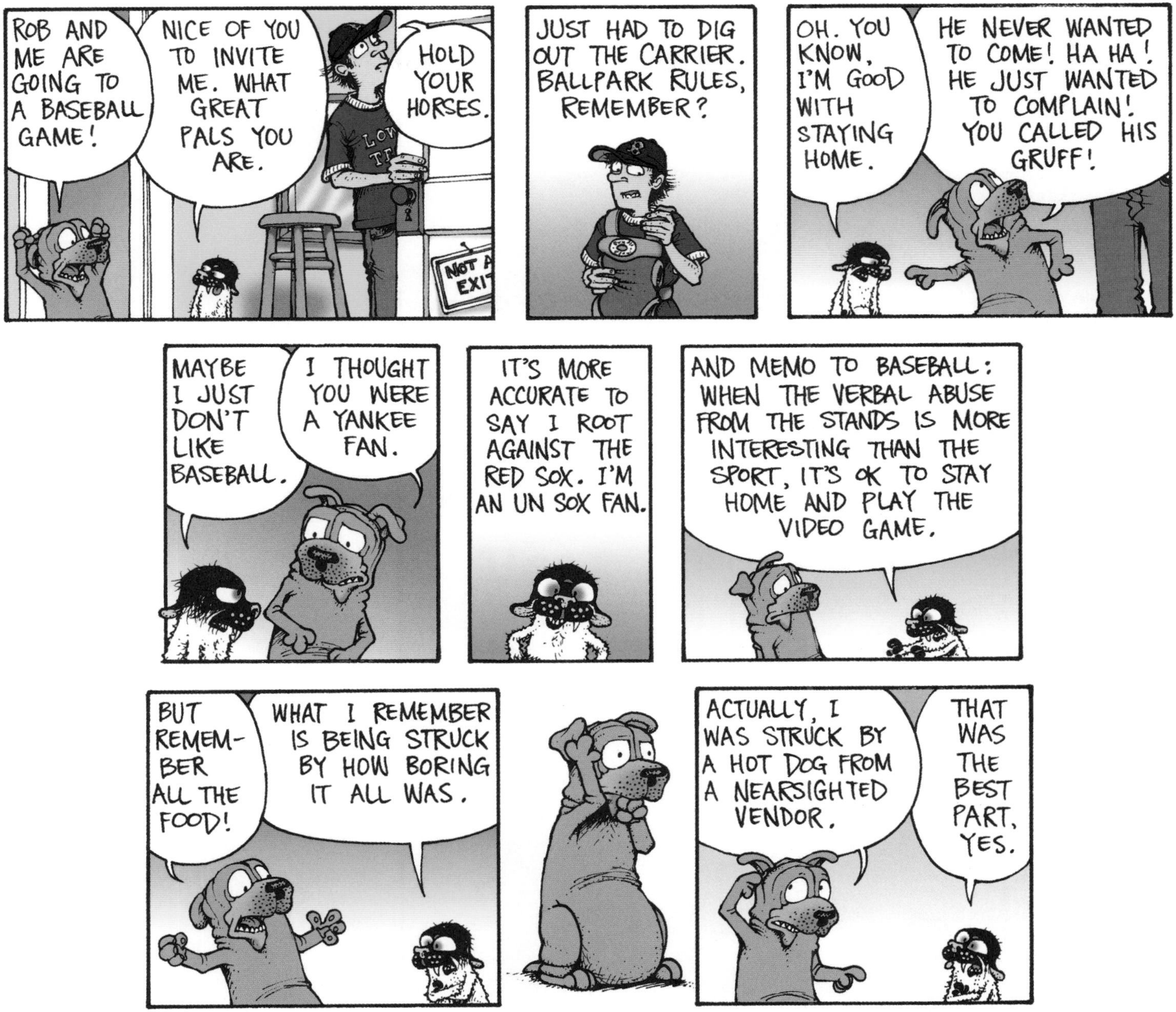
ROB AND ME ARE GOING TO A BASEBALL GAME!
NICE OF YOU TO INVITE ME. WHAT GREAT PALS YOU ARE.
HOLD YOUR HORSES.
JUST HAD TO DIG OUT THE CARRIER. BALLPARK RULES, REMEMBER?
OH. YOU KNOW, I'M GOOD WITH STAYING HOME.
HE NEVER WANTED TO COME! HA HA! HE JUST WANTED TO COMPLAIN! YOU CALLED HIS GRUFF!
MAYBE I JUST DON'T LIKE BASEBALL.
I THOUGHT YOU WERE A YANKEE FAN.
IT'S MORE ACCURATE TO SAY I ROOT AGAINST THE RED SOX. I'M AN UN SOX FAN.
AND MEMO TO BASEBALL: WHEN THE VERBAL ABUSE FROM THE STANDS IS MORE INTERESTING THAN THE SPORT, IT'S OK TO STAY HOME AND PLAY THE VIDEO GAME.
BUT REMEMBER ALL THE FOOD!
WHAT I REMEMBER IS BEING STRUCK BY HOW BORING IT ALL WAS.
ACTUALLY, I WAS STRUCK BY A HOT DOG FROM A NEARSIGHTED VENDOR.
THAT WAS THE BEST PART, YES.

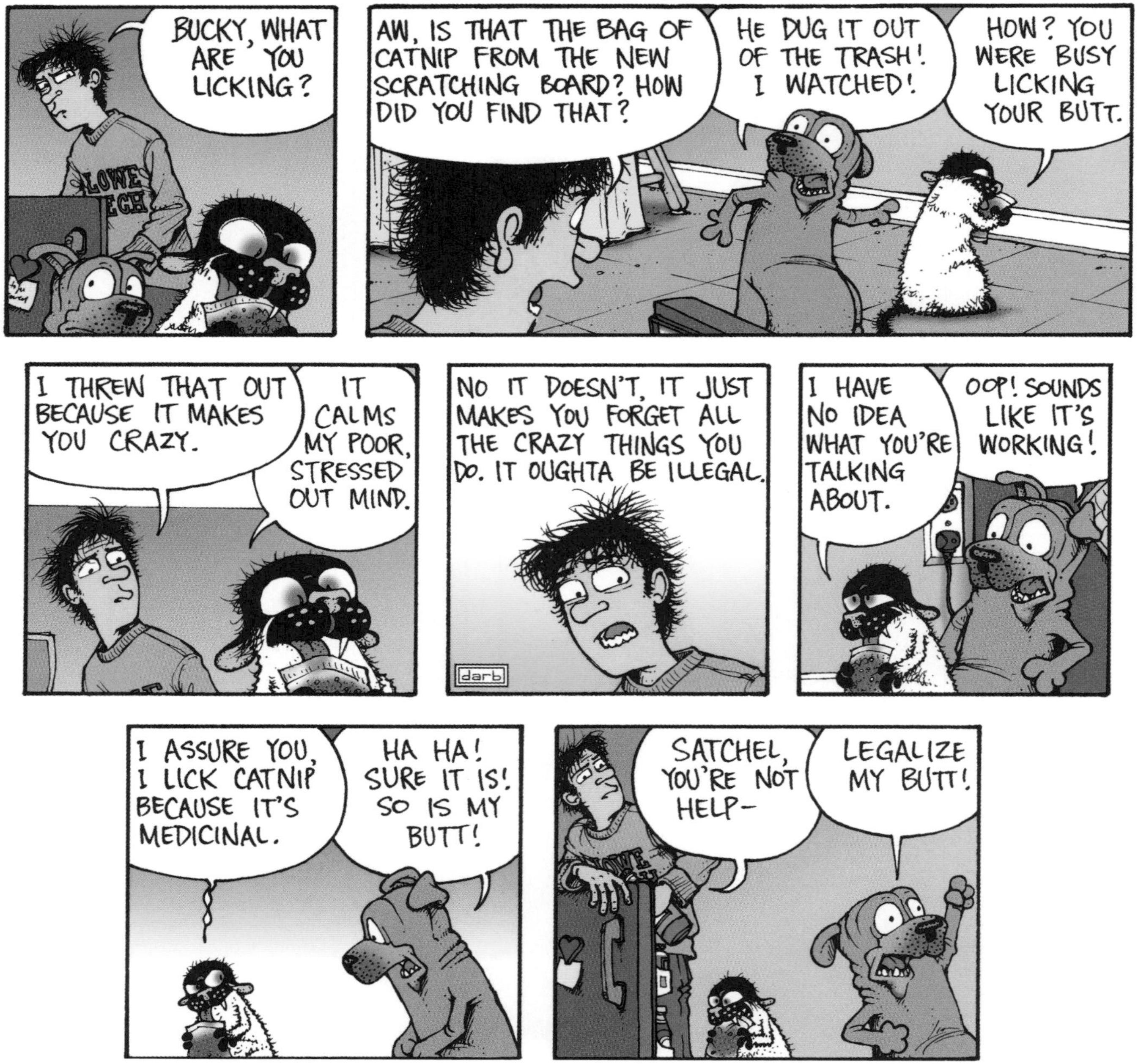
BUCKY, WHAT ARE YOU LICKING?
AW, IS THAT THE BAG OF CATNIP FROM THE NEW SCRATCHING BOARD? HOW DID YOU FIND THAT?
HE DUG IT OUT OF THE TRASH! I WATCHED!
HOW? YOU WERE BUSY LICKING YOUR BUTT.
I THREW THAT OUT BECAUSE IT MAKES YOU CRAZY.
IT CALMS MY POOR, STRESSED OUT MIND.
NO IT DOESN'T, IT JUST MAKES YOU FORGET ALL THE CRAZY THINGS YOU DO. IT OUGHTA BE ILLEGAL.
darb
I HAVE NO IDEA WHAT YOU'RE TALKING ABOUT.
OOP! SOUNDS LIKE IT'S WORKING!
I ASSURE YOU, I LICK CATNIP BECAUSE IT'S MEDICINAL.
HA HA! SURE IT IS! SO IS MY BUTT!
SATCHEL, YOU'RE NOT HELP-
LEGALIZE MY BUTT!

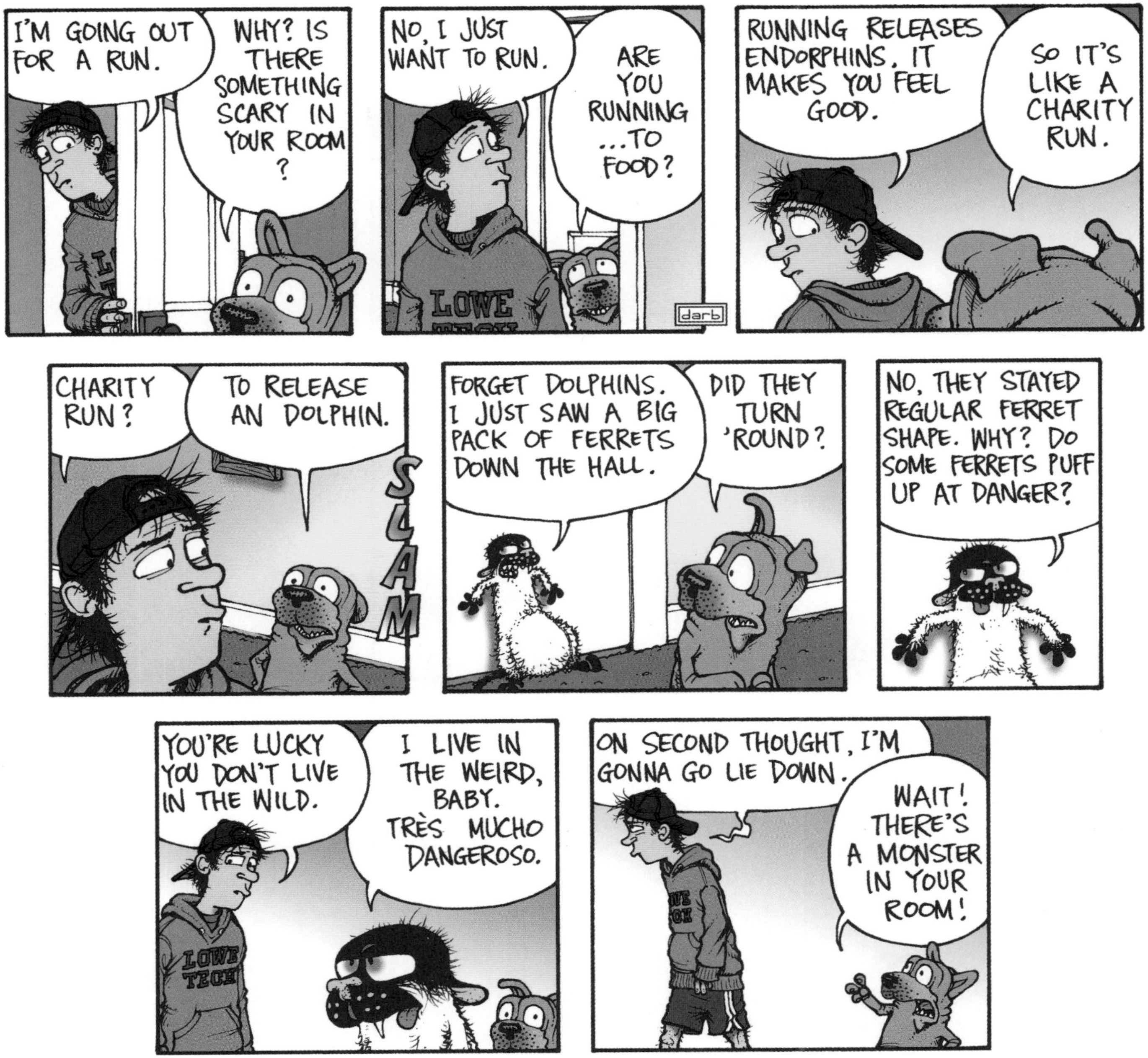
I'M GOING OUT FOR A RUN.
WHY? IS THERE SOMETHING SCARY IN YOUR ROOM?
NO, I JUST WANT TO RUN.
ARE YOU RUNNING ...TO FOOD?
RUNNING RELEASES ENDORPHINS. IT MAKES YOU FEEL GOOD.
SO IT'S LIKE A CHARITY RUN.
CHARITY RUN?
TO RELEASE AN DOLPHIN.
SLAM
FORGET DOLPHINS. I JUST SAW A BIG PACK OF FERRETS DOWN THE HALL.
DID THEY TURN 'ROUND?
NO, THEY STAYED REGULAR FERRET SHAPE. WHY? DO SOME FERRETS PUFF UP AT DANGER?
YOU'RE LUCKY YOU DON'T LIVE IN THE WILD.
I LIVE IN THE WEIRD, BABY. TRÈS MUCHO DANGEROSO.
ON SECOND THOUGHT, I'M GONNA GO LIE DOWN.
WAIT! THERE'S A MONSTER IN YOUR ROOM!

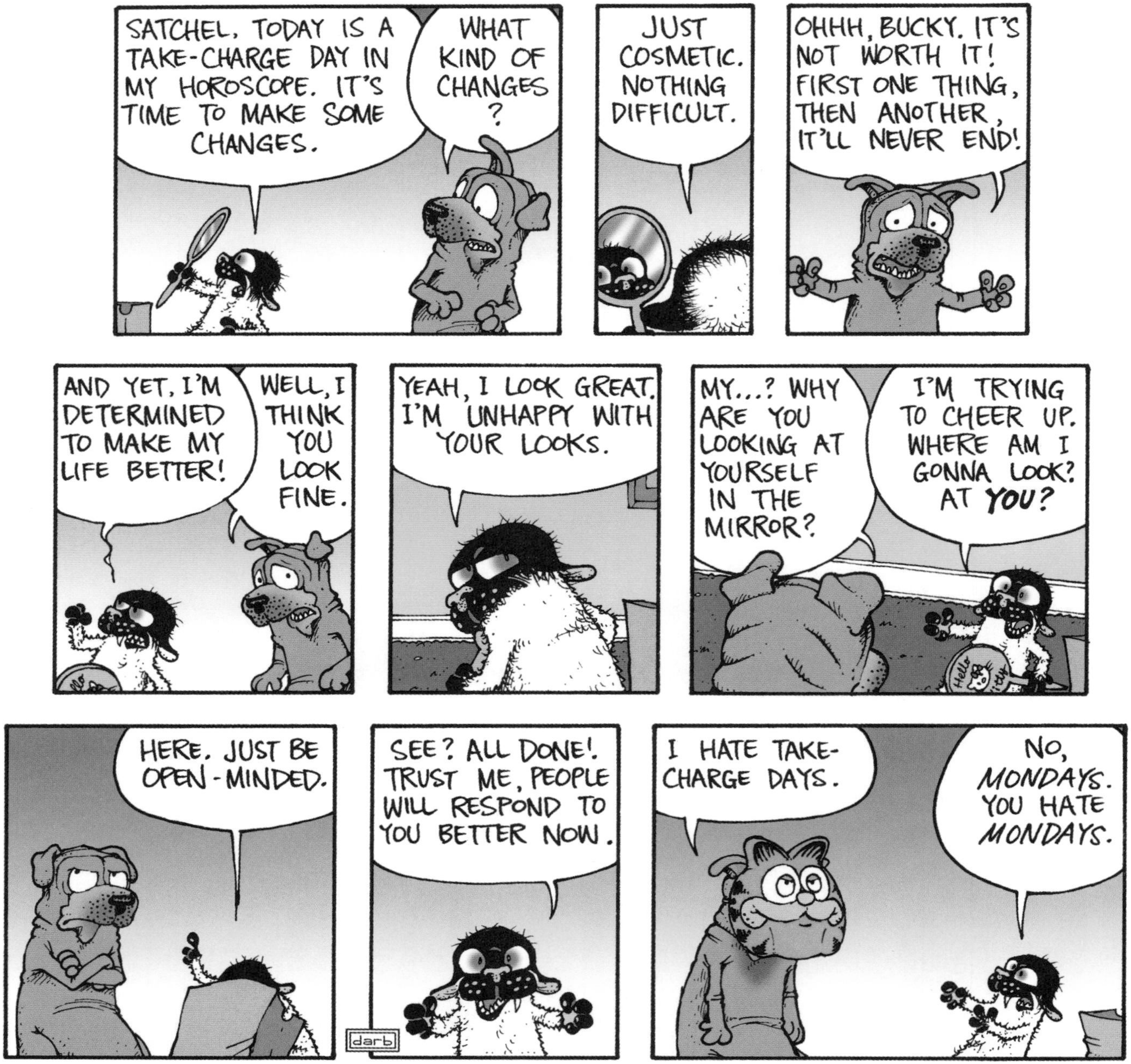
SATCHEL, TODAY IS A TAKE-CHARGE DAY IN MY HOROSCOPE. IT'S TIME TO MAKE SOME CHANGES.
WHAT KIND OF CHANGES?
JUST COSMETIC. NOTHING DIFFICULT.
OHHH, BUCKY. IT'S NOT WORTH IT! FIRST ONE THING, THEN ANOTHER, IT'LL NEVER END!
AND YET, I'M DETERMINED TO MAKE MY LIFE BETTER!
WELL, I THINK YOU LOOK FINE.
YEAH, I LOOK GREAT. I'M UNHAPPY WITH YOUR LOOKS.
MY...? WHY ARE YOU LOOKING AT YOURSELF IN THE MIRROR?
I'M TRYING TO CHEER UP. WHERE AM I GONNA LOOK? AT **YOU?**
HERE. JUST BE OPEN-MINDED.
darb
SEE? ALL DONE! TRUST ME, PEOPLE WILL RESPOND TO YOU BETTER NOW.
I HATE TAKE-CHARGE DAYS.
NO, *MONDAYS*. YOU HATE *MONDAYS*.

Panel 1: DID I HEAR A KNOCK? ROB'S IN THE SHOWER, I HAVE TO GET HIS FOOD.

I TOOK CARE OF IT.

Panel 2: OH... THANKS. WHERE IS IT?

I HAVE KINDLY STACKED TODAY'S DELIVERIES IN REVERSE CHRONOLOGIC ORDER.

Panel 3: AWW! YOU PUT DUMBBELLS ON ROB'S CHINESE FOOD? THAT'S WANTON DESTRUCTION!

Panel 4: I BELIEVE IT'S PRONOUNCED "*WONTON* DESTRUCTION."

ANYWAY, IT'S A PHILOSOPHICAL EXERCISE. I PROVED I HAVE FREE WILL.

darb

BUYCEPS

Panel 5: HAVING FREE WILL MEANS YOU ALSO HAVE THE FREEDOM TO *NOT*. ALL DOGS HAVE FREE WON'T.

AND ALL DOGS ARE DROOLING TOOLS.

Panel 6: I CHOOSE TO EXERCISE FREE WON'T AND NOT GET MAD.

I CHOOSE TO EXERCISE FREE MUSTARD SAUCE.

SOUND of SAUCE!

Panel 7: DEEP BREATH. I LOVE PEACE. AND A WISE WOMAN ONCE SAID *YOU BECOME THAT WHICH YOU LOVE.*

Panel 8: I THINK MY FREE WILL IS ABOUT TO DETERMINE THAT YOU LOVE PLUM SAUCE, TOO.

I'M STARTING TO GET A LITTLE FREE MAYBE-THE-*@#%-I-WILL AFTER ALL.

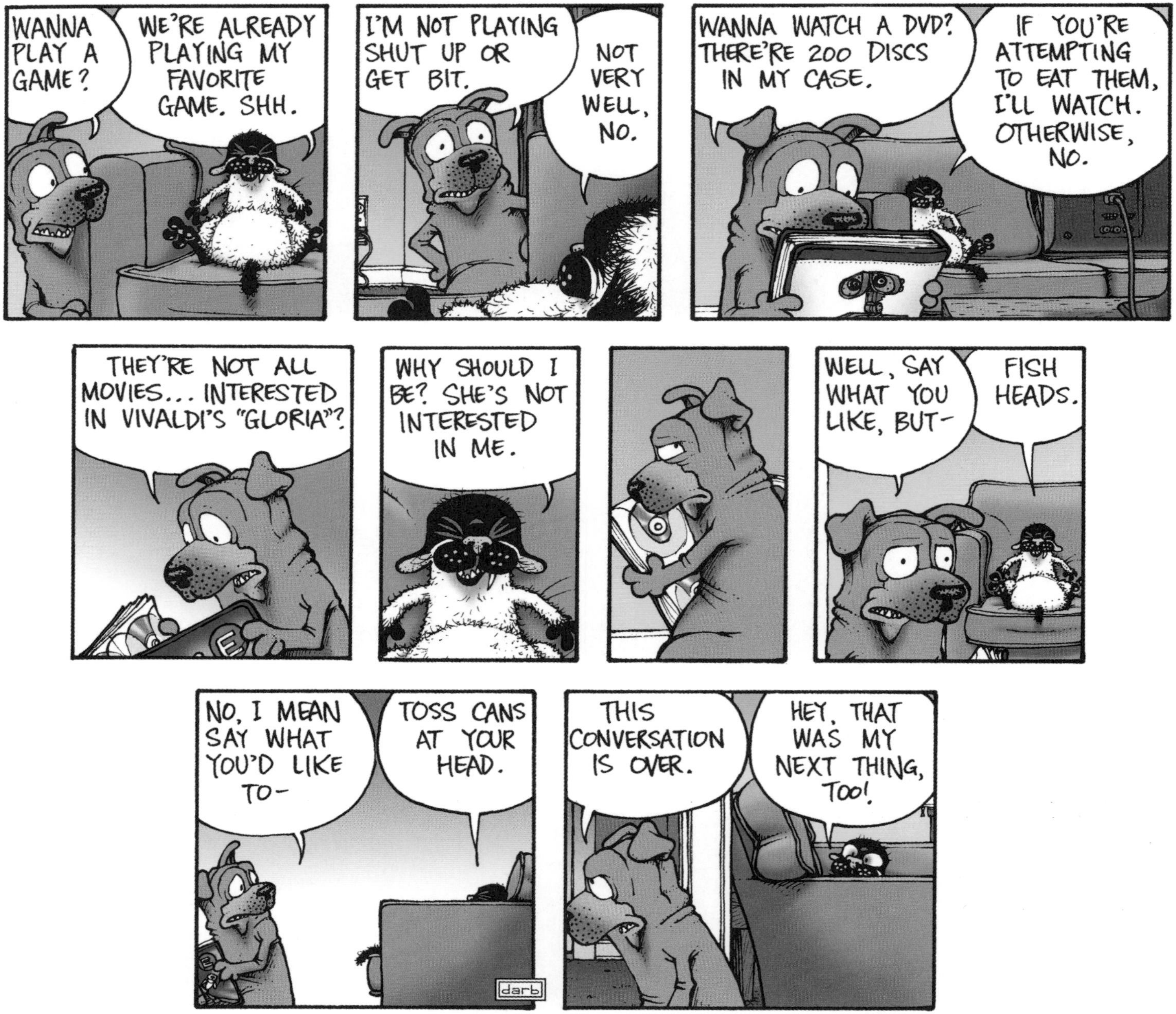
WANNA PLAY A GAME?
WE'RE ALREADY PLAYING MY FAVORITE GAME. SHH.
I'M NOT PLAYING SHUT UP OR GET BIT.
NOT VERY WELL, NO.
WANNA WATCH A DVD? THERE'RE 200 DISCS IN MY CASE.
IF YOU'RE ATTEMPTING TO EAT THEM, I'LL WATCH. OTHERWISE, NO.
THEY'RE NOT ALL MOVIES... INTERESTED IN VIVALDI'S "GLORIA"?
WHY SHOULD I BE? SHE'S NOT INTERESTED IN ME.
WELL, SAY WHAT YOU LIKE, BUT-
FISH HEADS.
NO, I MEAN SAY WHAT YOU'D LIKE TO-
TOSS CANS AT YOUR HEAD.
darb
THIS CONVERSATION IS OVER.
HEY, THAT WAS MY NEXT THING, TOO!

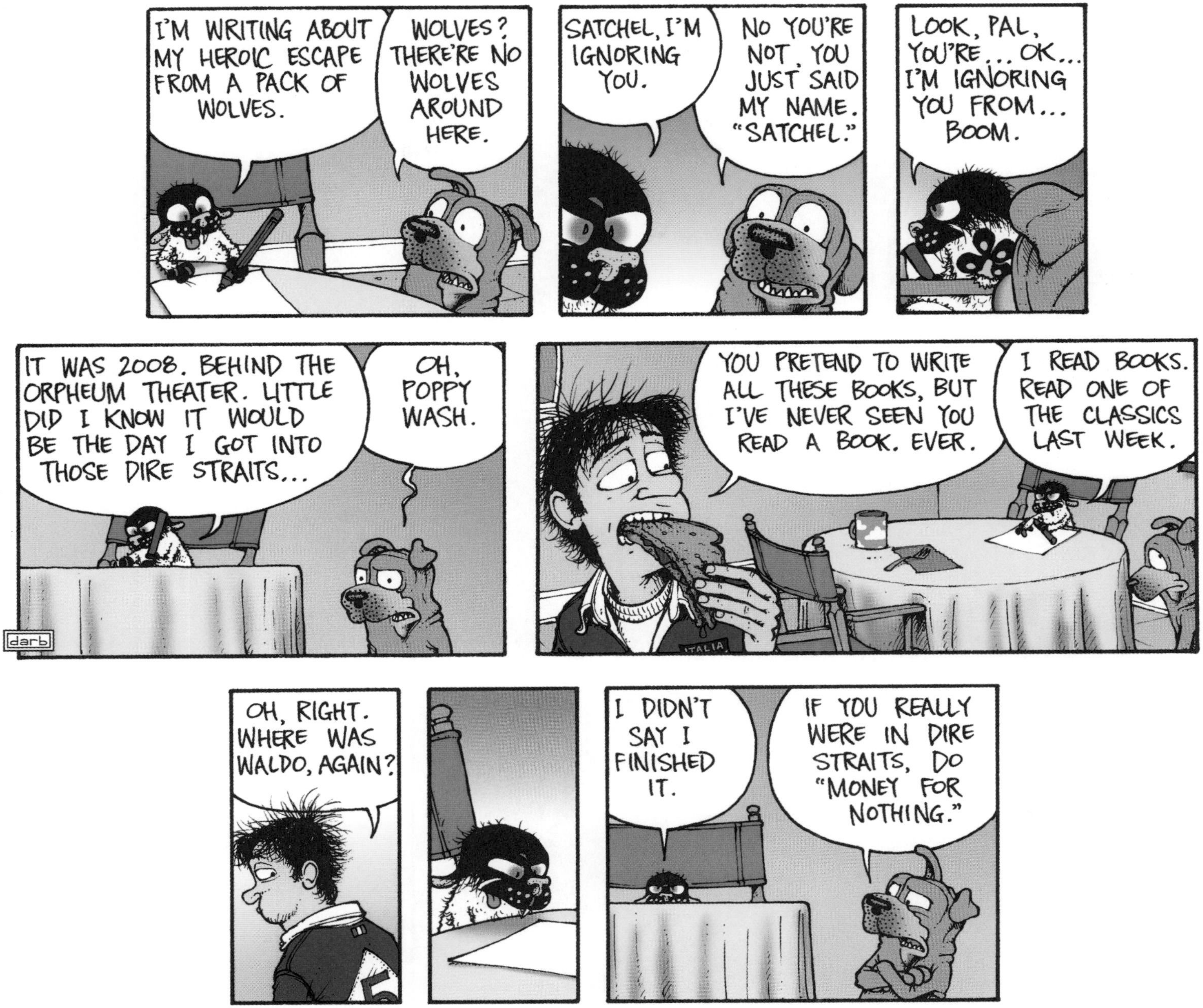
I'M WRITING ABOUT MY HEROIC ESCAPE FROM A PACK OF WOLVES.
WOLVES? THERE'RE NO WOLVES AROUND HERE.
SATCHEL, I'M IGNORING YOU.
NO YOU'RE NOT, YOU JUST SAID MY NAME. "SATCHEL."
LOOK, PAL, YOU'RE... OK... I'M IGNORING YOU FROM... BOOM.
IT WAS 2008. BEHIND THE ORPHEUM THEATER. LITTLE DID I KNOW IT WOULD BE THE DAY I GOT INTO THOSE DIRE STRAITS...
OH, POPPY WASH.
darb
YOU PRETEND TO WRITE ALL THESE BOOKS, BUT I'VE NEVER SEEN YOU READ A BOOK. EVER.
I READ BOOKS. READ ONE OF THE CLASSICS LAST WEEK.
ITALIA
OH, RIGHT. WHERE WAS WALDO, AGAIN?
I DIDN'T SAY I FINISHED IT.
IF YOU REALLY WERE IN DIRE STRAITS, DO "MONEY FOR NOTHING."

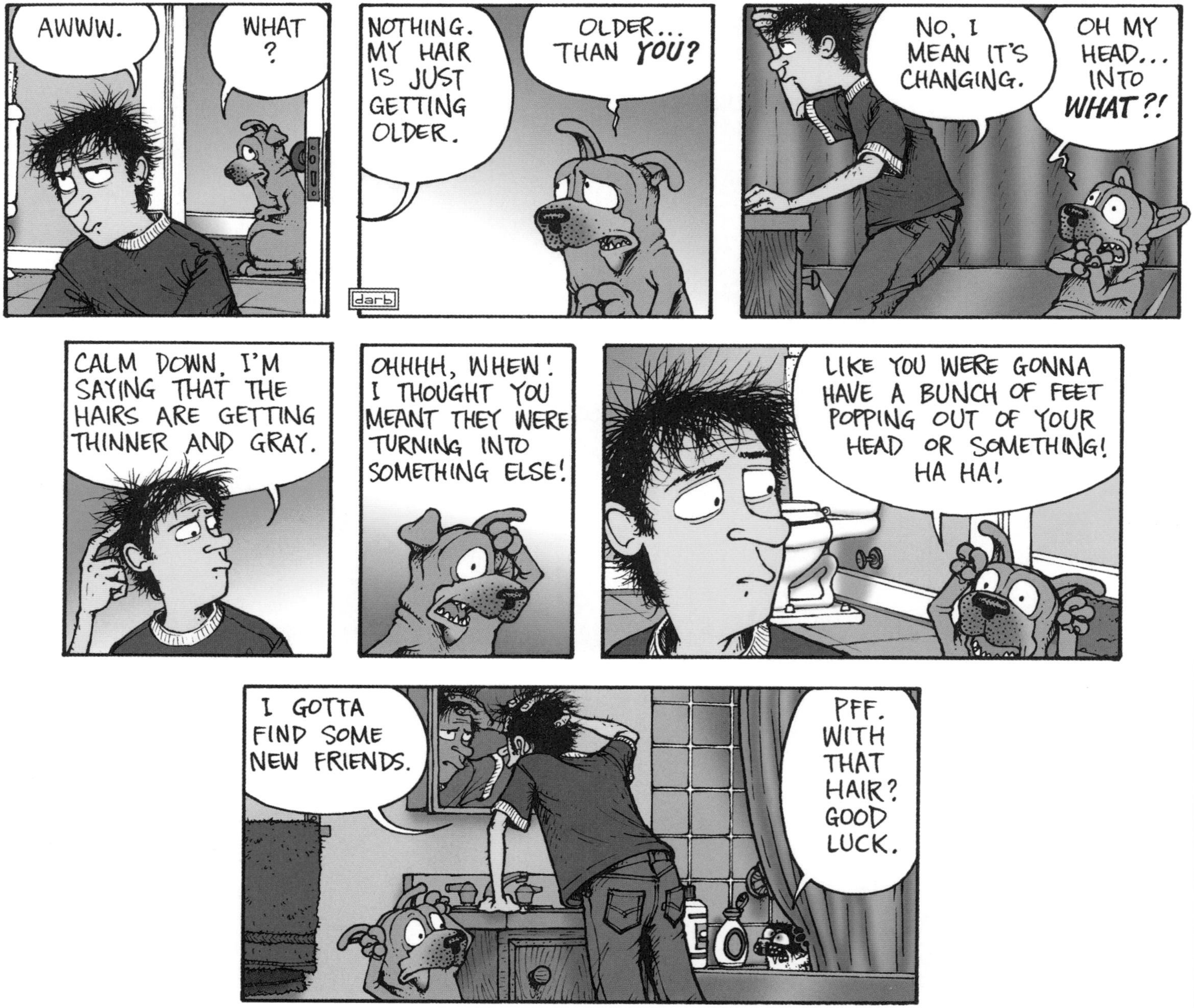
AWWW.
WHAT?
NOTHING. MY HAIR IS JUST GETTING OLDER.
OLDER... THAN YOU?
darb
NO, I MEAN IT'S CHANGING.
OH MY HEAD... INTO WHAT?!
CALM DOWN. I'M SAYING THAT THE HAIRS ARE GETTING THINNER AND GRAY.
OHHHH, WHEW! I THOUGHT YOU MEANT THEY WERE TURNING INTO SOMETHING ELSE!
LIKE YOU WERE GONNA HAVE A BUNCH OF FEET POPPING OUT OF YOUR HEAD OR SOMETHING! HA HA!
I GOTTA FIND SOME NEW FRIENDS.
PFF. WITH THAT HAIR? GOOD LUCK.

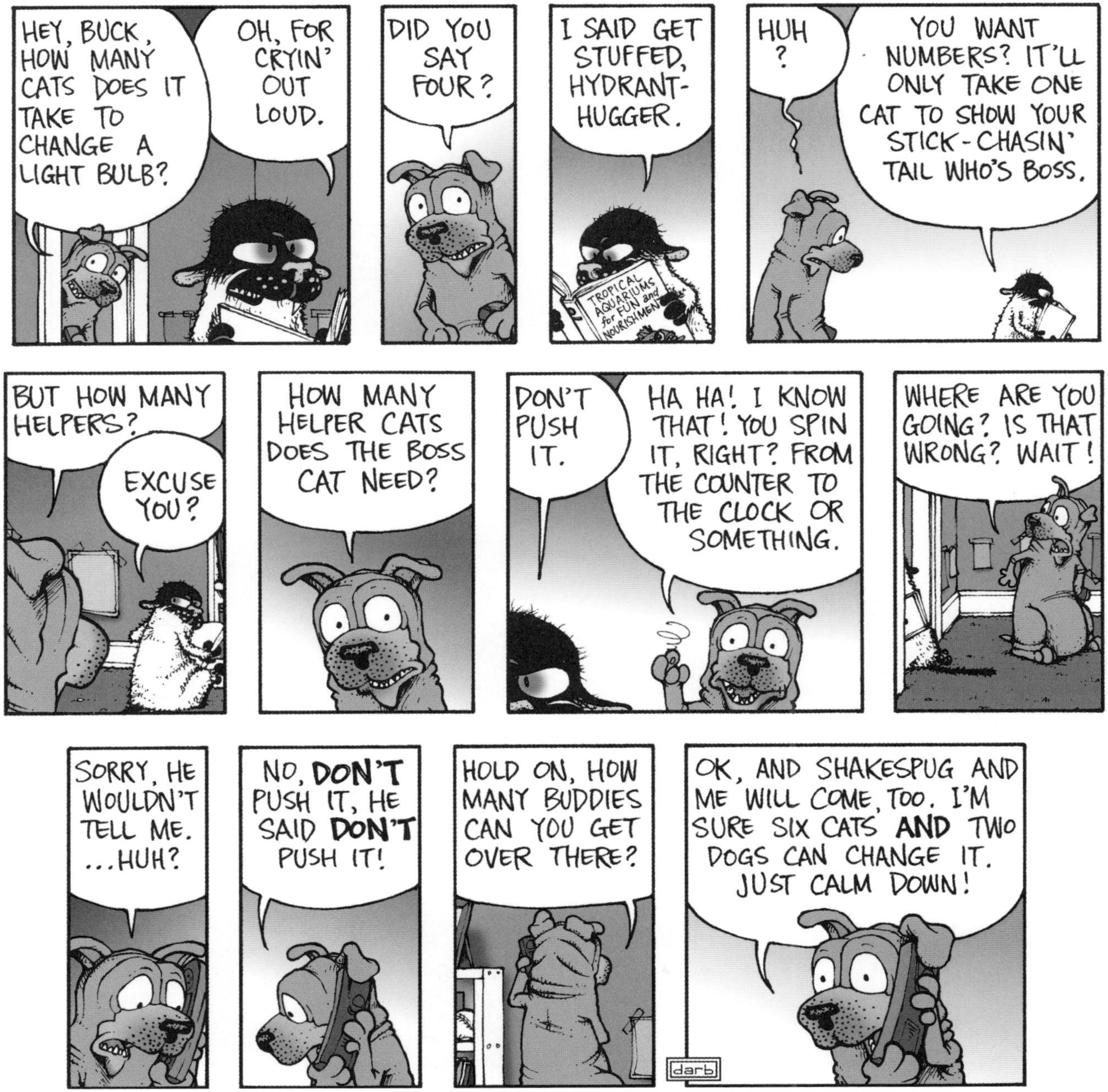
HEY, BUCK, HOW MANY CATS DOES IT TAKE TO CHANGE A LIGHT BULB?
OH, FOR CRYIN' OUT LOUD.
DID YOU SAY FOUR?
I SAID GET STUFFED, HYDRANT-HUGGER.
TROPICAL AQUARIUMS for FUN and NOURISHMENT
HUH?
YOU WANT NUMBERS? IT'LL ONLY TAKE ONE CAT TO SHOW YOUR STICK-CHASIN' TAIL WHO'S BOSS.
BUT HOW MANY HELPERS?
EXCUSE YOU?
HOW MANY HELPER CATS DOES THE BOSS CAT NEED?
DON'T PUSH IT.
HA HA! I KNOW THAT! YOU SPIN IT, RIGHT? FROM THE COUNTER TO THE CLOCK OR SOMETHING.
WHERE ARE YOU GOING? IS THAT WRONG? WAIT!
SORRY, HE WOULDN'T TELL ME. ...HUH?
NO, **DON'T** PUSH IT, HE SAID **DON'T** PUSH IT!
HOLD ON, HOW MANY BUDDIES CAN YOU GET OVER THERE?
darb
OK, AND SHAKESPUG AND ME WILL COME, TOO. I'M SURE SIX CATS **AND** TWO DOGS CAN CHANGE IT. JUST CALM DOWN!

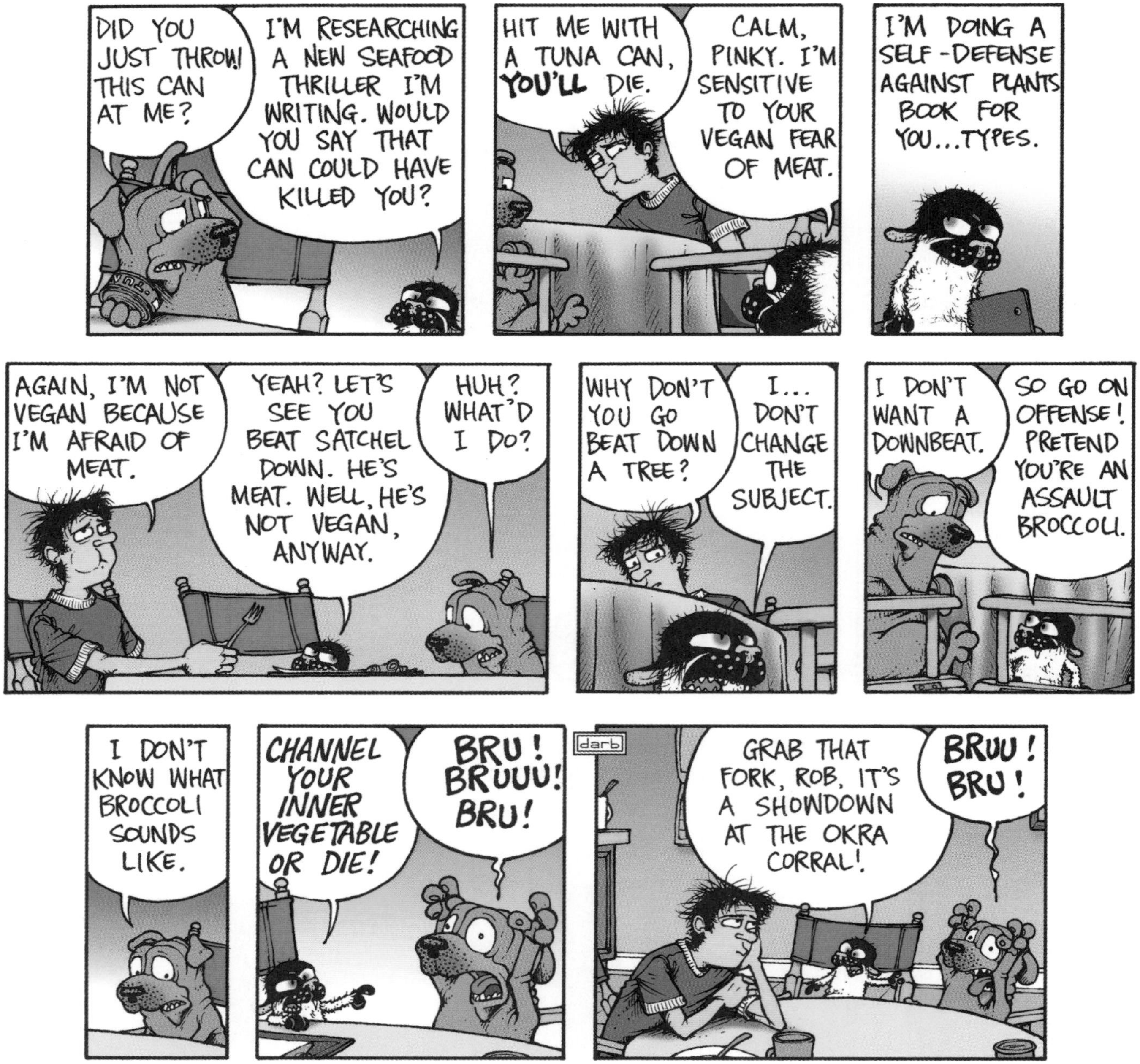

DID YOU JUST THROW THIS CAN AT ME?
I'M RESEARCHING A NEW SEAFOOD THRILLER I'M WRITING. WOULD YOU SAY THAT CAN COULD HAVE KILLED YOU?
HIT ME WITH A TUNA CAN, YOU'LL DIE.
CALM, PINKY. I'M SENSITIVE TO YOUR VEGAN FEAR OF MEAT.
I'M DOING A SELF-DEFENSE AGAINST PLANTS BOOK FOR YOU...TYPES.
AGAIN, I'M NOT VEGAN BECAUSE I'M AFRAID OF MEAT.
YEAH? LET'S SEE YOU BEAT SATCHEL DOWN. HE'S MEAT. WELL, HE'S NOT VEGAN, ANYWAY.
HUH? WHAT'D I DO?
WHY DON'T YOU GO BEAT DOWN A TREE?
I... DON'T CHANGE THE SUBJECT.
I DON'T WANT A DOWNBEAT.
SO GO ON OFFENSE! PRETEND YOU'RE AN ASSAULT BROCCOLI.
I DON'T KNOW WHAT BROCCOLI SOUNDS LIKE.
CHANNEL YOUR INNER VEGETABLE OR DIE!
BRU! BRUUU! BRU!
darb
GRAB THAT FORK, ROB, IT'S A SHOWDOWN AT THE OKRA CORRAL!
BRUU! BRU!

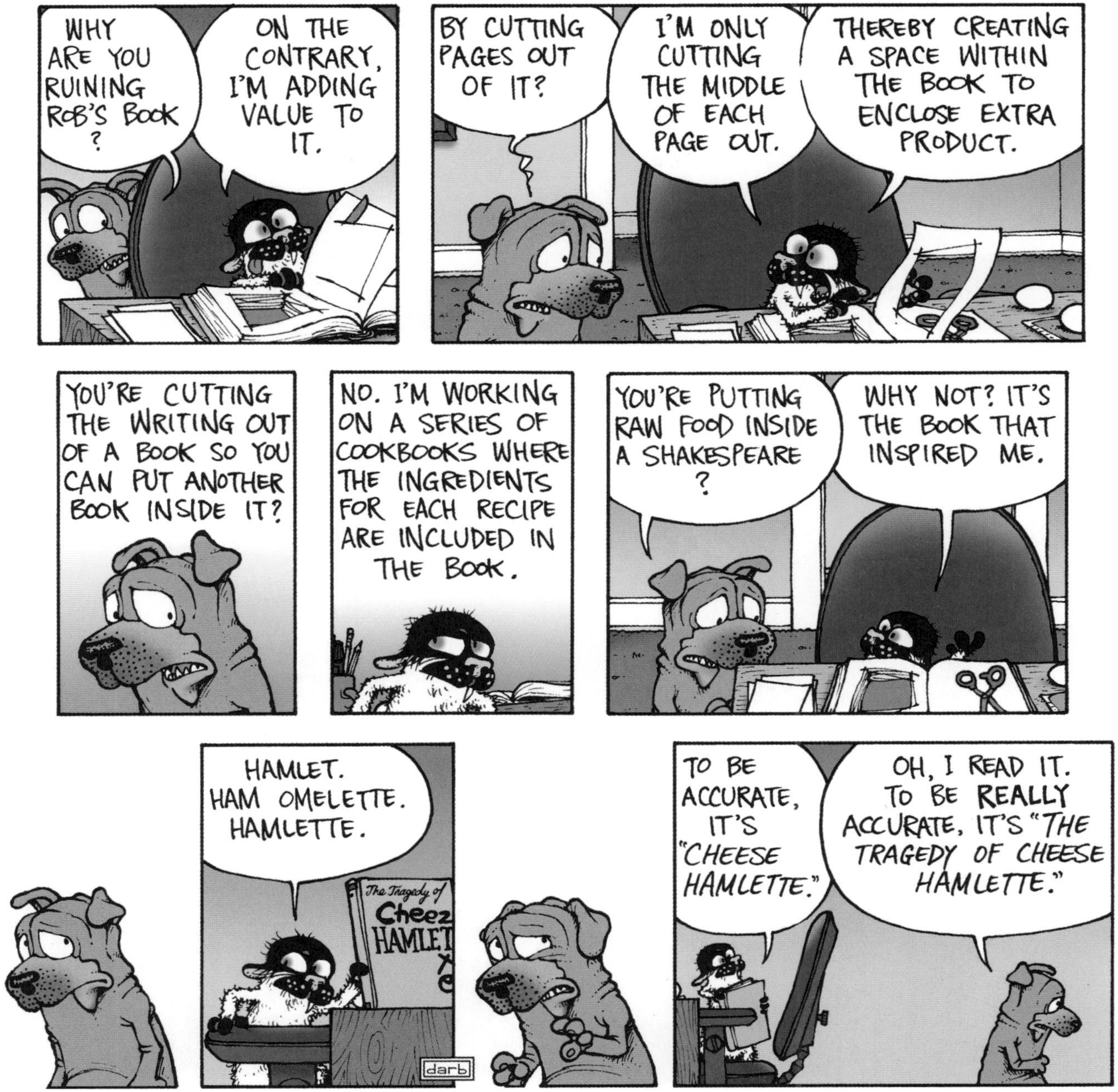
WHY ARE YOU RUINING ROB'S BOOK ?
ON THE CONTRARY, I'M ADDING VALUE TO IT.
BY CUTTING PAGES OUT OF IT?
I'M ONLY CUTTING THE MIDDLE OF EACH PAGE OUT.
THEREBY CREATING A SPACE WITHIN THE BOOK TO ENCLOSE EXTRA PRODUCT.
YOU'RE CUTTING THE WRITING OUT OF A BOOK SO YOU CAN PUT ANOTHER BOOK INSIDE IT?
NO. I'M WORKING ON A SERIES OF COOKBOOKS WHERE THE INGREDIENTS FOR EACH RECIPE ARE INCLUDED IN THE BOOK.
YOU'RE PUTTING RAW FOOD INSIDE A SHAKESPEARE ?
WHY NOT? IT'S THE BOOK THAT INSPIRED ME.
HAMLET. HAM OMELETTE. HAMLETTE.
The Tragedy of Cheez HAMLET
darb
TO BE ACCURATE, IT'S "CHEESE HAMLETTE."
OH, I READ IT. TO BE **REALLY** ACCURATE, IT'S "*THE TRAGEDY OF CHEESE HAMLETTE.*"

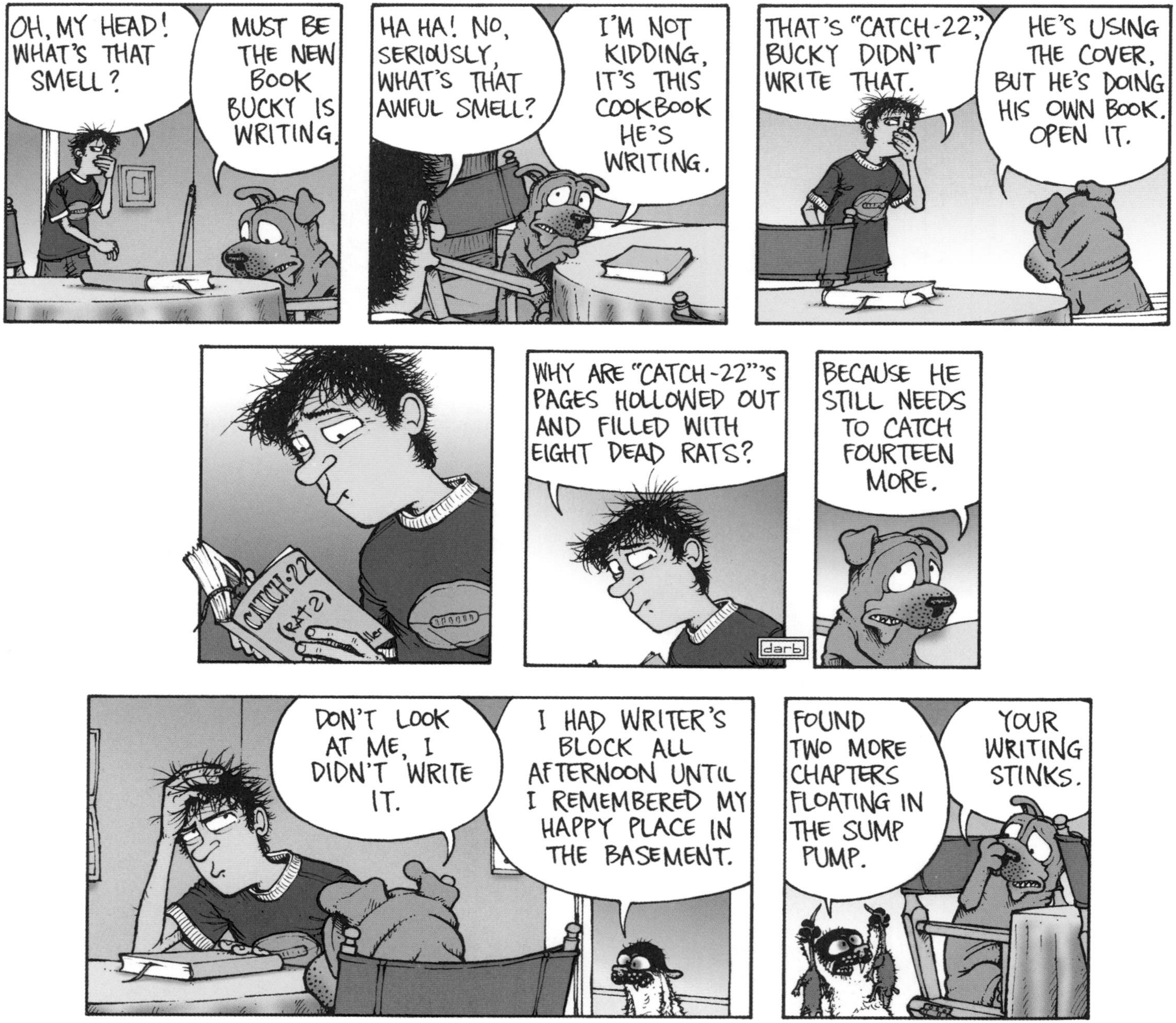
OH, MY HEAD! WHAT'S THAT SMELL?
MUST BE THE NEW BOOK BUCKY IS WRITING.
HA HA! NO, SERIOUSLY, WHAT'S THAT AWFUL SMELL?
I'M NOT KIDDING, IT'S THIS COOKBOOK HE'S WRITING.
THAT'S "CATCH-22," BUCKY DIDN'T WRITE THAT.
HE'S USING THE COVER, BUT HE'S DOING HIS OWN BOOK. OPEN IT.
CATCH-22
WHY ARE "CATCH-22"'s PAGES HOLLOWED OUT AND FILLED WITH EIGHT DEAD RATS?
darb
BECAUSE HE STILL NEEDS TO CATCH FOURTEEN MORE.
DON'T LOOK AT ME, I DIDN'T WRITE IT.
I HAD WRITER'S BLOCK ALL AFTERNOON UNTIL I REMEMBERED MY HAPPY PLACE IN THE BASEMENT.
FOUND TWO MORE CHAPTERS FLOATING IN THE SUMP PUMP.
YOUR WRITING STINKS.

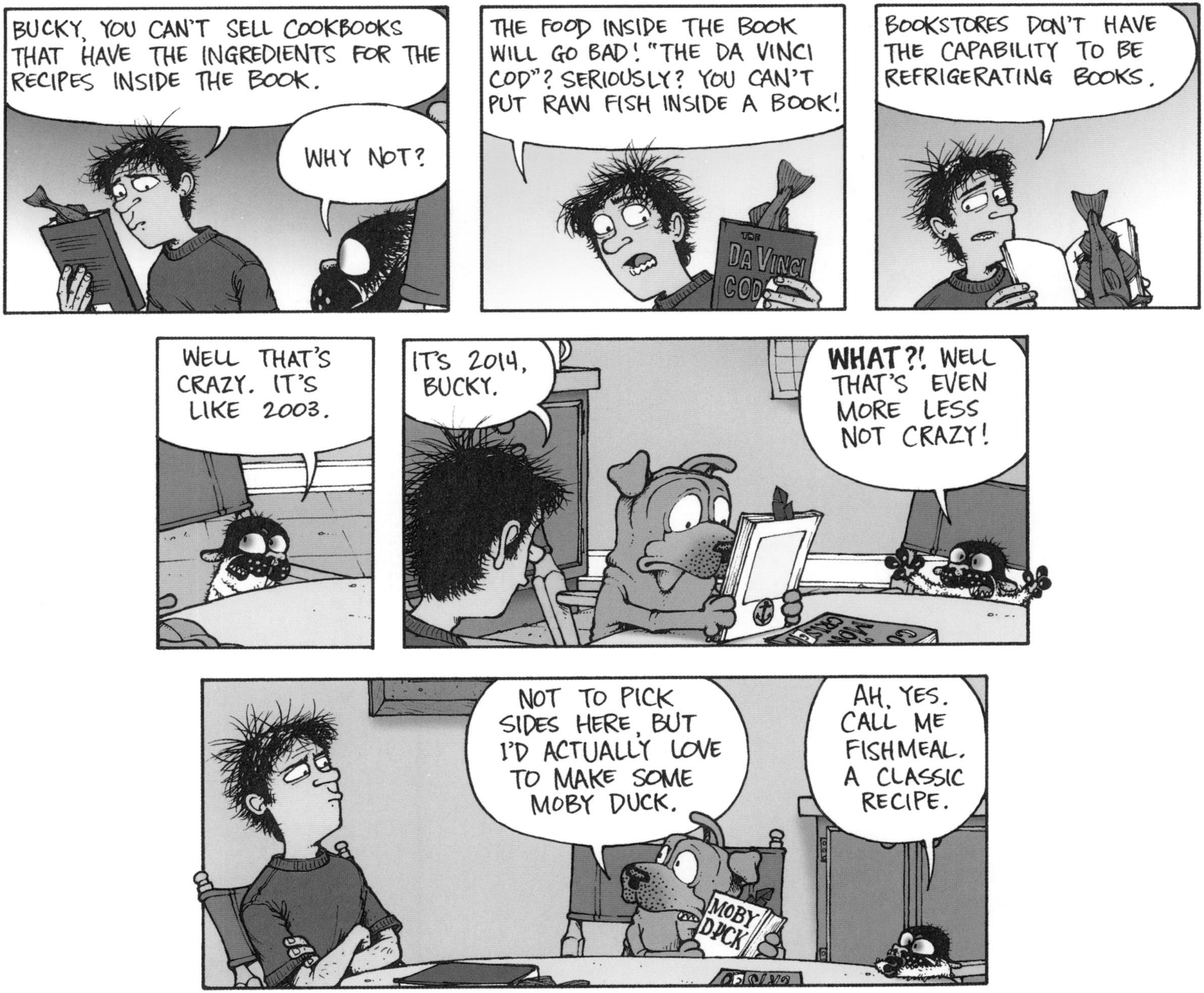
BUCKY, YOU CAN'T SELL COOKBOOKS THAT HAVE THE INGREDIENTS FOR THE RECIPES INSIDE THE BOOK.
WHY NOT?
THE FOOD INSIDE THE BOOK WILL GO BAD! "THE DA VINCI COD"? SERIOUSLY? YOU CAN'T PUT RAW FISH INSIDE A BOOK!
THE DA VINCI COD
BOOKSTORES DON'T HAVE THE CAPABILITY TO BE REFRIGERATING BOOKS.
WELL THAT'S CRAZY. IT'S LIKE 2003.
IT'S 2014, BUCKY.
WHAT?! WELL THAT'S EVEN MORE LESS NOT CRAZY!
NOT TO PICK SIDES HERE, BUT I'D ACTUALLY LOVE TO MAKE SOME MOBY DUCK.
AH, YES. CALL ME FISHMEAL. A CLASSIC RECIPE.
MOBY DUCK

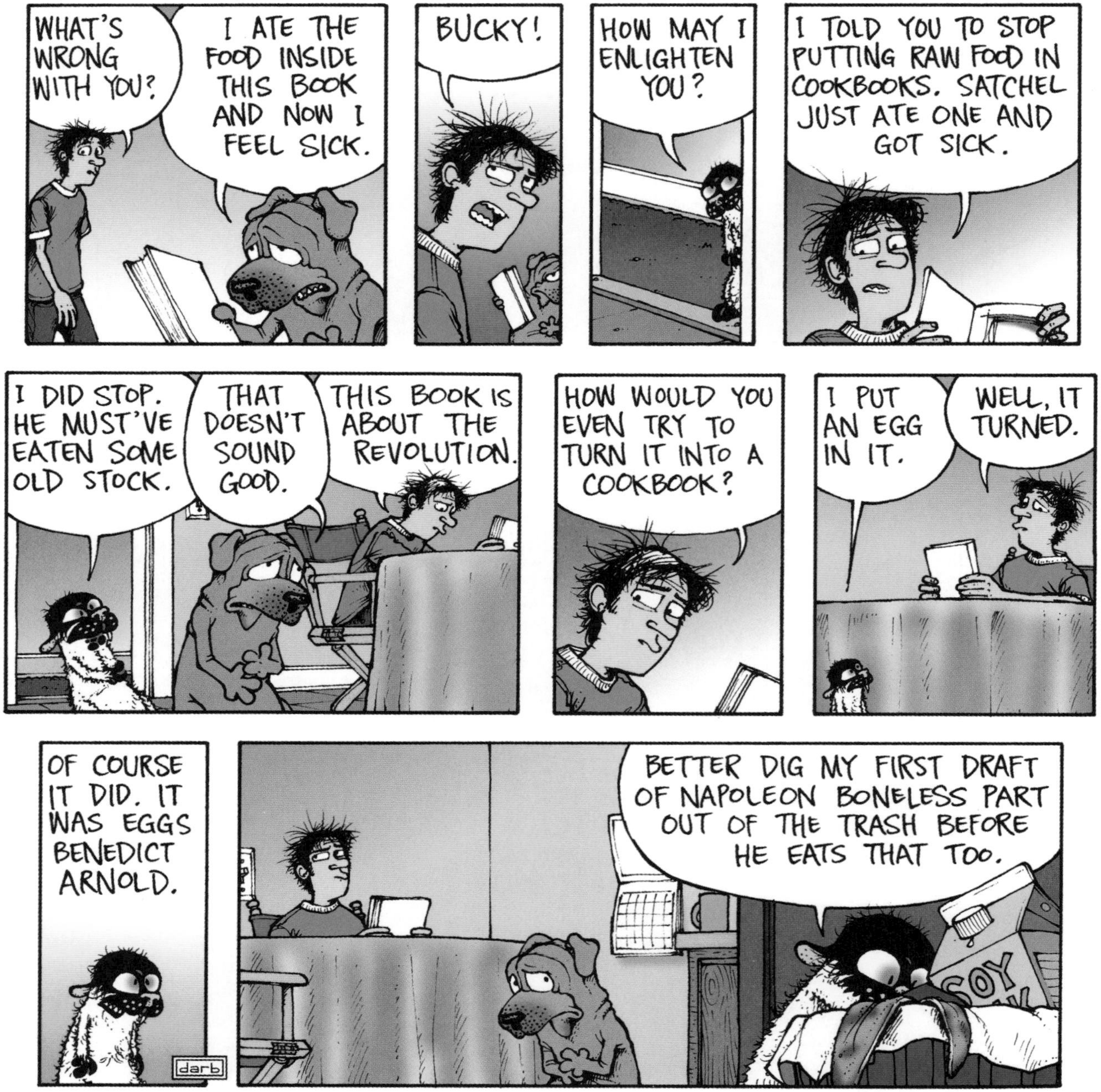
WHAT'S WRONG WITH YOU?
I ATE THE FOOD INSIDE THIS BOOK AND NOW I FEEL SICK.
BUCKY!
HOW MAY I ENLIGHTEN YOU?
I TOLD YOU TO STOP PUTTING RAW FOOD IN COOKBOOKS. SATCHEL JUST ATE ONE AND GOT SICK.
I DID STOP. HE MUST'VE EATEN SOME OLD STOCK.
THAT DOESN'T SOUND GOOD.
THIS BOOK IS ABOUT THE REVOLUTION.
HOW WOULD YOU EVEN TRY TO TURN IT INTO A COOKBOOK?
I PUT AN EGG IN IT.
WELL, IT TURNED.
OF COURSE IT DID. IT WAS EGGS BENEDICT ARNOLD.
BETTER DIG MY FIRST DRAFT OF NAPOLEON BONELESS PART OUT OF THE TRASH BEFORE HE EATS THAT TOO.
SOY
darb

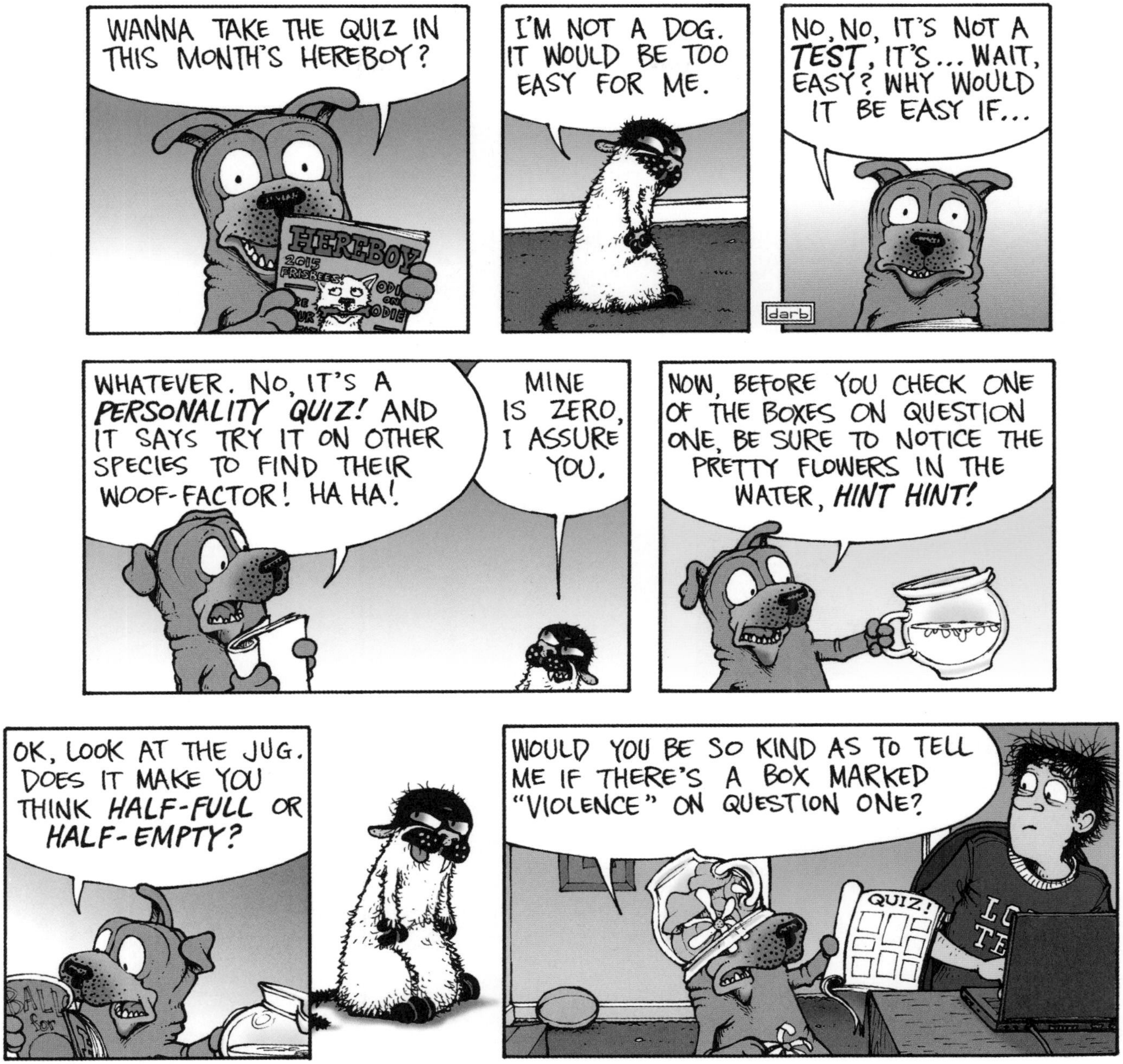
WANNA TAKE THE QUIZ IN THIS MONTH'S HEREBOY?
HEREBOY
I'M NOT A DOG. IT WOULD BE TOO EASY FOR ME.
NO, NO, IT'S NOT A ***TEST***, IT'S... WAIT, EASY? WHY WOULD IT BE EASY IF...
WHATEVER. NO, IT'S A ***PERSONALITY QUIZ!*** AND IT SAYS TRY IT ON OTHER SPECIES TO FIND THEIR WOOF-FACTOR! HA HA!
MINE IS ZERO, I ASSURE YOU.
NOW, BEFORE YOU CHECK ONE OF THE BOXES ON QUESTION ONE, BE SURE TO NOTICE THE PRETTY FLOWERS IN THE WATER, ***HINT HINT!***
OK, LOOK AT THE JUG. DOES IT MAKE YOU THINK ***HALF-FULL*** OR ***HALF-EMPTY?***
WOULD YOU BE SO KIND AS TO TELL ME IF THERE'S A BOX MARKED "VIOLENCE" ON QUESTION ONE?
QUIZ!

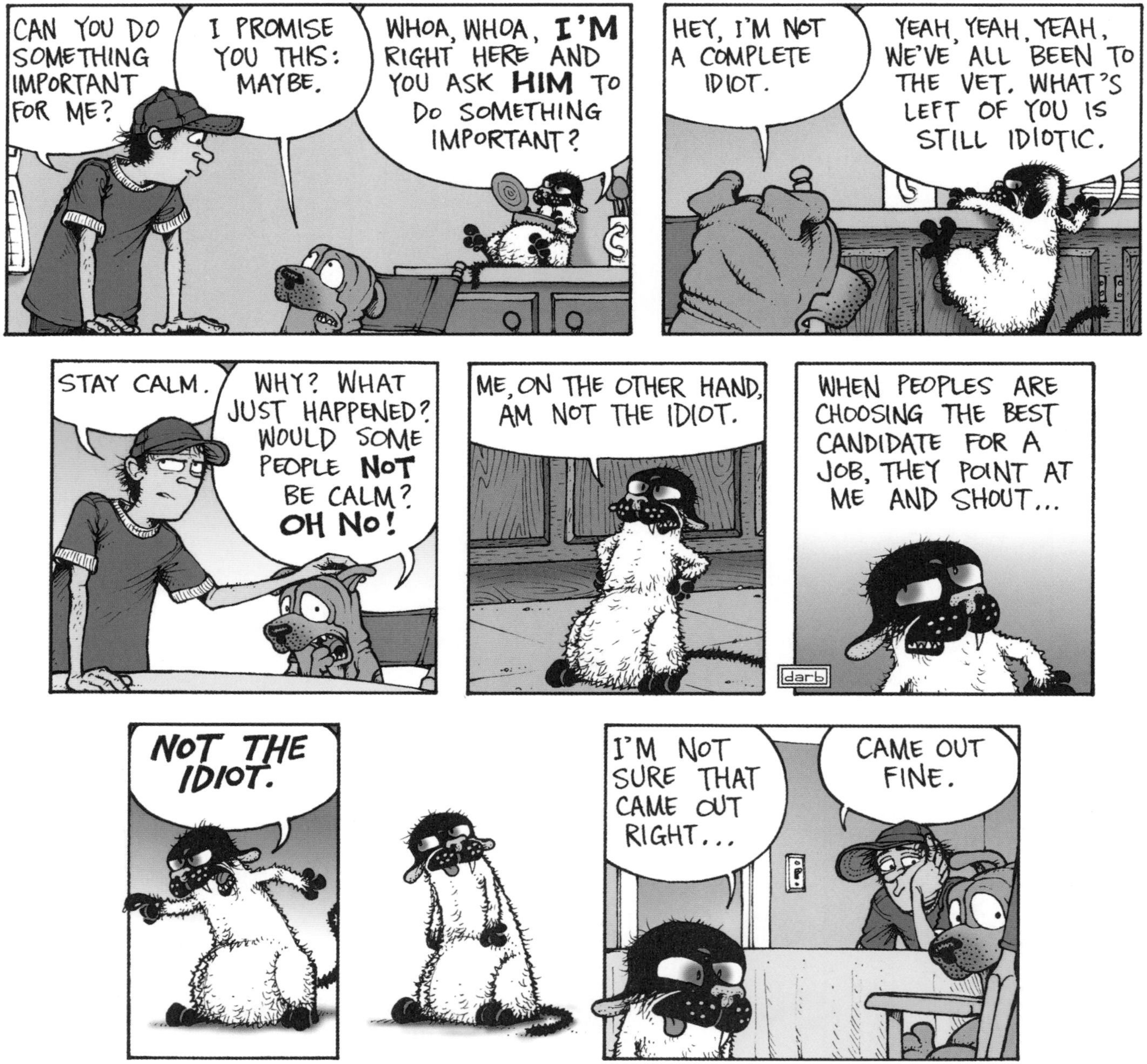
CAN YOU DO SOMETHING IMPORTANT FOR ME?
I PROMISE YOU THIS: MAYBE.
WHOA, WHOA, I'M RIGHT HERE AND YOU ASK HIM TO DO SOMETHING IMPORTANT?
HEY, I'M NOT A COMPLETE IDIOT.
YEAH, YEAH, YEAH, WE'VE ALL BEEN TO THE VET. WHAT'S LEFT OF YOU IS STILL IDIOTIC.
STAY CALM.
WHY? WHAT JUST HAPPENED? WOULD SOME PEOPLE NOT BE CALM? OH NO!
ME, ON THE OTHER HAND, AM NOT THE IDIOT.
WHEN PEOPLES ARE CHOOSING THE BEST CANDIDATE FOR A JOB, THEY POINT AT ME AND SHOUT...
darb
NOT THE IDIOT.
I'M NOT SURE THAT CAME OUT RIGHT...
CAME OUT FINE.

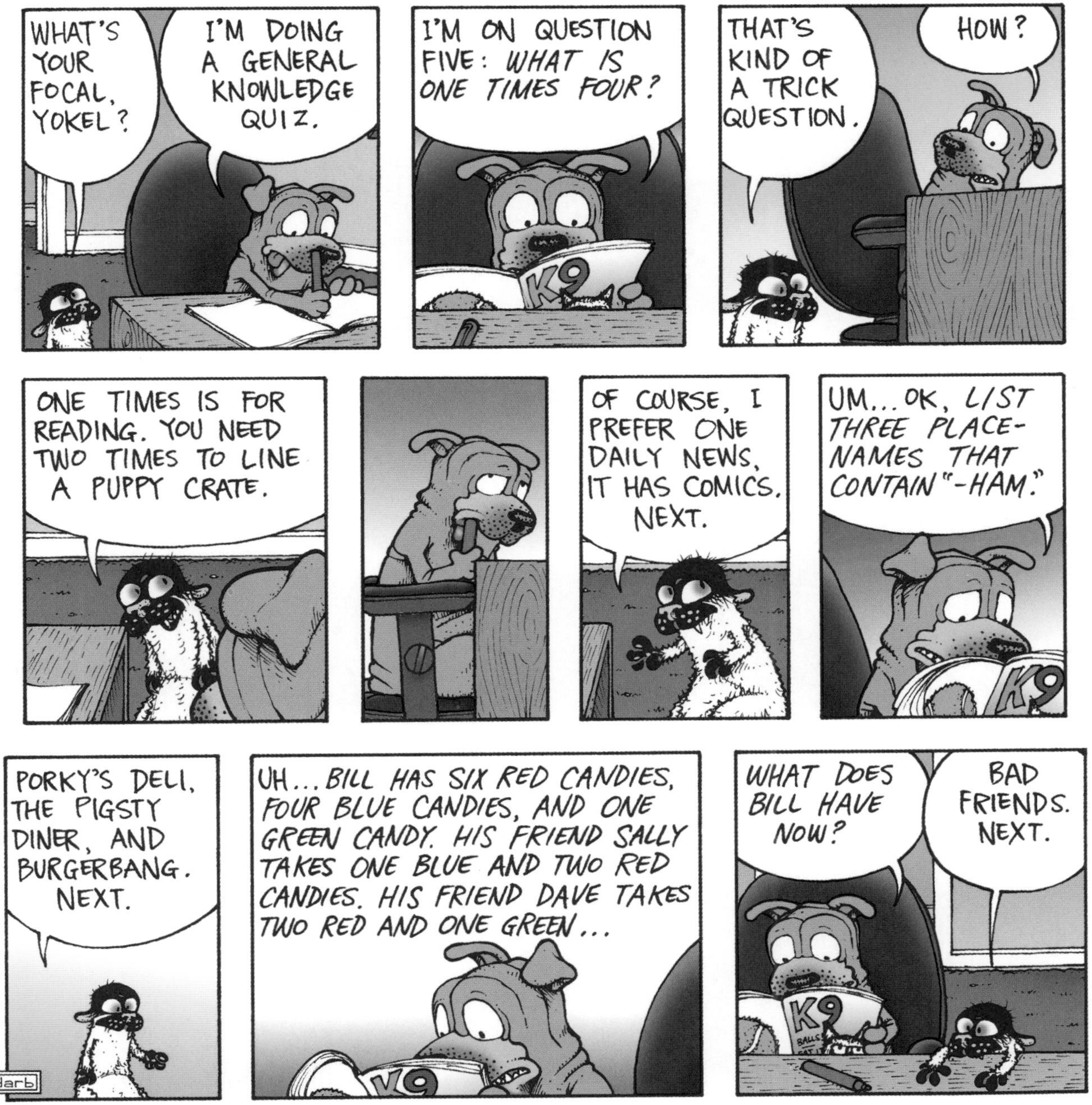
WHAT'S YOUR FOCAL, YOKEL?
I'M DOING A GENERAL KNOWLEDGE QUIZ.
I'M ON QUESTION FIVE: *WHAT IS ONE TIMES FOUR?*
THAT'S KIND OF A TRICK QUESTION.
HOW?
ONE TIMES IS FOR READING. YOU NEED TWO TIMES TO LINE A PUPPY CRATE.
OF COURSE, I PREFER ONE DAILY NEWS, IT HAS COMICS. NEXT.
UM... OK, *LIST THREE PLACE-NAMES THAT CONTAIN "-HAM."*
K9
PORKY'S DELI, THE PIGSTY DINER, AND BURGERBANG. NEXT.
darb
UH... *BILL HAS SIX RED CANDIES, FOUR BLUE CANDIES, AND ONE GREEN CANDY. HIS FRIEND SALLY TAKES ONE BLUE AND TWO RED CANDIES. HIS FRIEND DAVE TAKES TWO RED AND ONE GREEN...*
WHAT DOES BILL HAVE NOW?
BAD FRIENDS. NEXT.

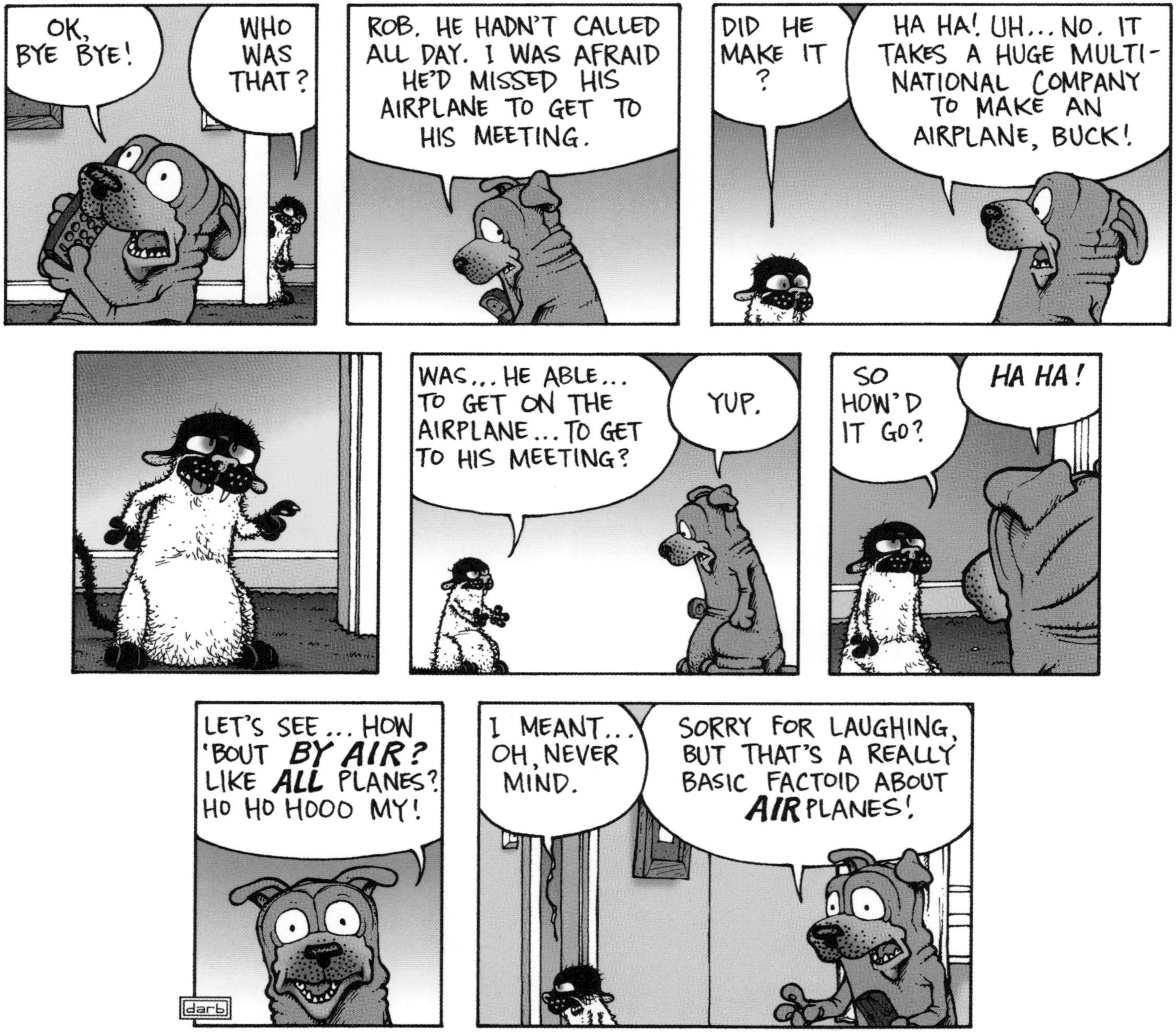
OK, BYE BYE!
WHO WAS THAT?
ROB. HE HADN'T CALLED ALL DAY. I WAS AFRAID HE'D MISSED HIS AIRPLANE TO GET TO HIS MEETING.
DID HE MAKE IT?
HA HA! UH... NO. IT TAKES A HUGE MULTI-NATIONAL COMPANY TO MAKE AN AIRPLANE, BUCK!
WAS... HE ABLE... TO GET ON THE AIRPLANE... TO GET TO HIS MEETING?
YUP.
SO HOW'D IT GO?
HA HA!
LET'S SEE... HOW 'BOUT BY AIR? LIKE ALL PLANES? HO HO HOOO MY!
darb
I MEANT... OH, NEVER MIND.
SORRY FOR LAUGHING, BUT THAT'S A REALLY BASIC FACTOID ABOUT AIRPLANES!

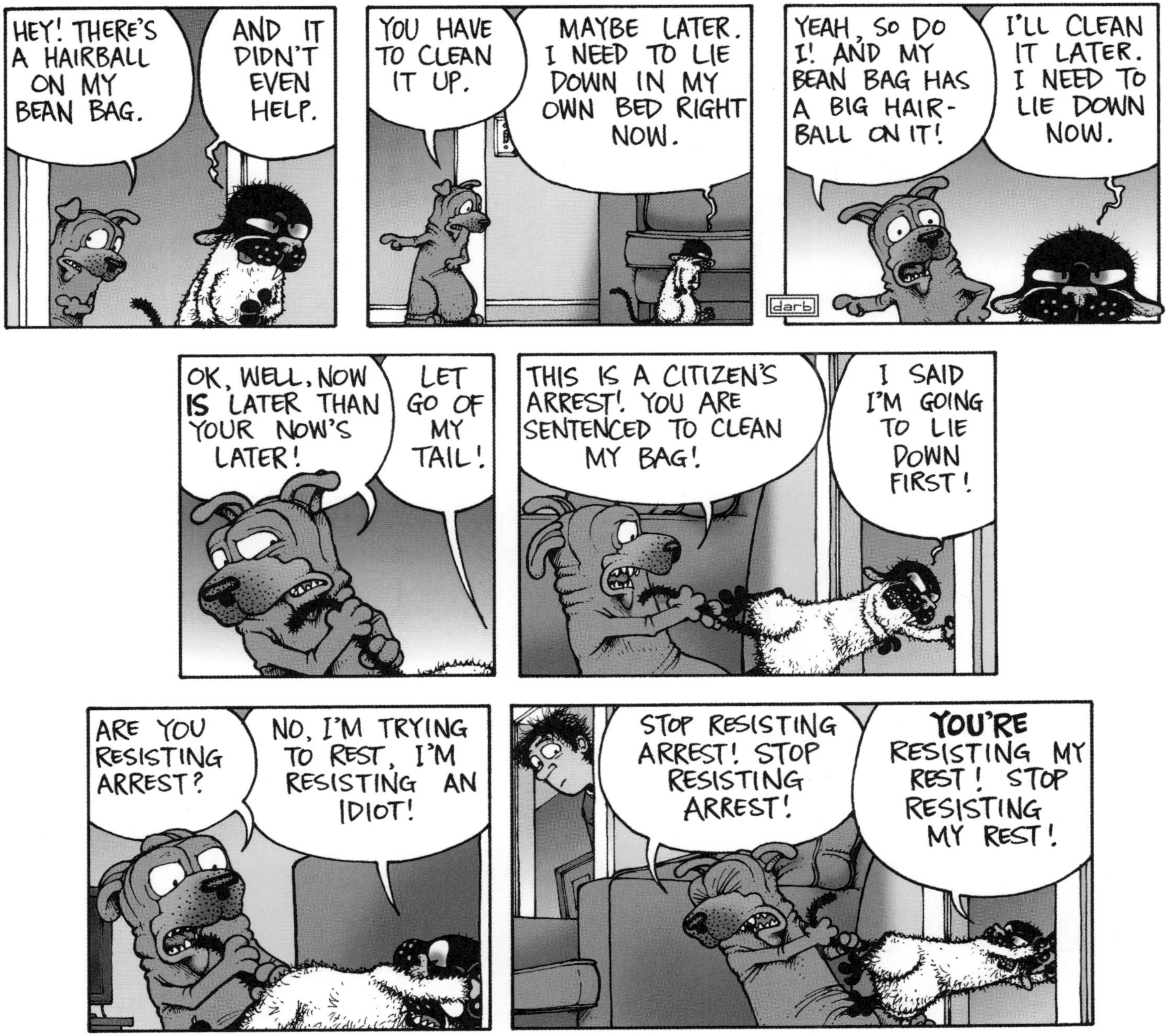
HEY! THERE'S A HAIRBALL ON MY BEAN BAG.
AND IT DIDN'T EVEN HELP.
YOU HAVE TO CLEAN IT UP.
MAYBE LATER. I NEED TO LIE DOWN IN MY OWN BED RIGHT NOW.
YEAH, SO DO I! AND MY BEAN BAG HAS A BIG HAIR-BALL ON IT!
I'LL CLEAN IT LATER. I NEED TO LIE DOWN NOW.
darb
OK, WELL, NOW **IS** LATER THAN YOUR NOW'S LATER!
LET GO OF MY TAIL!
THIS IS A CITIZEN'S ARREST! YOU ARE SENTENCED TO CLEAN MY BAG!
I SAID I'M GOING TO LIE DOWN FIRST!
ARE YOU RESISTING ARREST?
NO, I'M TRYING TO REST, I'M RESISTING AN IDIOT!
STOP RESISTING ARREST! STOP RESISTING ARREST!
YOU'RE RESISTING MY REST! STOP RESISTING MY REST!

MORNIN' ZZ. OR ARE YOU TOP? I ALWAYS FORGET.

I THINK I HAVE TO CALL IN SICK TODAY.

DID SATCHEL GET YOU SICK?

IT DOESN'T WORK LIKE THAT, BUCKY.

I KNOW. IT JUST SAID IT WAS CALLING IN SICK.

IT?

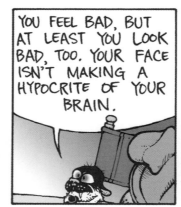

AT LEAST YOUR INSIDE IS CONSISTENT WITH YOUR OUTSIDE.

WHAT?

YOU FEEL BAD, BUT AT LEAST YOU LOOK BAD, TOO. YOUR FACE ISN'T MAKING A HYPOCRITE OF YOUR BRAIN.

AS THE CAR DEALERS SAY, YOUR SERIAL NUMBERS MATCH.

YOU MAY BE AN UNCLEAN SICKO, BUT AT LEAST YOU'RE NOT A LIAR.

IS THAT SUPPOSED TO BE SOME WEIRD GLASS HALF FULL PHILOSOPHY?

I PREFER THE EMPTY GLASS, YOU CAN'T GET FREE DRINKS IF YOUR GLASS IS ALREADY FULL, ROB.

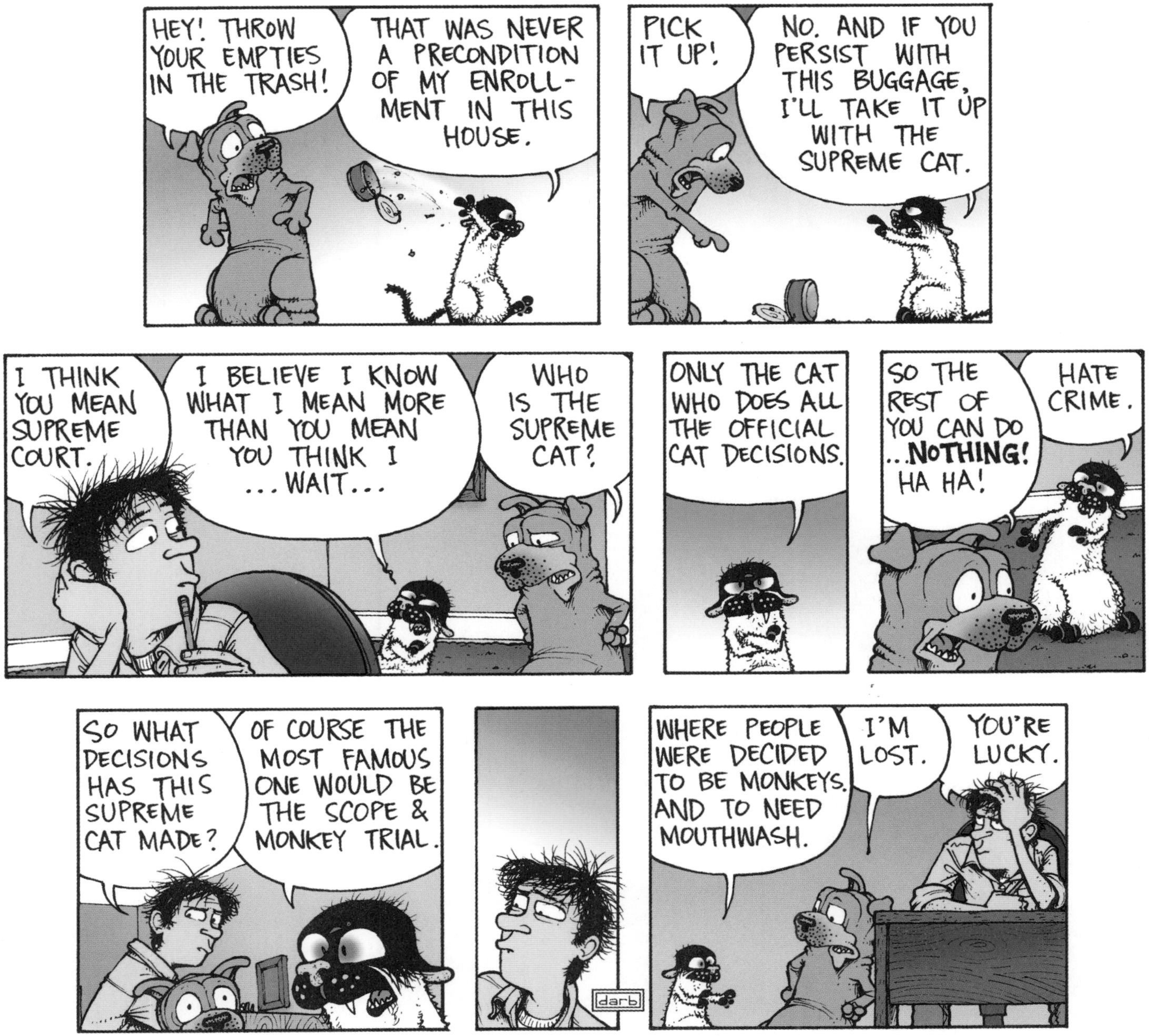
HEY! THROW YOUR EMPTIES IN THE TRASH!
THAT WAS NEVER A PRECONDITION OF MY ENROLL- MENT IN THIS HOUSE.
PICK IT UP!
NO. AND IF YOU PERSIST WITH THIS BUGGAGE, I'LL TAKE IT UP WITH THE SUPREME CAT.
I THINK YOU MEAN SUPREME COURT.
I BELIEVE I KNOW WHAT I MEAN MORE THAN YOU MEAN YOU THINK I ...WAIT...
WHO IS THE SUPREME CAT?
ONLY THE CAT WHO DOES ALL THE OFFICIAL CAT DECISIONS.
SO THE REST OF YOU CAN DO ...**NOTHING!** HA HA!
HATE CRIME.
SO WHAT DECISIONS HAS THIS SUPREME CAT MADE?
OF COURSE THE MOST FAMOUS ONE WOULD BE THE SCOPE & MONKEY TRIAL.
darb
WHERE PEOPLE WERE DECIDED TO BE MONKEYS. AND TO NEED MOUTHWASH.
I'M LOST.
YOU'RE LUCKY.

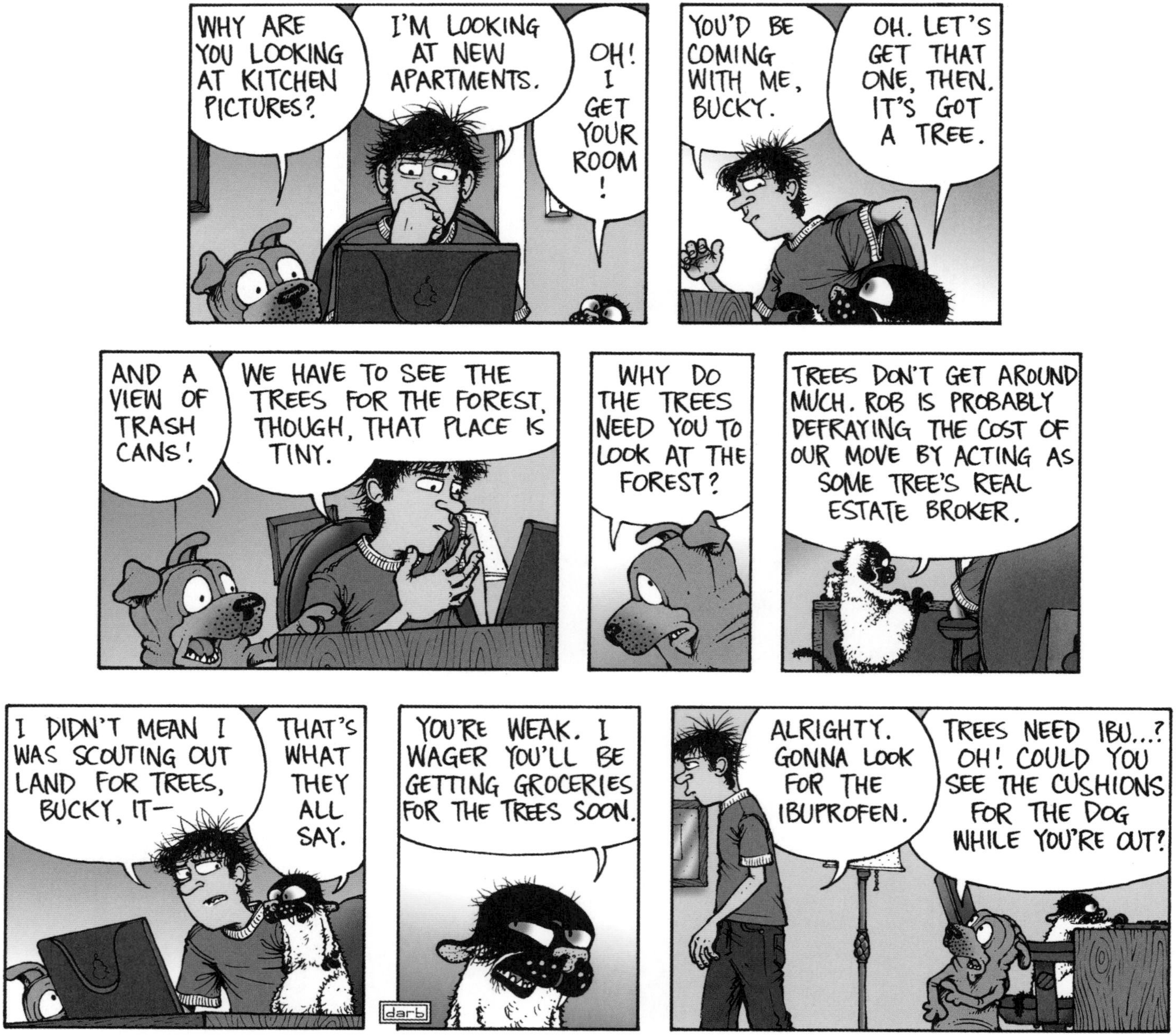
WHY ARE YOU LOOKING AT KITCHEN PICTURES?
I'M LOOKING AT NEW APARTMENTS.
OH! I GET YOUR ROOM!
YOU'D BE COMING WITH ME, BUCKY.
OH. LET'S GET THAT ONE, THEN. IT'S GOT A TREE.
AND A VIEW OF TRASH CANS!
WE HAVE TO SEE THE TREES FOR THE FOREST, THOUGH. THAT PLACE IS TINY.
WHY DO THE TREES NEED YOU TO LOOK AT THE FOREST?
TREES DON'T GET AROUND MUCH. ROB IS PROBABLY DEFRAYING THE COST OF OUR MOVE BY ACTING AS SOME TREE'S REAL ESTATE BROKER.
I DIDN'T MEAN I WAS SCOUTING OUT LAND FOR TREES, BUCKY, IT—
THAT'S WHAT THEY ALL SAY.
YOU'RE WEAK. I WAGER YOU'LL BE GETTING GROCERIES FOR THE TREES SOON.
darb
ALRIGHTY. GONNA LOOK FOR THE IBUPROFEN.
TREES NEED IBU...? OH! COULD YOU SEE THE CUSHIONS FOR THE DOG WHILE YOU'RE OUT?

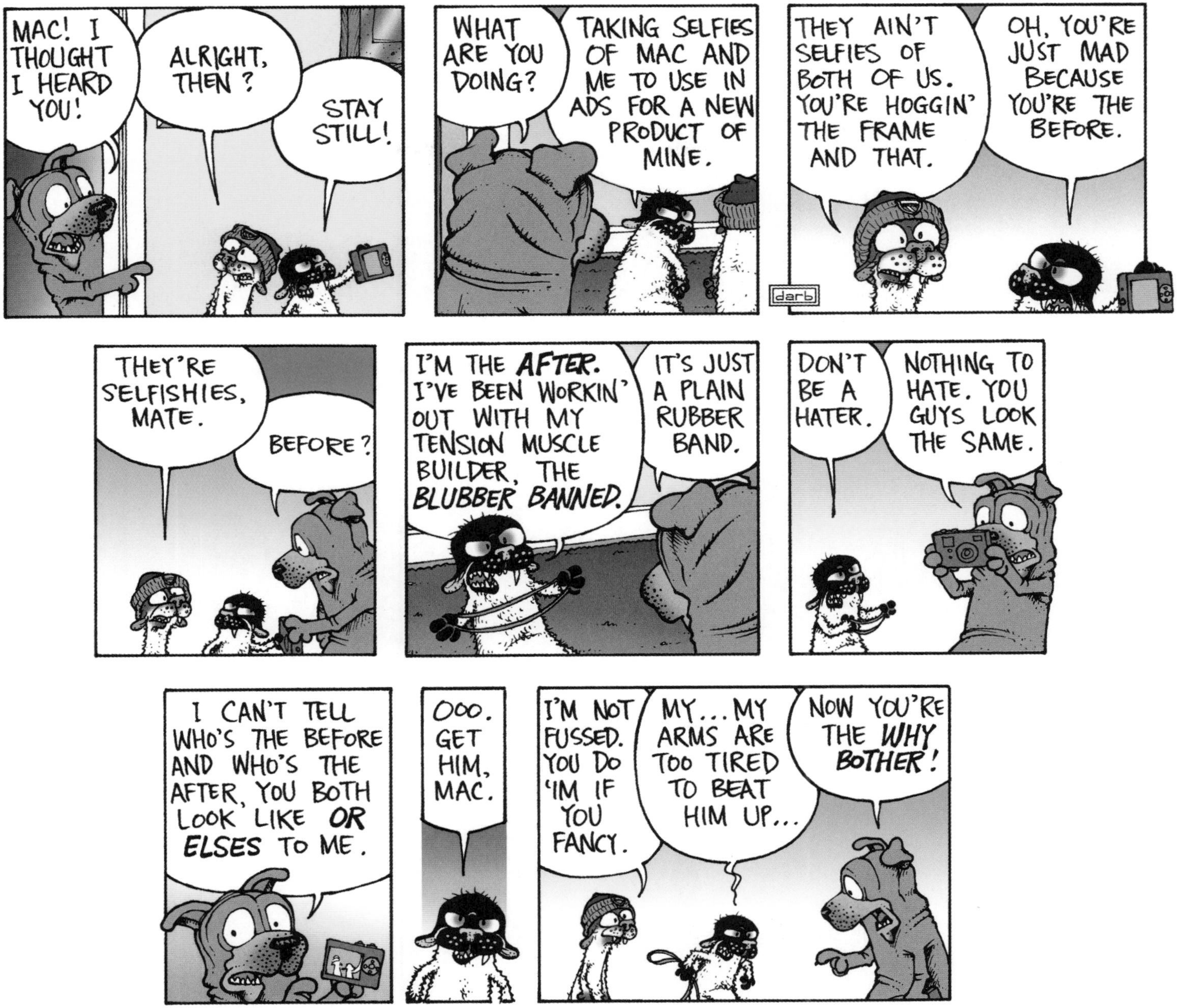
MAC! I THOUGHT I HEARD YOU!
ALRIGHT, THEN ?
STAY STILL!
WHAT ARE YOU DOING?
TAKING SELFIES OF MAC AND ME TO USE IN ADS FOR A NEW PRODUCT OF MINE.
THEY AIN'T SELFIES OF BOTH OF US. YOU'RE HOGGIN' THE FRAME AND THAT.
OH, YOU'RE JUST MAD BECAUSE YOU'RE THE BEFORE.
darb
THEY'RE SELFISHIES, MATE.
BEFORE?
I'M THE AFTER. I'VE BEEN WORKIN' OUT WITH MY TENSION MUSCLE BUILDER, THE BLUBBER BANNED.
IT'S JUST A PLAIN RUBBER BAND.
DON'T BE A HATER.
NOTHING TO HATE. YOU GUYS LOOK THE SAME.
I CAN'T TELL WHO'S THE BEFORE AND WHO'S THE AFTER, YOU BOTH LOOK LIKE OR ELSES TO ME.
OOO. GET HIM, MAC.
I'M NOT FUSSED. YOU DO 'IM IF YOU FANCY.
MY... MY ARMS ARE TOO TIRED TO BEAT HIM UP...
NOW YOU'RE THE WHY BOTHER!

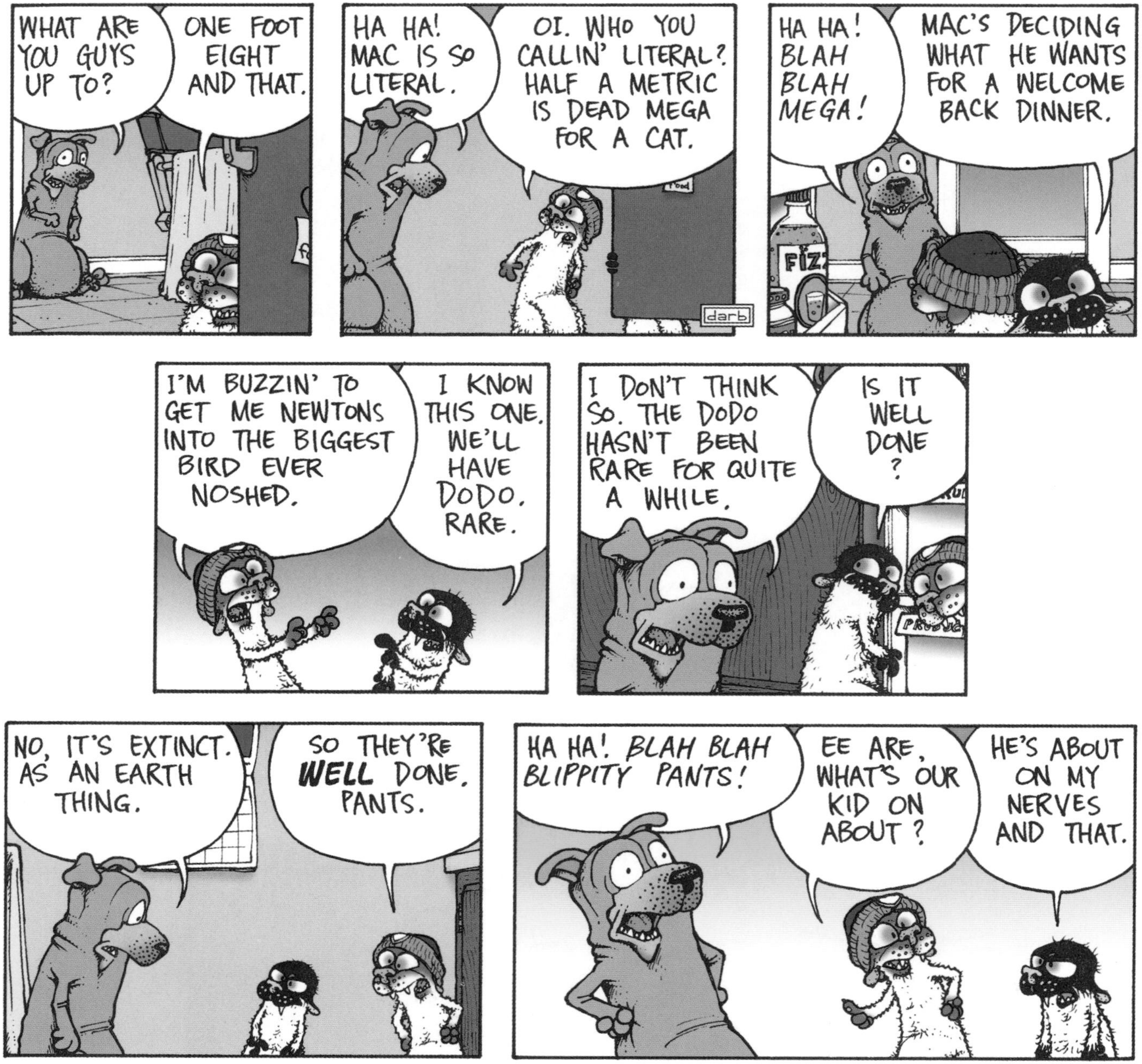
WHAT ARE YOU GUYS UP TO?
ONE FOOT EIGHT AND THAT.
HA HA! MAC IS SO LITERAL.
OI. WHO YOU CALLIN' LITERAL? HALF A METRIC IS DEAD MEGA FOR A CAT.
darb
HA HA! BLAH BLAH MEGA!
MAC'S DECIDING WHAT HE WANTS FOR A WELCOME BACK DINNER.
FIZZ
I'M BUZZIN' TO GET ME NEWTONS INTO THE BIGGEST BIRD EVER NOSHED.
I KNOW THIS ONE. WE'LL HAVE DODO. RARE.
I DON'T THINK SO. THE DODO HASN'T BEEN RARE FOR QUITE A WHILE.
IS IT WELL DONE ?
NO, IT'S EXTINCT. AS AN EARTH THING.
SO THEY'RE **WELL** DONE. PANTS.
HA HA! *BLAH BLAH BLIPPITY PANTS!*
EE ARE, WHAT'S OUR KID ON ABOUT ?
HE'S ABOUT ON MY NERVES AND THAT.

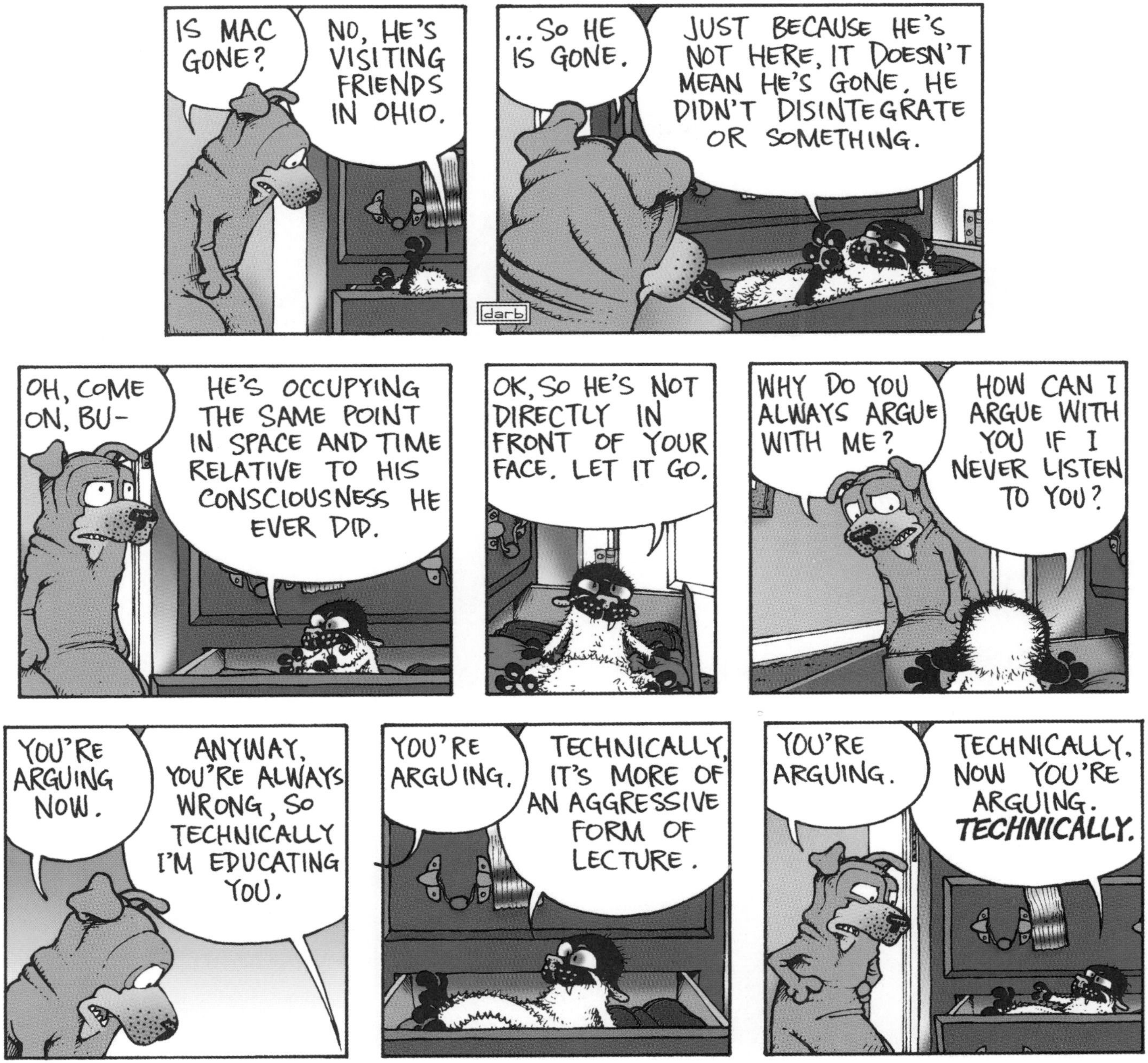
IS MAC GONE?
NO, HE'S VISITING FRIENDS IN OHIO.
...SO HE IS GONE.
JUST BECAUSE HE'S NOT HERE, IT DOESN'T MEAN HE'S GONE. HE DIDN'T DISINTEGRATE OR SOMETHING.
darb
OH, COME ON, BU-
HE'S OCCUPYING THE SAME POINT IN SPACE AND TIME RELATIVE TO HIS CONSCIOUSNESS HE EVER DID.
OK, SO HE'S NOT DIRECTLY IN FRONT OF YOUR FACE. LET IT GO.
WHY DO YOU ALWAYS ARGUE WITH ME?
HOW CAN I ARGUE WITH YOU IF I NEVER LISTEN TO YOU?
YOU'RE ARGUING NOW.
ANYWAY, YOU'RE ALWAYS WRONG, SO TECHNICALLY I'M EDUCATING YOU.
YOU'RE ARGUING.
TECHNICALLY, IT'S MORE OF AN AGGRESSIVE FORM OF LECTURE.
YOU'RE ARGUING.
TECHNICALLY. NOW YOU'RE ARGUING. *TECHNICALLY.*

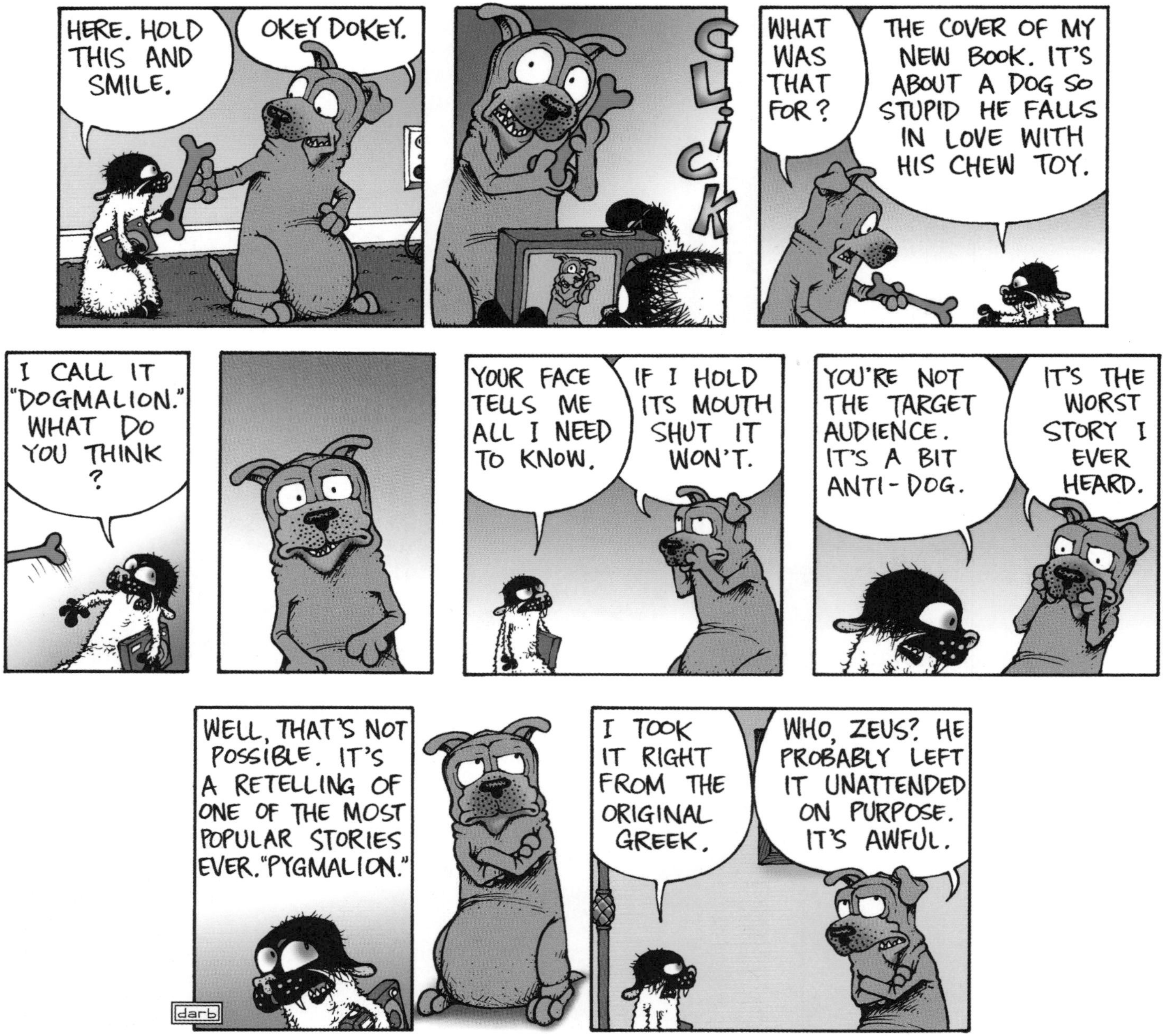
HERE. HOLD THIS AND SMILE.
OKEY DOKEY.
CLICK
WHAT WAS THAT FOR?
THE COVER OF MY NEW BOOK. IT'S ABOUT A DOG SO STUPID HE FALLS IN LOVE WITH HIS CHEW TOY.
I CALL IT "DOGMALION." WHAT DO YOU THINK?
YOUR FACE TELLS ME ALL I NEED TO KNOW.
IF I HOLD ITS MOUTH SHUT IT WON'T.
YOU'RE NOT THE TARGET AUDIENCE. IT'S A BIT ANTI-DOG.
IT'S THE WORST STORY I EVER HEARD.
WELL, THAT'S NOT POSSIBLE. IT'S A RETELLING OF ONE OF THE MOST POPULAR STORIES EVER. "PYGMALION."
darb
I TOOK IT RIGHT FROM THE ORIGINAL GREEK.
WHO, ZEUS? HE PROBABLY LEFT IT UNATTENDED ON PURPOSE. IT'S AWFUL.

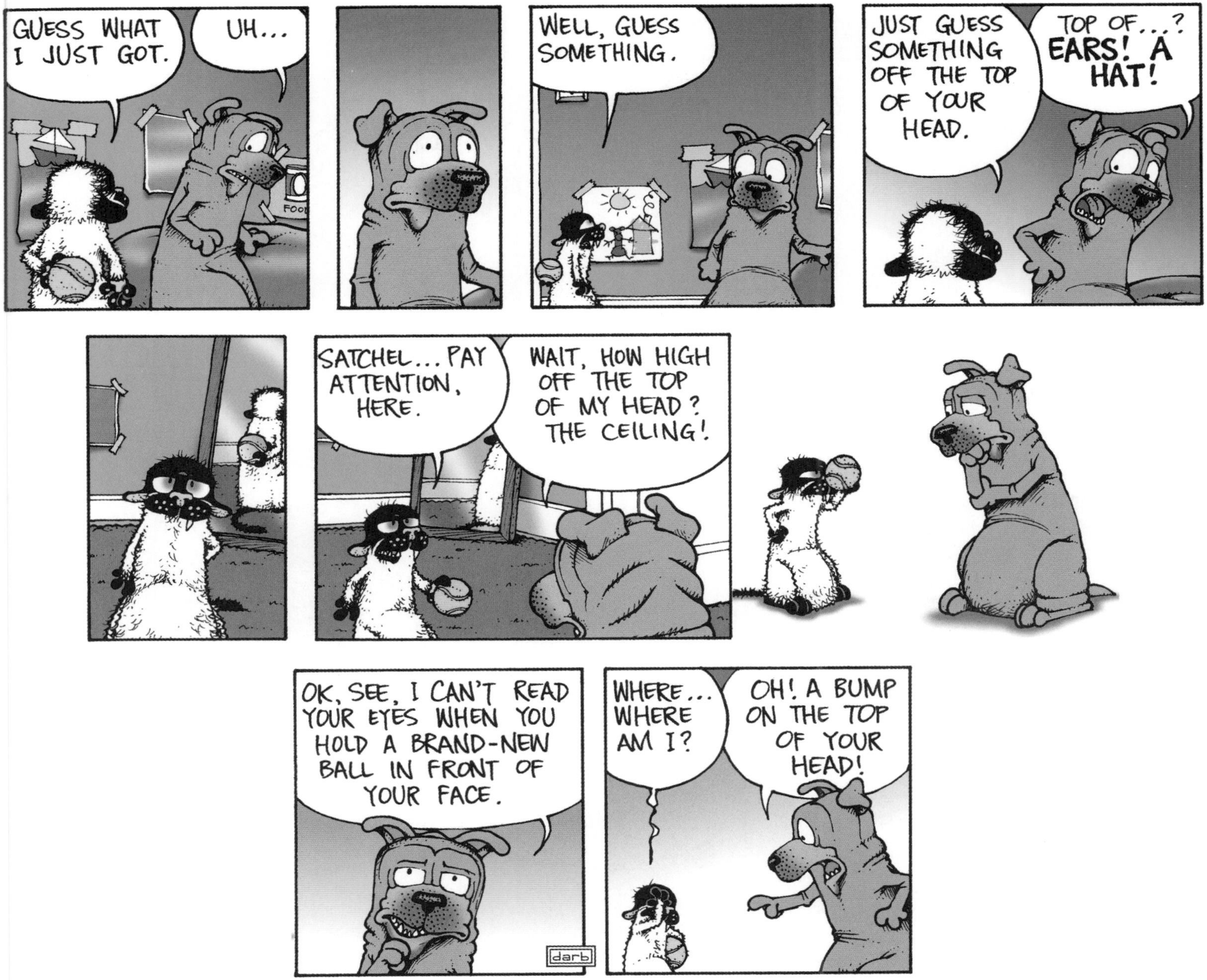
GUESS WHAT I JUST GOT.
UH...
FOOD
WELL, GUESS SOMETHING.
JUST GUESS SOMETHING OFF THE TOP OF YOUR HEAD.
TOP OF...? EARS! A HAT!
SATCHEL... PAY ATTENTION, HERE.
WAIT, HOW HIGH OFF THE TOP OF MY HEAD? THE CEILING!
OK, SEE, I CAN'T READ YOUR EYES WHEN YOU HOLD A BRAND-NEW BALL IN FRONT OF YOUR FACE.
darb
WHERE... WHERE AM I?
OH! A BUMP ON THE TOP OF YOUR HEAD!

THE AQUARIUM GOT HIT WITH REEF DISEASE. WORD IS THEIR DUMPSTERS LOOK LIKE A FRENCH NUCLEAR TEST.

SO YOU'RE GOING TO WRAP DEAD FISH IN THAT MAP TO TAKE HOME?

NO, I'M FINDING THE AQUARIUM. IT'S DOWN-TOWN, RIGHT?

FORGET THE MAP. GET A TAXI.

WHAT'S THAT SUPPOSED TO MEAN?

I'M NOT SAYIN'. YOU'D GET MAD AND I'D HAVE TO HIDE IN A PLACE YOU'D NEVER BE ABLE TO FIND ME...

...LIKE RIGHT BEHIND YOU! HA HA!

OH. THIS AGAIN. LOOK, MY SENSE OF DIRECTION IS JUST AS GOOD AS A DOG'S.

YOU CAN'T FIND YOUR WAY OUT OF A PAPER BAG.

FOR THE LAST TIME, I *LIKE* SLEEPING IN BAGS!

WHEN I GO IN THEM, I'M *NOT TRYING* TO GET OUT.

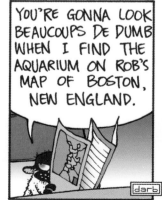

YOU'RE GONNA LOOK BEAUCOUPS DE DUMB WHEN I FIND THE AQUARIUM ON ROB'S MAP OF BOSTON, NEW ENGLAND.

darb

FOR NOW I'LL WATCH YOU LOOK FOR IT ON MAC'S MAP OF BOSTON, LINCOLNSHIRE. OLD ENGLAND.

TELL ME MORE OF THIS TAXI OF WHICH YOU SPEAK.

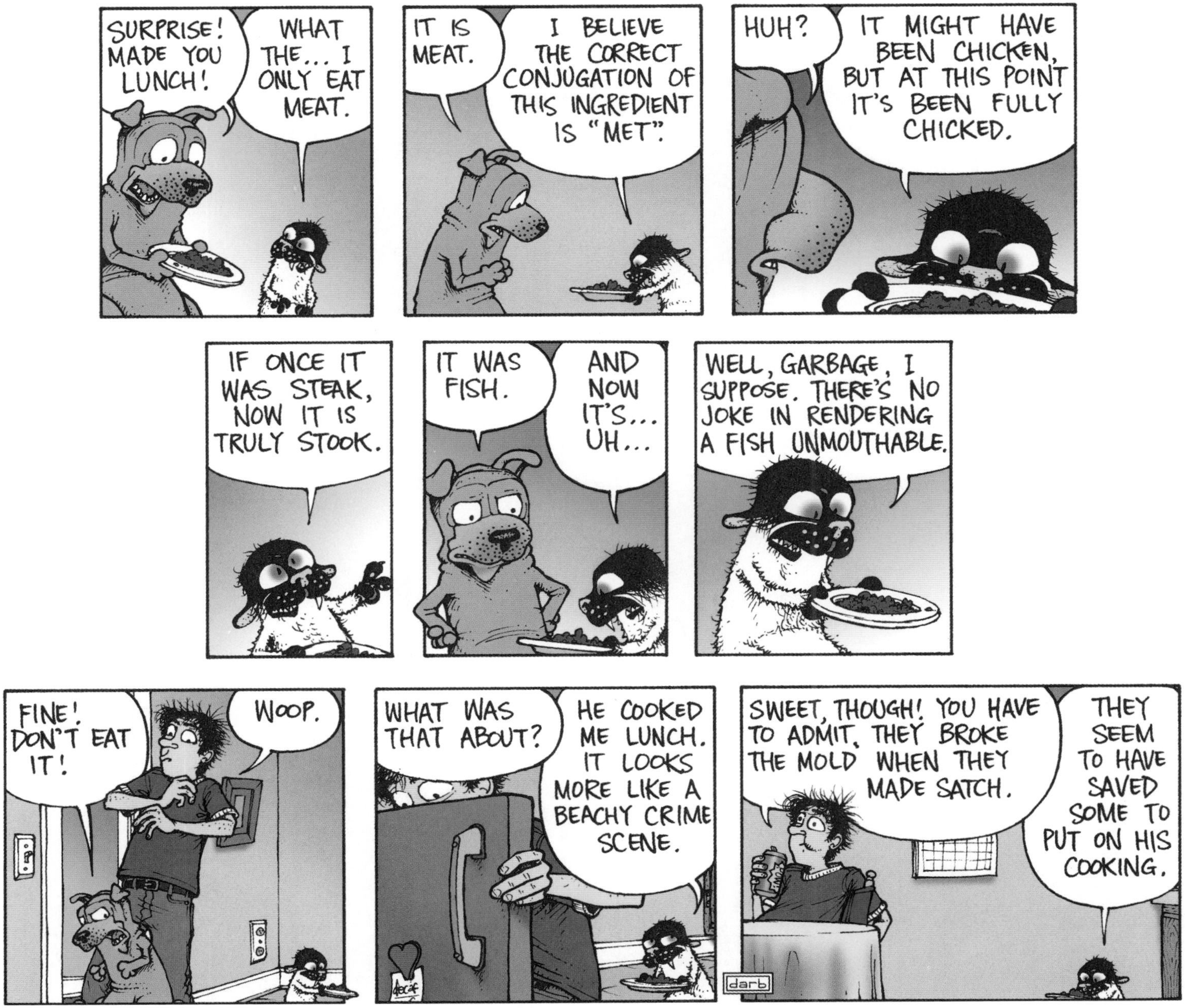
SURPRISE! MADE YOU LUNCH!
WHAT THE... I ONLY EAT MEAT.
IT IS MEAT.
I BELIEVE THE CORRECT CONJUGATION OF THIS INGREDIENT IS "MET".
HUH?
IT MIGHT HAVE BEEN CHICKEN, BUT AT THIS POINT IT'S BEEN FULLY CHICKED.
IF ONCE IT WAS STEAK, NOW IT IS TRULY STOOK.
IT WAS FISH.
AND NOW IT'S... UH...
WELL, GARBAGE, I SUPPOSE. THERE'S NO JOKE IN RENDERING A FISH UNMOUTHABLE.
FINE! DON'T EAT IT!
WOOP.
WHAT WAS THAT ABOUT?
HE COOKED ME LUNCH. IT LOOKS MORE LIKE A BEACHY CRIME SCENE.
darb
SWEET, THOUGH! YOU HAVE TO ADMIT, THEY BROKE THE MOLD WHEN THEY MADE SATCH.
THEY SEEM TO HAVE SAVED SOME TO PUT ON HIS COOKING.

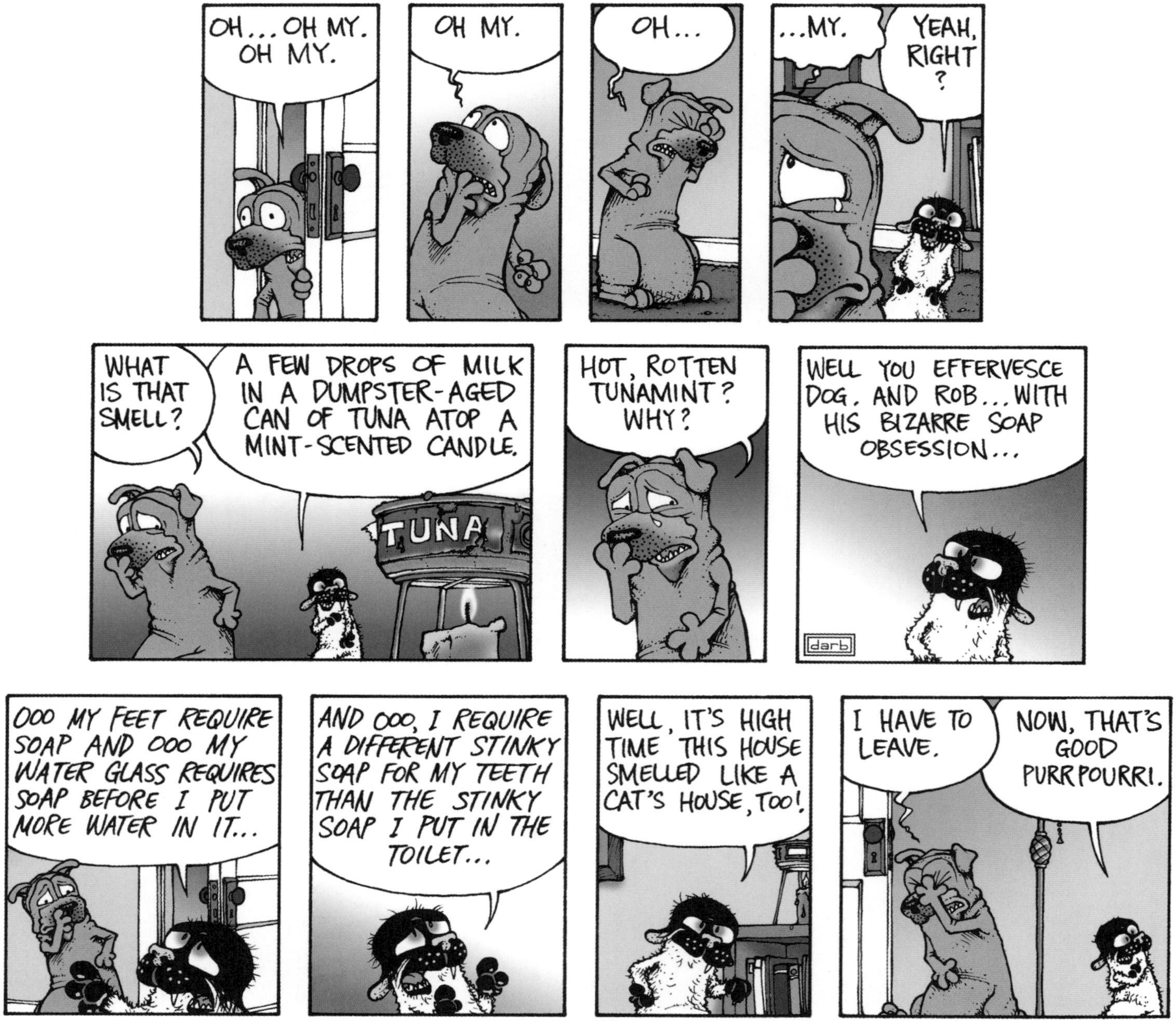
OH... OH MY. OH MY.
OH MY.
OH...
...MY.
YEAH, RIGHT?
WHAT IS THAT SMELL?
A FEW DROPS OF MILK IN A DUMPSTER-AGED CAN OF TUNA ATOP A MINT-SCENTED CANDLE.
TUNA
HOT, ROTTEN TUNAMINT? WHY?
WELL YOU EFFERVESCE DOG. AND ROB... WITH HIS BIZARRE SOAP OBSESSION...
darb
OOO MY FEET REQUIRE SOAP AND OOO MY WATER GLASS REQUIRES SOAP BEFORE I PUT MORE WATER IN IT...
AND OOO, I REQUIRE A DIFFERENT STINKY SOAP FOR MY TEETH THAN THE STINKY SOAP I PUT IN THE TOILET...
WELL, IT'S HIGH TIME THIS HOUSE SMELLED LIKE A CAT'S HOUSE, TOO!
I HAVE TO LEAVE.
NOW, THAT'S GOOD PURRPOURRI.

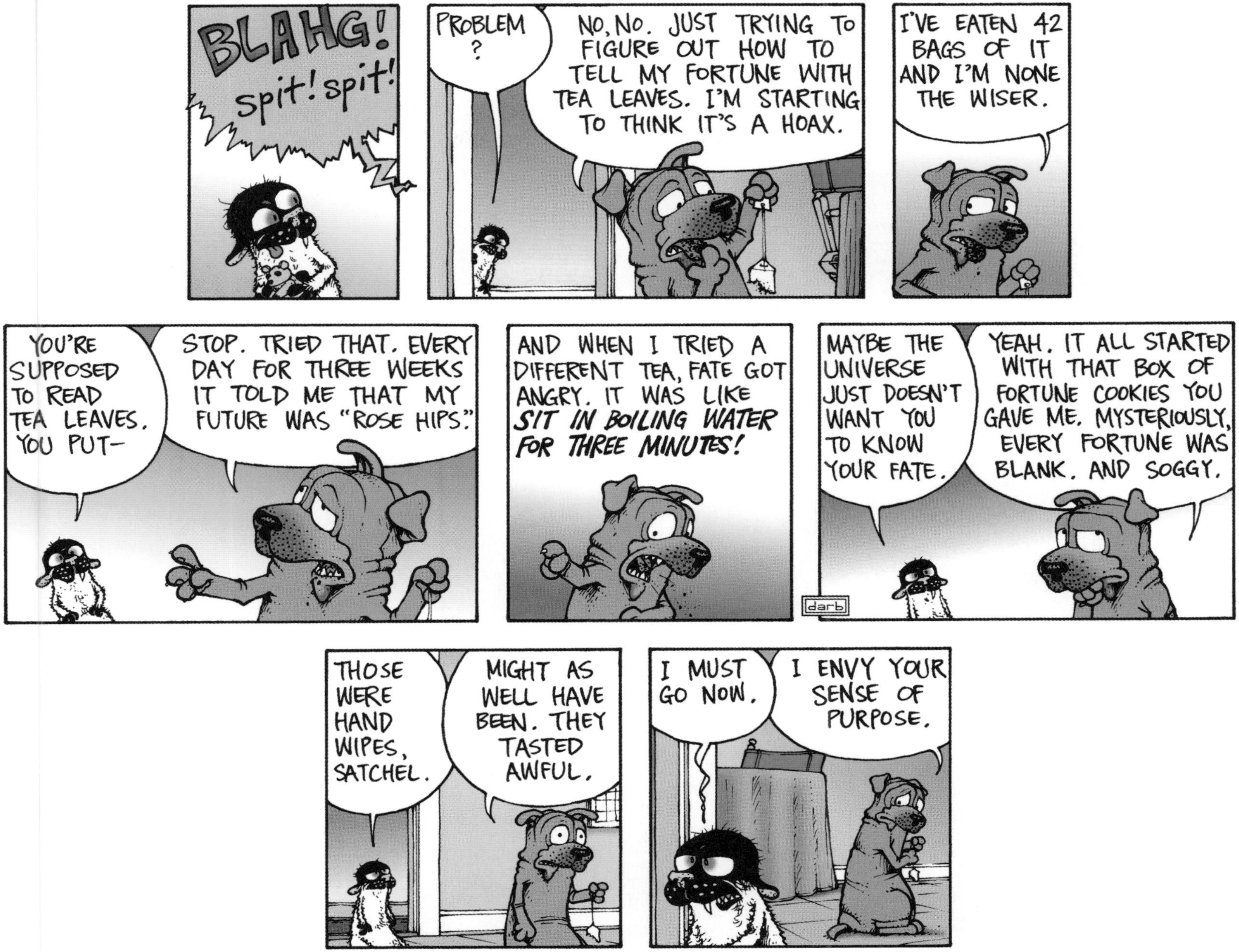
BLAHG!
spit! spit!
PROBLEM ?
NO, NO. JUST TRYING TO FIGURE OUT HOW TO TELL MY FORTUNE WITH TEA LEAVES. I'M STARTING TO THINK IT'S A HOAX.
I'VE EATEN 42 BAGS OF IT AND I'M NONE THE WISER.
YOU'RE SUPPOSED TO READ TEA LEAVES. YOU PUT—
STOP. TRIED THAT. EVERY DAY FOR THREE WEEKS IT TOLD ME THAT MY FUTURE WAS "ROSE HIPS."
AND WHEN I TRIED A DIFFERENT TEA, FATE GOT ANGRY. IT WAS LIKE *SIT IN BOILING WATER FOR THREE MINUTES!*
MAYBE THE UNIVERSE JUST DOESN'T WANT YOU TO KNOW YOUR FATE.
YEAH. IT ALL STARTED WITH THAT BOX OF FORTUNE COOKIES YOU GAVE ME. MYSTERIOUSLY, EVERY FORTUNE WAS BLANK. AND SOGGY.
darb
THOSE WERE HAND WIPES, SATCHEL.
MIGHT AS WELL HAVE BEEN. THEY TASTED AWFUL.
I MUST GO NOW.
I ENVY YOUR SENSE OF PURPOSE.

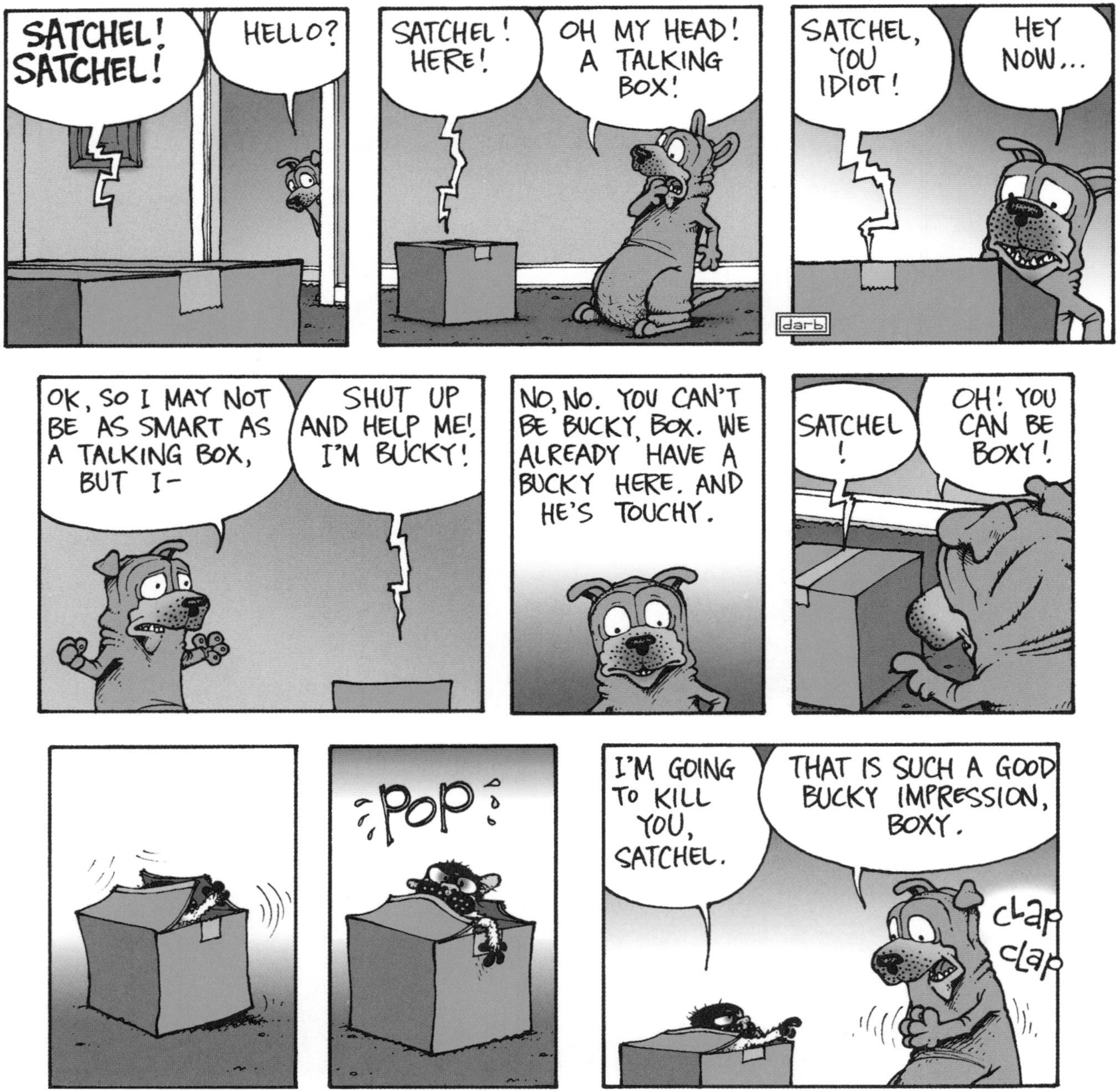
SATCHEL! SATCHEL!
HELLO?
SATCHEL! HERE!
OH MY HEAD! A TALKING BOX!
SATCHEL, YOU IDIOT!
HEY NOW...
darb
OK, SO I MAY NOT BE AS SMART AS A TALKING BOX, BUT I-
SHUT UP AND HELP ME! I'M BUCKY!
NO, NO. YOU CAN'T BE BUCKY, BOX. WE ALREADY HAVE A BUCKY HERE. AND HE'S TOUCHY.
SATCHEL!
OH! YOU CAN BE BOXY!
POP
I'M GOING TO KILL YOU, SATCHEL.
THAT IS SUCH A GOOD BUCKY IMPRESSION, BOXY.
CLAP CLAP

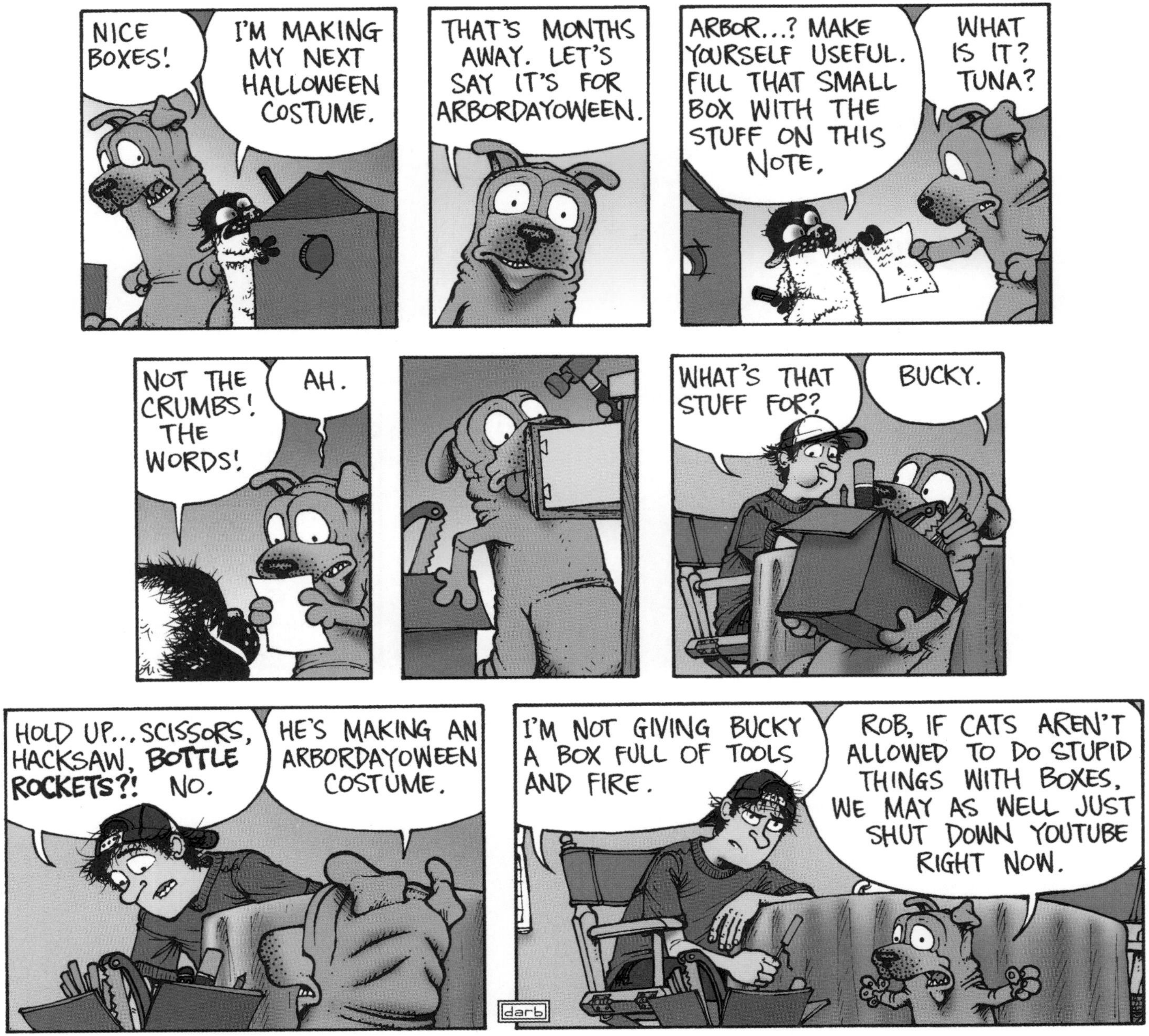
NICE BOXES!
I'M MAKING MY NEXT HALLOWEEN COSTUME.
THAT'S MONTHS AWAY. LET'S SAY IT'S FOR ARBORDAYOWEEN.
ARBOR...? MAKE YOURSELF USEFUL. FILL THAT SMALL BOX WITH THE STUFF ON THIS NOTE.
WHAT IS IT? TUNA?
NOT THE CRUMBS! THE WORDS!
AH.
WHAT'S THAT STUFF FOR?
BUCKY.
HOLD UP... SCISSORS, HACKSAW, **BOTTLE ROCKETS?!** NO.
HE'S MAKING AN ARBORDAYOWEEN COSTUME.
I'M NOT GIVING BUCKY A BOX FULL OF TOOLS AND FIRE.
ROB, IF CATS AREN'T ALLOWED TO DO STUPID THINGS WITH BOXES, WE MAY AS WELL JUST SHUT DOWN YOUTUBE RIGHT NOW.
darb

Panel 1: AH. YOU'RE MAKING THE SHOPPING LIST. / NEED SOMETHING?

Panel 2: WE'RE OUT OF THESE.

Panel 3: THE MEGALUX, ULTRAPLUSH, SOLAR HEATED, MULTI-PET SUPERBED?

Panel 4: THAT'S CORRECT. / YOU AND FIVE FRIENDS WILL LUXURIATE IN STYLE AS...

Panel 5: WAIT, YOU DON'T NEED THIS. YOU HAVE NO FRIENDS. THIS MUST BE FOR DOGS. / WHAT?! I HAVE PLENTY OF FRIENDS.

Panel 6: CATS DON'T HAVE FRIENDS. THEY HAVE CO-CONSPIRATORS. / HEY, I GET CARDS ON HOLIDAYS JUST LIKE YOU.

Panel 7: YEAH. FROM SATCHEL. YOU CAN'T PROVE YOUR LIKEABILITY WITH DOGS. DOGS LIKE EVERYBODY. HITLER HAD DOGS.

Panel 8: LOOK, IF YOU'LL SHARE THIS MEGABED THING WITH SATCHEL, I'LL GET IT FOR YOU.

Panel 9: (silent)

Panel 10: I'LL BE IN THE SOCK DRAWER. / AW.

darb

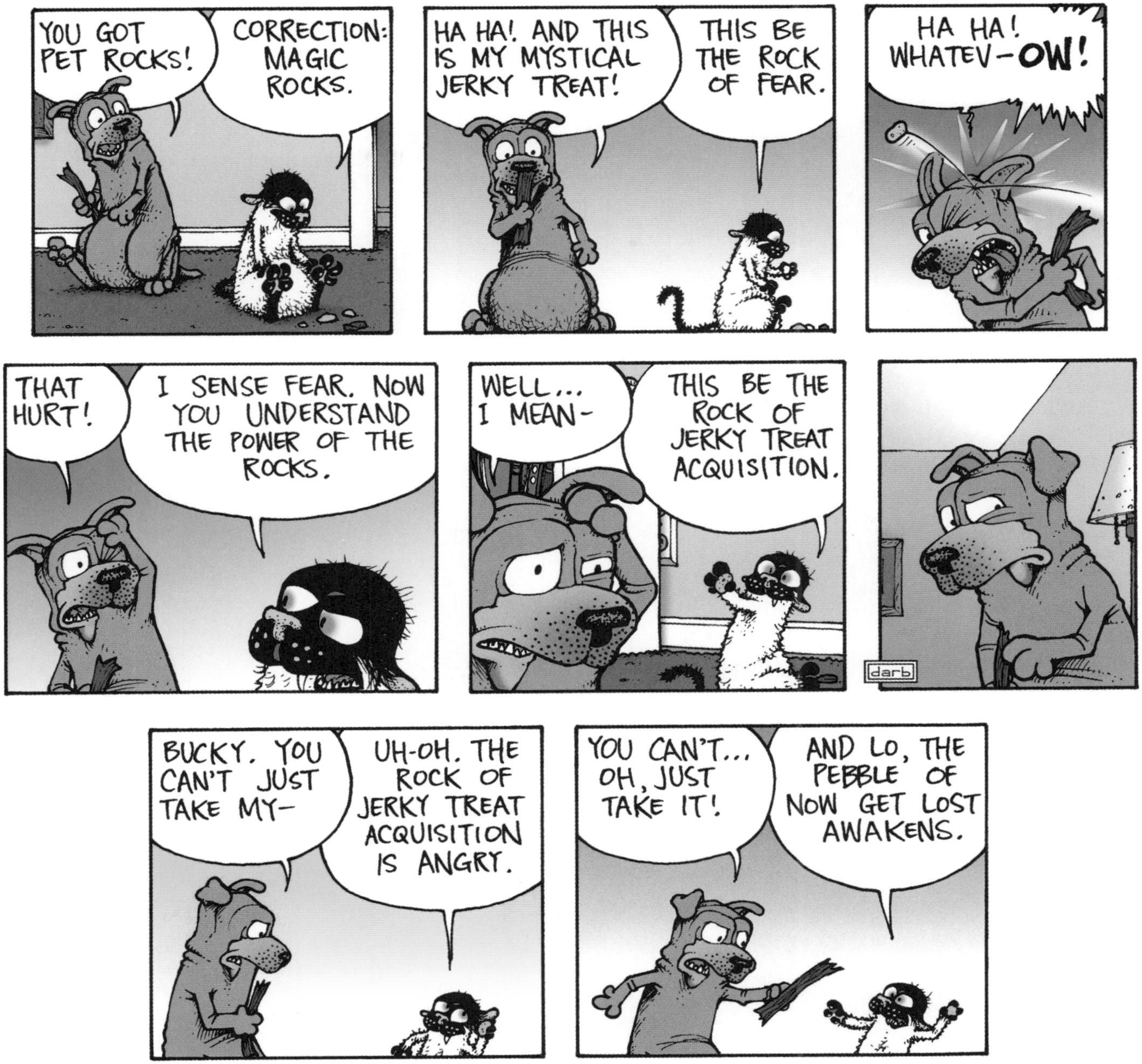
YOU GOT PET ROCKS!
CORRECTION: MAGIC ROCKS.
HA HA! AND THIS IS MY MYSTICAL JERKY TREAT!
THIS BE THE ROCK OF FEAR.
HA HA! WHATEV-OW!
THAT HURT!
I SENSE FEAR. NOW YOU UNDERSTAND THE POWER OF THE ROCKS.
WELL... I MEAN-
THIS BE THE ROCK OF JERKY TREAT ACQUISITION.
darb
BUCKY. YOU CAN'T JUST TAKE MY-
UH-OH. THE ROCK OF JERKY TREAT ACQUISITION IS ANGRY.
YOU CAN'T... OH, JUST TAKE IT!
AND LO, THE PEBBLE OF NOW GET LOST AWAKENS.

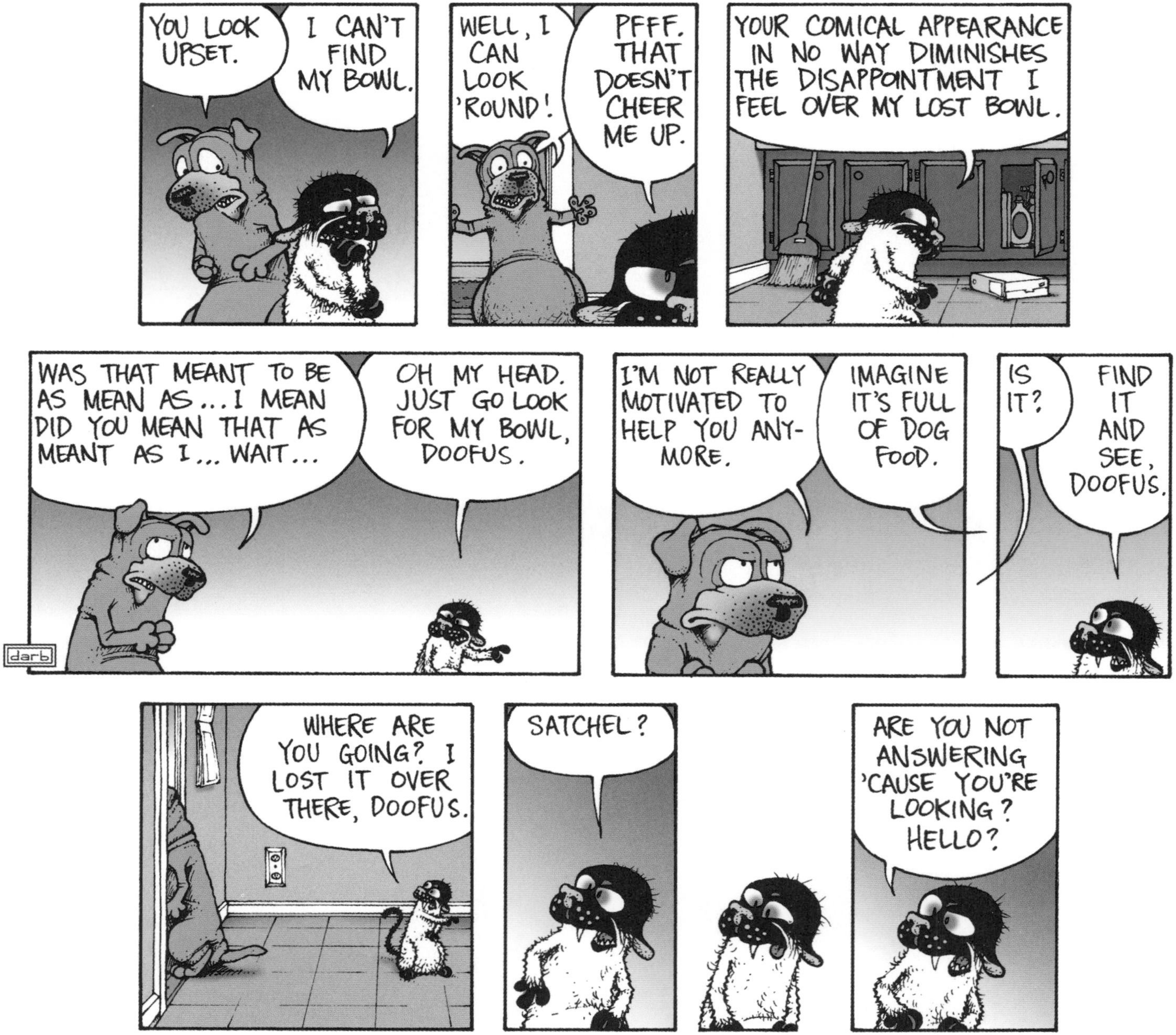
YOU LOOK UPSET.
I CAN'T FIND MY BOWL.
WELL, I CAN LOOK 'ROUND!
PFFF. THAT DOESN'T CHEER ME UP.
YOUR COMICAL APPEARANCE IN NO WAY DIMINISHES THE DISAPPOINTMENT I FEEL OVER MY LOST BOWL.
WAS THAT MEANT TO BE AS MEAN AS... I MEAN DID YOU MEAN THAT AS MEANT AS I... WAIT...
OH MY HEAD. JUST GO LOOK FOR MY BOWL, DOOFUS.
darb
I'M NOT REALLY MOTIVATED TO HELP YOU ANY-MORE.
IMAGINE IT'S FULL OF DOG FOOD.
IS IT?
FIND IT AND SEE, DOOFUS.
WHERE ARE YOU GOING? I LOST IT OVER THERE, DOOFUS.
SATCHEL?
ARE YOU NOT ANSWERING 'CAUSE YOU'RE LOOKING? HELLO?

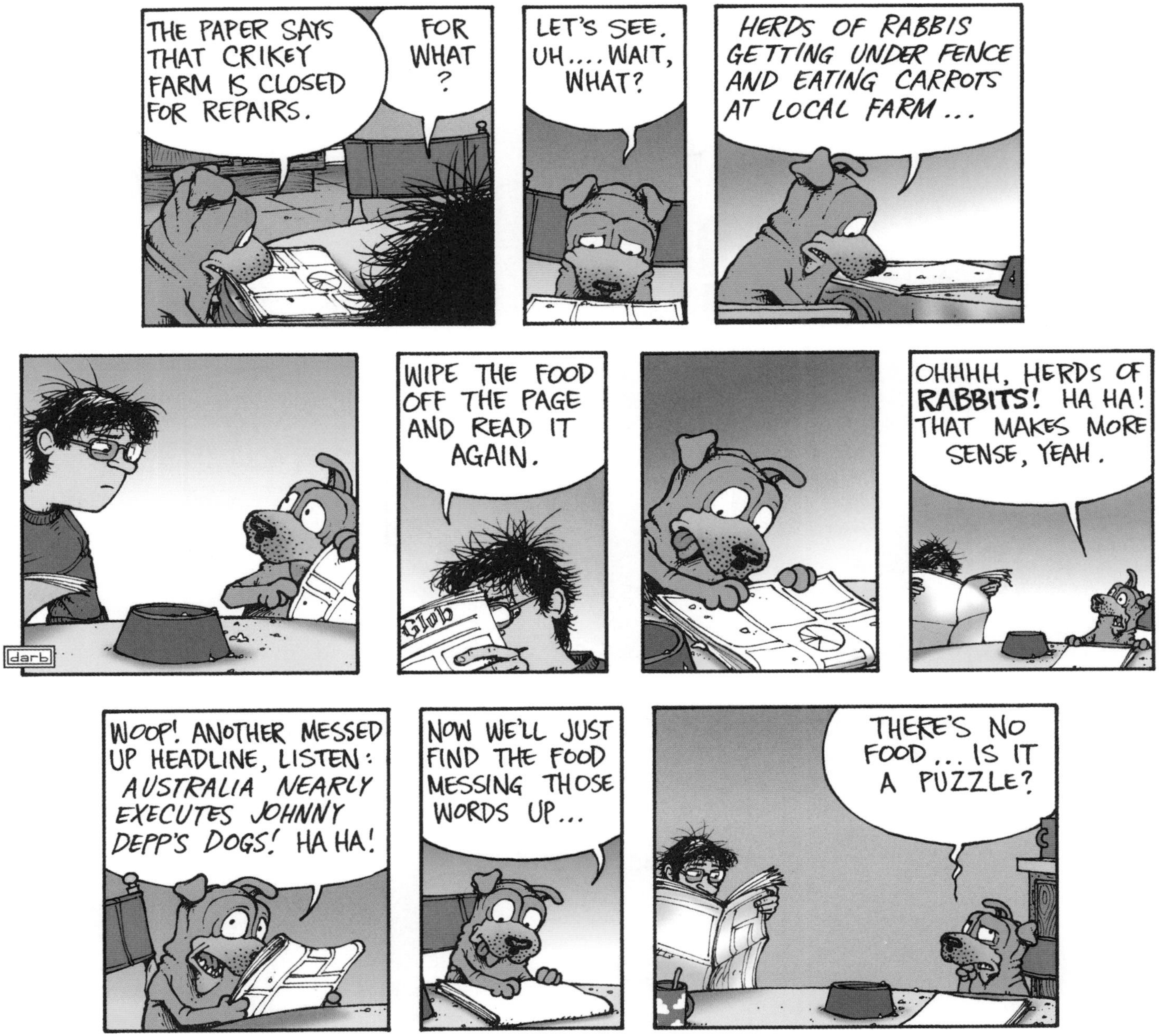
THE PAPER SAYS THAT CRIKEY FARM IS CLOSED FOR REPAIRS.
FOR WHAT ?
LET'S SEE. UH.... WAIT, WHAT?
HERDS OF RABBIS GETTING UNDER FENCE AND EATING CARROTS AT LOCAL FARM ...
darb
WIPE THE FOOD OFF THE PAGE AND READ IT AGAIN.
Glob
OHHHH, HERDS OF RABBITS! HA HA! THAT MAKES MORE SENSE, YEAH.
WOOP! ANOTHER MESSED UP HEADLINE, LISTEN: AUSTRALIA NEARLY EXECUTES JOHNNY DEPP'S DOGS! HA HA!
NOW WE'LL JUST FIND THE FOOD MESSING THOSE WORDS UP...
THERE'S NO FOOD... IS IT A PUZZLE?

Panel 1: NEW RATTLE TOY! SWEET!

I SCORED IT FROM THAT NEW NEIGHBOR.

Panel 2: NEW? NO ONE'S MOVED IN OR OUT FOR AGES.

NOT NEW *MOVED*, MORE LIKE NEW *EXISTING*.

Panel 3: ...LIKE A BABY? WAIT, YOU STOLE A TOY FROM THE NEW BOWE BABY?!

Panel 4: RELAX. I'M NO IDIOT. KID WAS SLEEPING. AT NO TIME WAS I IN REAL DANGER.

Panel 5: THE BABY'S A MINOR, BUCKY, THAT'S ILLEGAL!

Panel 6: HEY, IT'S NOT MY FAULT.

HOW IS IT NOT YOUR FAULT?!

Panel 7: *I'M* NOT THE ONE SENDING BABIES DOWN THE MINES!

NO, HE'S NOT A MINER OF THE EARTH, HE'S...UH... ...HM.

Panel 8: WELL, IF THAT THING IS AN ALIEN, EARTH HAS NOTHING TO FEAR. IT'S PATHETIC.

STOP SAYING "*IT*." IS THE BABY A BOY OR A GIRL?

Panel 9: PF. WHO KNOWS. THEY ALL LOOK THE SAME.

WELL THAT'S ...UM... BABYIST, SURELY.

rattle

darb

60

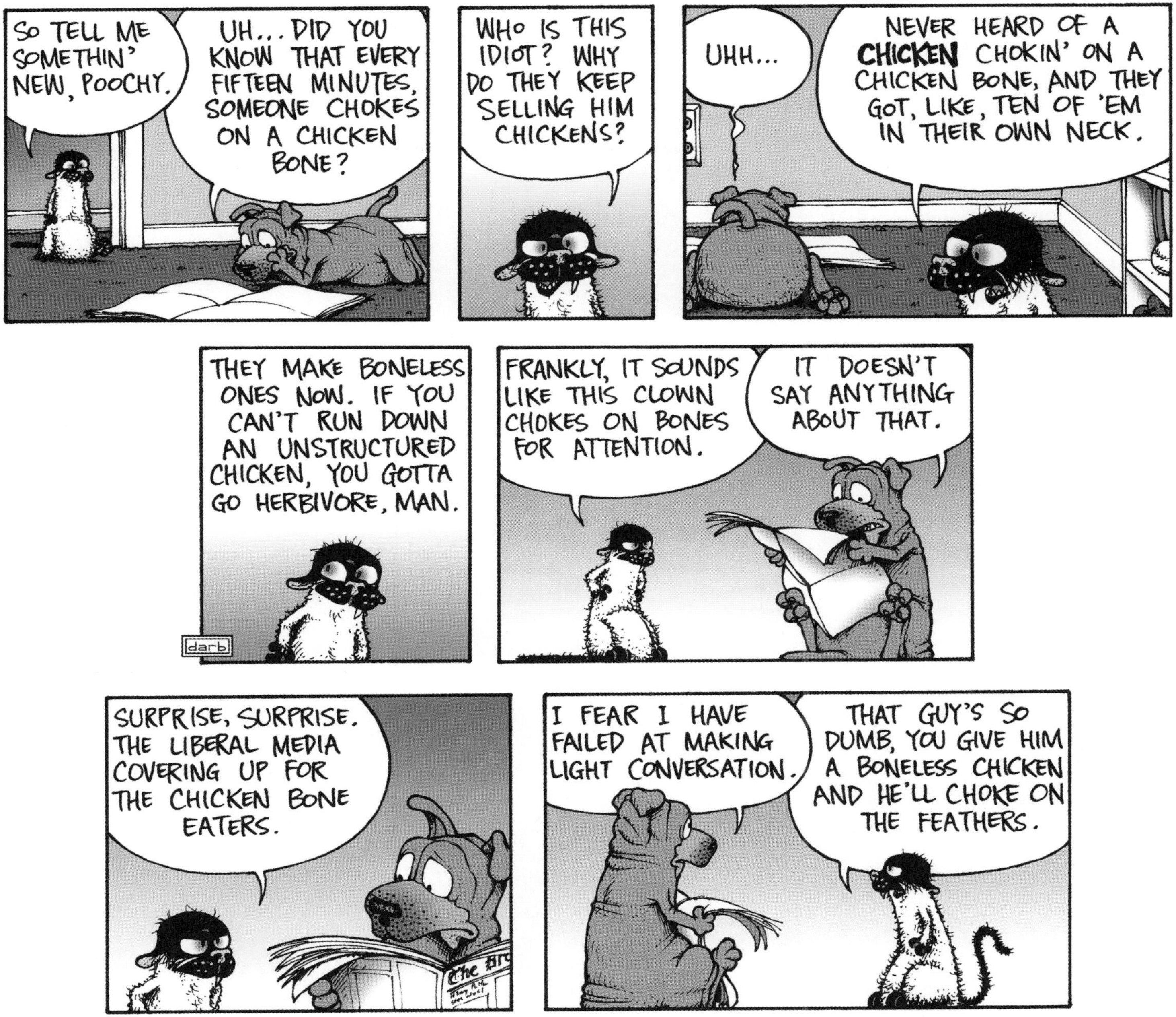
SO TELL ME SOMETHIN' NEW, POOCHY.
UH... DID YOU KNOW THAT EVERY FIFTEEN MINUTES, SOMEONE CHOKES ON A CHICKEN BONE?
WHO IS THIS IDIOT? WHY DO THEY KEEP SELLING HIM CHICKENS?
UHH...
NEVER HEARD OF A CHICKEN CHOKIN' ON A CHICKEN BONE, AND THEY GOT, LIKE, TEN OF 'EM IN THEIR OWN NECK.
THEY MAKE BONELESS ONES NOW. IF YOU CAN'T RUN DOWN AN UNSTRUCTURED CHICKEN, YOU GOTTA GO HERBIVORE, MAN.
darb
FRANKLY, IT SOUNDS LIKE THIS CLOWN CHOKES ON BONES FOR ATTENTION.
IT DOESN'T SAY ANYTHING ABOUT THAT.
SURPRISE, SURPRISE. THE LIBERAL MEDIA COVERING UP FOR THE CHICKEN BONE EATERS.
I FEAR I HAVE FAILED AT MAKING LIGHT CONVERSATION.
THAT GUY'S SO DUMB, YOU GIVE HIM A BONELESS CHICKEN AND HE'LL CHOKE ON THE FEATHERS.

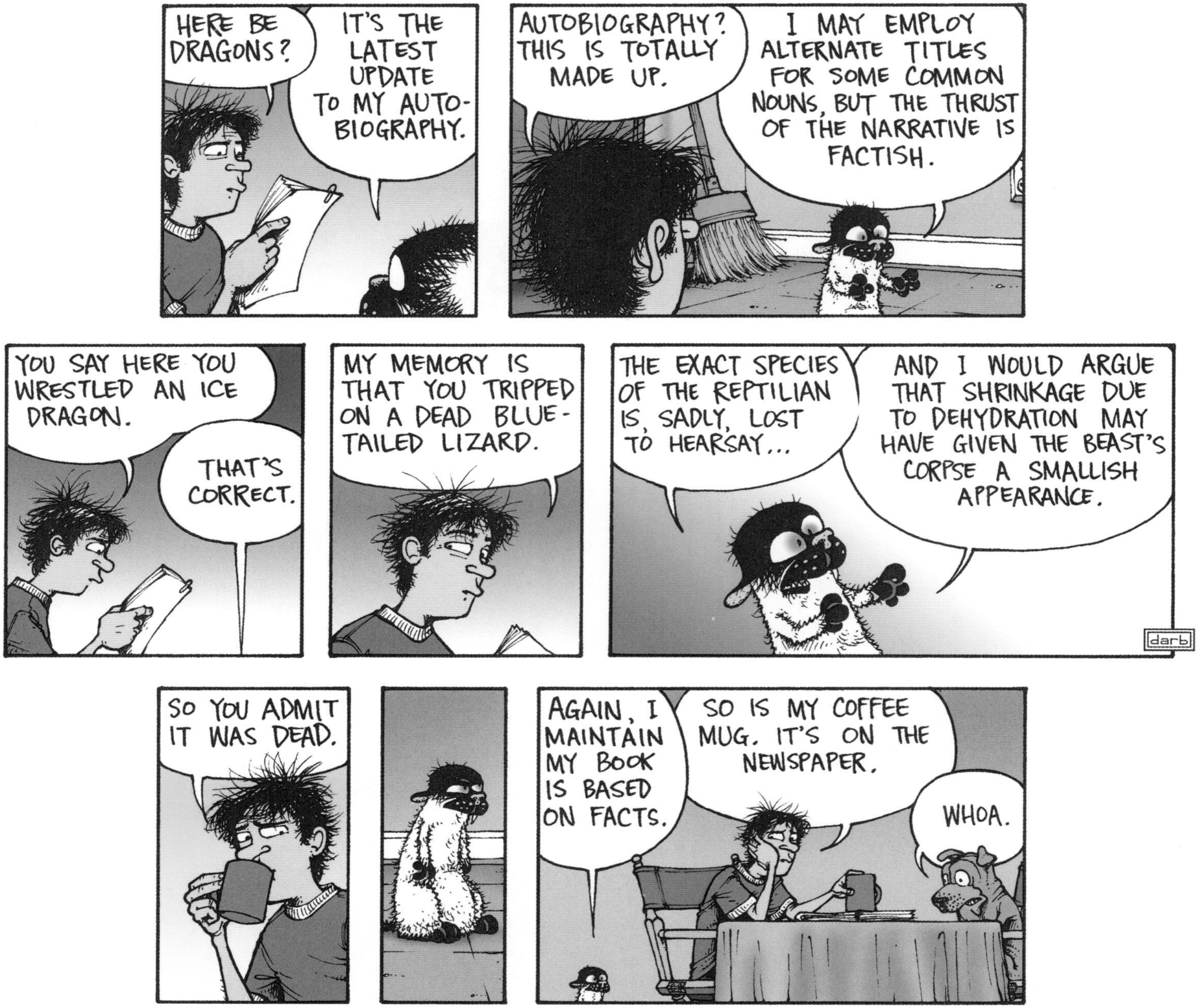
HERE BE DRAGONS?
IT'S THE LATEST UPDATE TO MY AUTO-BIOGRAPHY.
AUTOBIOGRAPHY? THIS IS TOTALLY MADE UP.
I MAY EMPLOY ALTERNATE TITLES FOR SOME COMMON NOUNS, BUT THE THRUST OF THE NARRATIVE IS FACTISH.
YOU SAY HERE YOU WRESTLED AN ICE DRAGON.
THAT'S CORRECT.
MY MEMORY IS THAT YOU TRIPPED ON A DEAD BLUE-TAILED LIZARD.
THE EXACT SPECIES OF THE REPTILIAN IS, SADLY, LOST TO HEARSAY...
AND I WOULD ARGUE THAT SHRINKAGE DUE TO DEHYDRATION MAY HAVE GIVEN THE BEAST'S CORPSE A SMALLISH APPEARANCE.
darb
SO YOU ADMIT IT WAS DEAD.
AGAIN, I MAINTAIN MY BOOK IS BASED ON FACTS.
SO IS MY COFFEE MUG. IT'S ON THE NEWSPAPER.
WHOA.

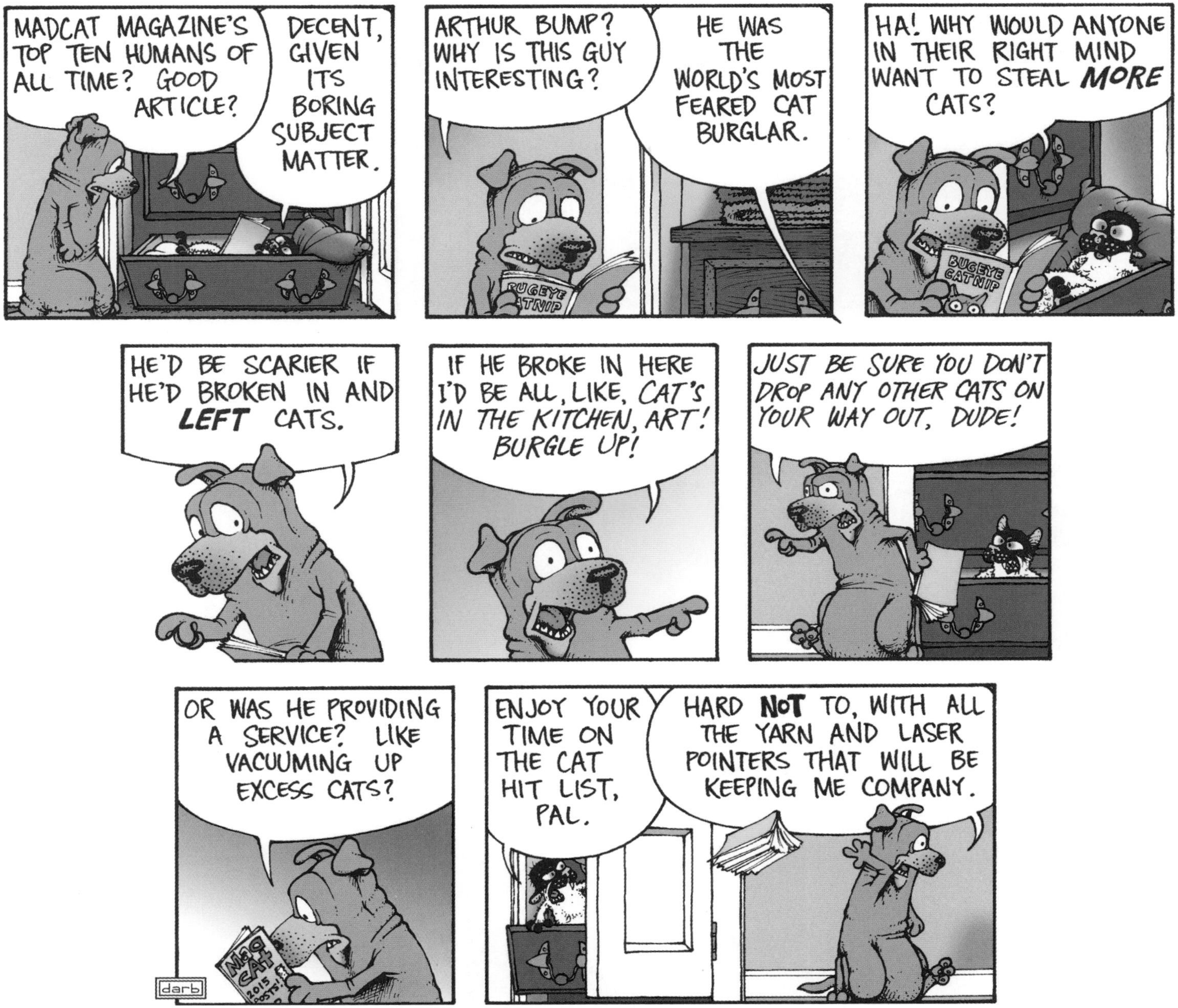
MADCAT MAGAZINE'S TOP TEN HUMANS OF ALL TIME? GOOD ARTICLE?
DECENT, GIVEN ITS BORING SUBJECT MATTER.
ARTHUR BUMP? WHY IS THIS GUY INTERESTING?
HE WAS THE WORLD'S MOST FEARED CAT BURGLAR.
BUGEYE CATNIP
HA! WHY WOULD ANYONE IN THEIR RIGHT MIND WANT TO STEAL **MORE** CATS?
BUGEYE CATNIP
HE'D BE SCARIER IF HE'D BROKEN IN AND **LEFT** CATS.
IF HE BROKE IN HERE I'D BE ALL, LIKE, *CAT'S IN THE KITCHEN, ART! BURGLE UP!*
JUST BE SURE YOU DON'T DROP ANY OTHER CATS ON YOUR WAY OUT, DUDE!
OR WAS HE PROVIDING A SERVICE? LIKE VACUUMING UP EXCESS CATS?
MAD CAT 2015
darb
ENJOY YOUR TIME ON THE CAT HIT LIST, PAL.
HARD **NOT** TO, WITH ALL THE YARN AND LASER POINTERS THAT WILL BE KEEPING ME COMPANY.

Panel 1: I AM INCENSED WITH MY FOOD. / NO WORRIES. WITH MY ALLERGIES, I CAN'T SMELL ANYTHING.

Panel 2: THEY CHANGED MY FAVORITE TREATS! LOOK!

Panel 3: WHAT AM I LOOKING FOR, NOW? / RIGHT THERE!, CHEMICALS! PINK NUMBER TWO!

Panel 4: BUT THAT'S IN THE OLD ONE, NOT THE NEW ONE. / EXACTLY! AND THE NEW ONES ARE AWFUL!

Panel 5: THE BAG STILL SAYS ATLANTIC SALMON...

Panel 6: BUT THEY TASTE MORE LIKE SOME JUNK PACIFIC CHUM SALMON WHO GOT RUN OVER BY AN OIL TANKER IN THE STRAIT OF TARTARY!

Panel 7: CLEARLY, THE PINK NUMBER TWO WAS THE TASTE NUMBER ONE.

Panel 8: SO I NEED SOME HELP COMPLETING MY COMPLAINY LETTER. / EASY. GET A PEN AND SOME PAPER: "DEAR—

Panel 9: AND WHERE AM I SUPPOSED TO FIND A STAMP, *DARLING?*

Panel 10: NO, DEAR— / I SUGGEST YOU TAKE THIS MORE SERIOUSLY, SNOOKUMS.

darb

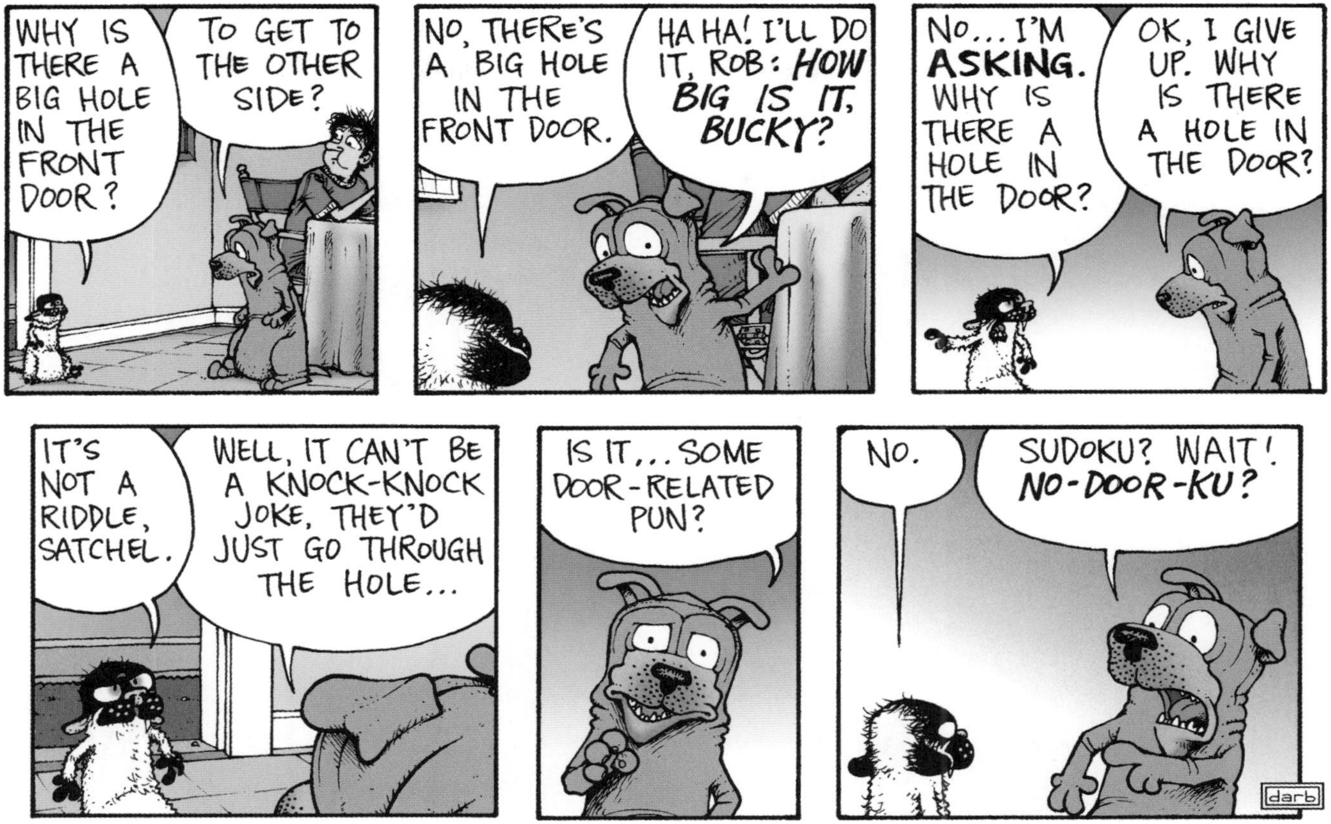
WHY IS THERE A BIG HOLE IN THE FRONT DOOR?
TO GET TO THE OTHER SIDE?
NO, THERE'S A BIG HOLE IN THE FRONT DOOR.
HA HA! I'LL DO IT, ROB: HOW BIG IS IT, BUCKY?
NO... I'M ASKING. WHY IS THERE A HOLE IN THE DOOR?
OK, I GIVE UP. WHY IS THERE A HOLE IN THE DOOR?
IT'S NOT A RIDDLE, SATCHEL.
WELL, IT CAN'T BE A KNOCK-KNOCK JOKE, THEY'D JUST GO THROUGH THE HOLE...
IS IT... SOME DOOR-RELATED PUN?
NO.
SUDOKU? WAIT! NO-DOOR-KU?
darb
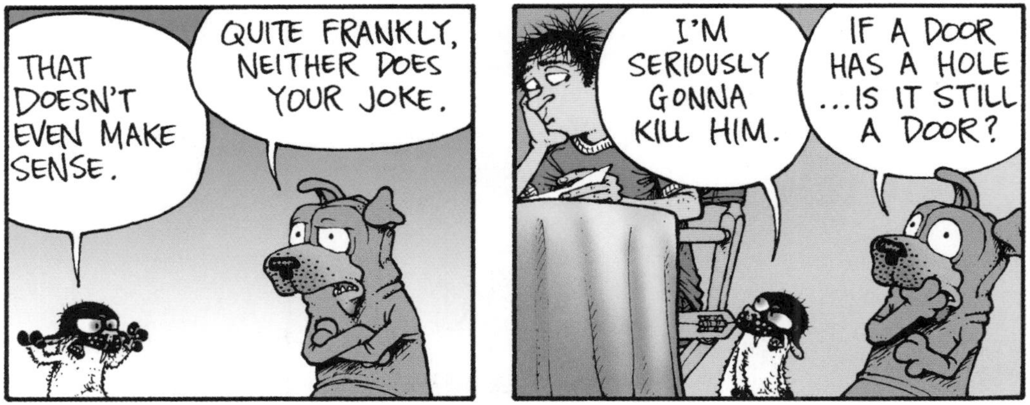
THAT DOESN'T EVEN MAKE SENSE.
QUITE FRANKLY, NEITHER DOES YOUR JOKE.
I'M SERIOUSLY GONNA KILL HIM.
IF A DOOR HAS A HOLE ...IS IT STILL A DOOR?

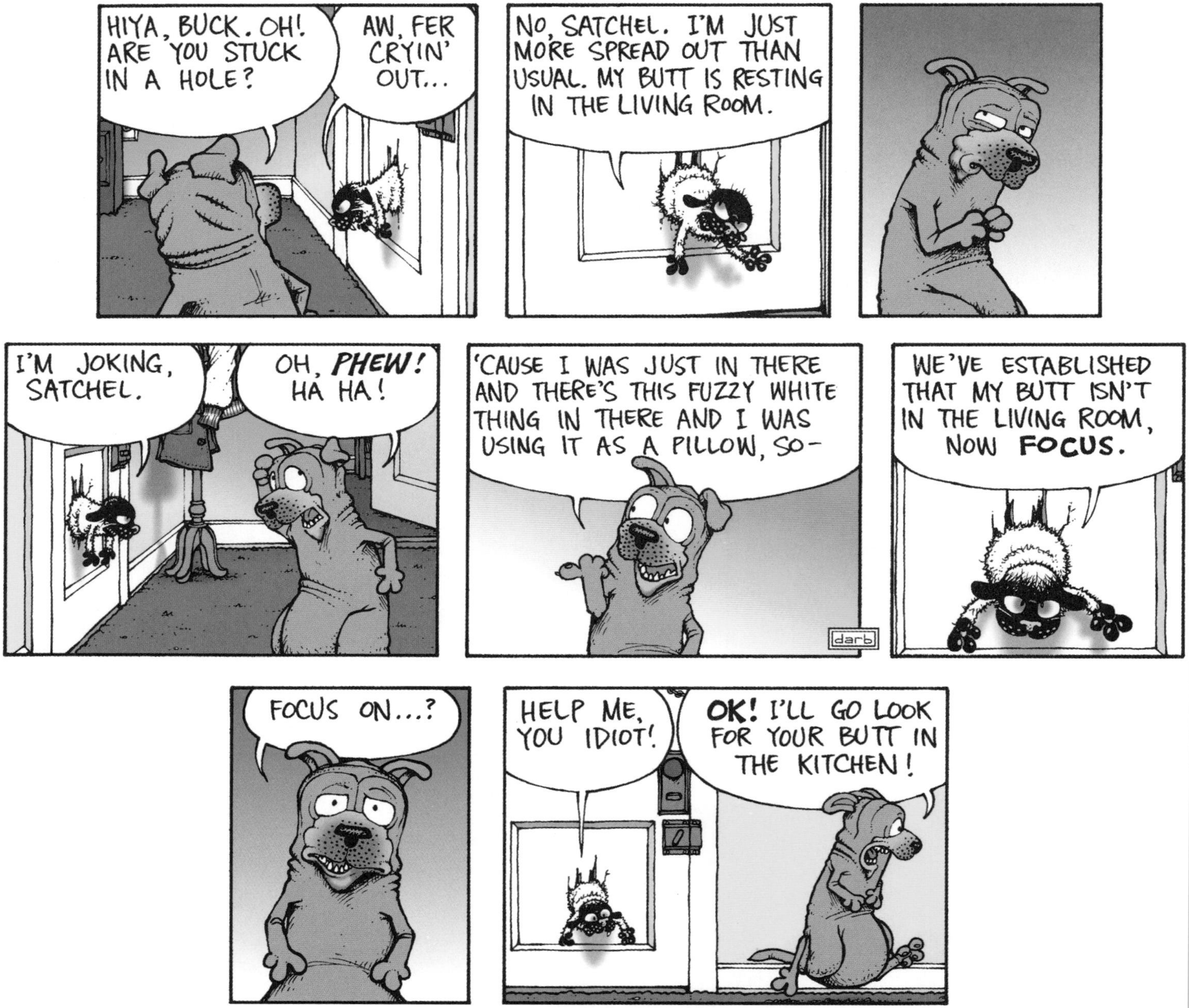
HIYA, BUCK. OH! ARE YOU STUCK IN A HOLE?
AW, FER CRYIN' OUT...
NO, SATCHEL. I'M JUST MORE SPREAD OUT THAN USUAL. MY BUTT IS RESTING IN THE LIVING ROOM.
I'M JOKING, SATCHEL.
OH, PHEW! HA HA!
'CAUSE I WAS JUST IN THERE AND THERE'S THIS FUZZY WHITE THING IN THERE AND I WAS USING IT AS A PILLOW, SO-
darb
WE'VE ESTABLISHED THAT MY BUTT ISN'T IN THE LIVING ROOM, NOW FOCUS.
FOCUS ON...?
HELP ME, YOU IDIOT!
OK! I'LL GO LOOK FOR YOUR BUTT IN THE KITCHEN!

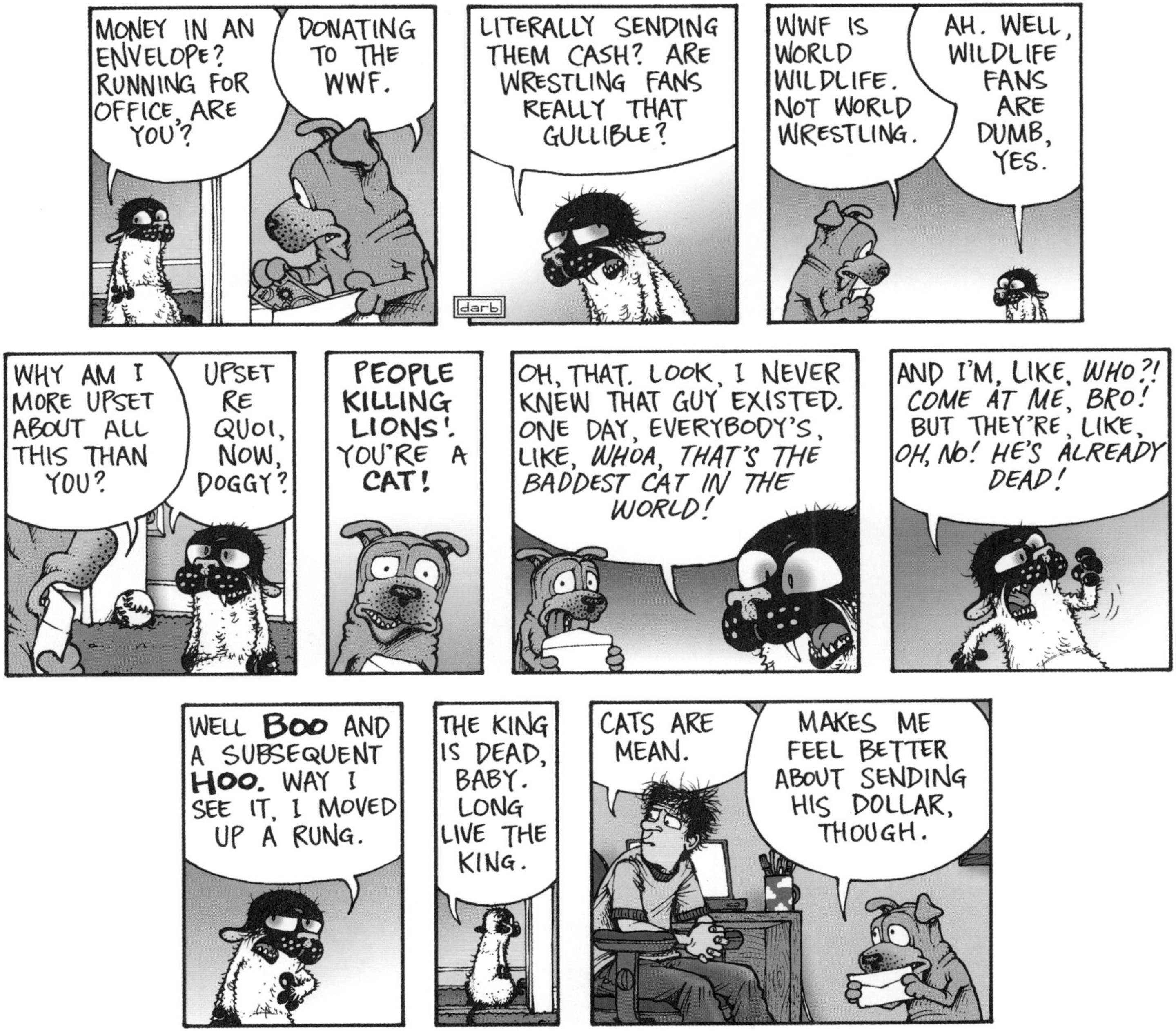
MONEY IN AN ENVELOPE? RUNNING FOR OFFICE, ARE YOU?
DONATING TO THE WWF.
LITERALLY SENDING THEM CASH? ARE WRESTLING FANS REALLY THAT GULLIBLE?
darb
WWF IS WORLD WILDLIFE. NOT WORLD WRESTLING.
AH. WELL, WILDLIFE FANS ARE DUMB, YES.
WHY AM I MORE UPSET ABOUT ALL THIS THAN YOU?
UPSET RE QUOI, NOW, DOGGY?
PEOPLE KILLING LIONS! YOU'RE A CAT!
OH, THAT. LOOK, I NEVER KNEW THAT GUY EXISTED. ONE DAY, EVERYBODY'S, LIKE, WHOA, THAT'S THE BADDEST CAT IN THE WORLD!
AND I'M, LIKE, WHO?! COME AT ME, BRO! BUT THEY'RE, LIKE, OH, NO! HE'S ALREADY DEAD!
WELL BOO AND A SUBSEQUENT HOO. WAY I SEE IT, I MOVED UP A RUNG.
THE KING IS DEAD, BABY. LONG LIVE THE KING.
CATS ARE MEAN.
MAKES ME FEEL BETTER ABOUT SENDING HIS DOLLAR, THOUGH.

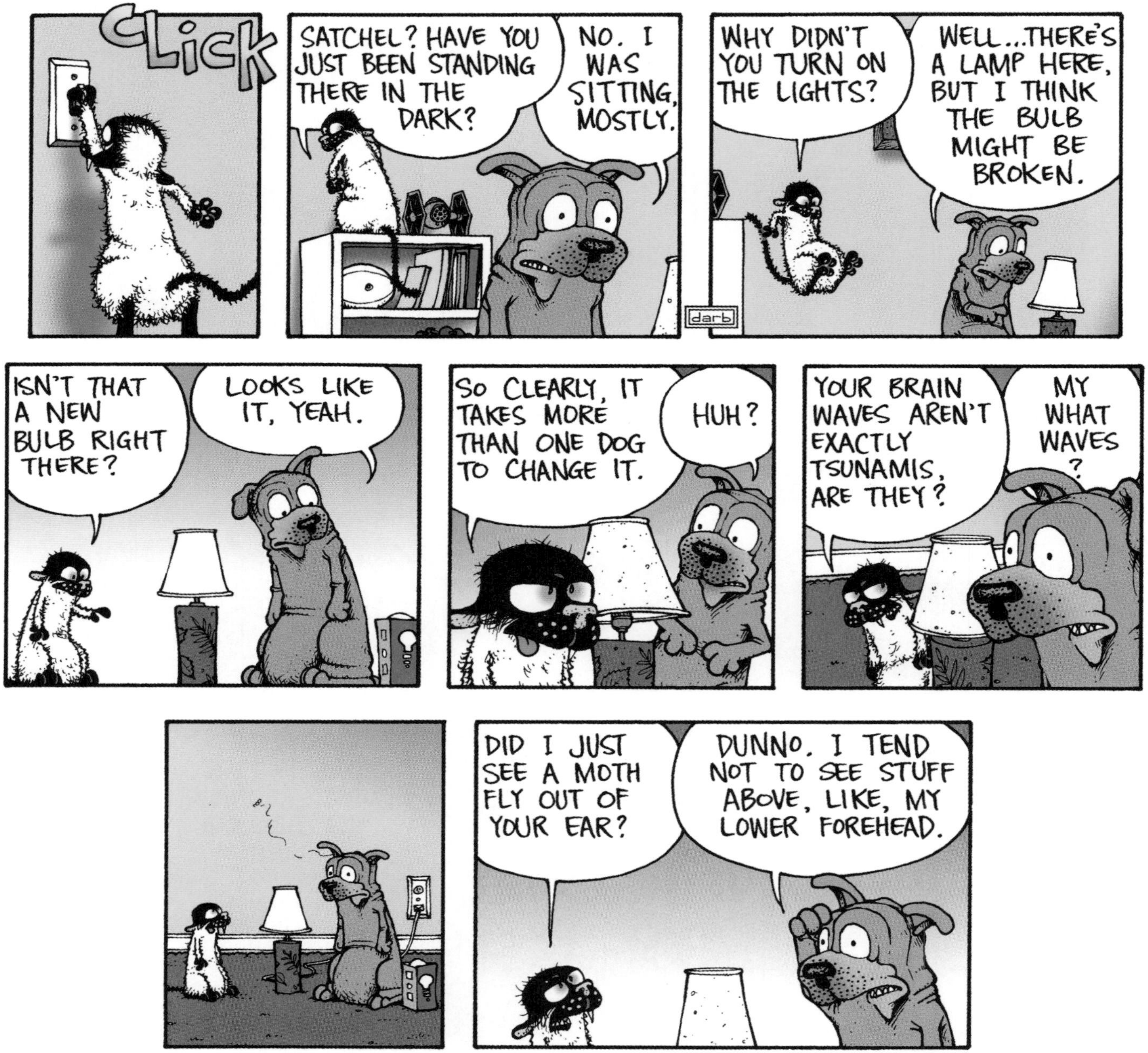
CLICK
SATCHEL? HAVE YOU JUST BEEN STANDING THERE IN THE DARK?
NO. I WAS SITTING, MOSTLY.
darb
WHY DIDN'T YOU TURN ON THE LIGHTS?
WELL...THERE'S A LAMP HERE, BUT I THINK THE BULB MIGHT BE BROKEN.
ISN'T THAT A NEW BULB RIGHT THERE?
LOOKS LIKE IT, YEAH.
SO CLEARLY, IT TAKES MORE THAN ONE DOG TO CHANGE IT.
HUH?
YOUR BRAIN WAVES AREN'T EXACTLY TSUNAMIS, ARE THEY?
MY WHAT WAVES?
DID I JUST SEE A MOTH FLY OUT OF YOUR EAR?
DUNNO. I TEND NOT TO SEE STUFF ABOVE, LIKE, MY LOWER FOREHEAD.

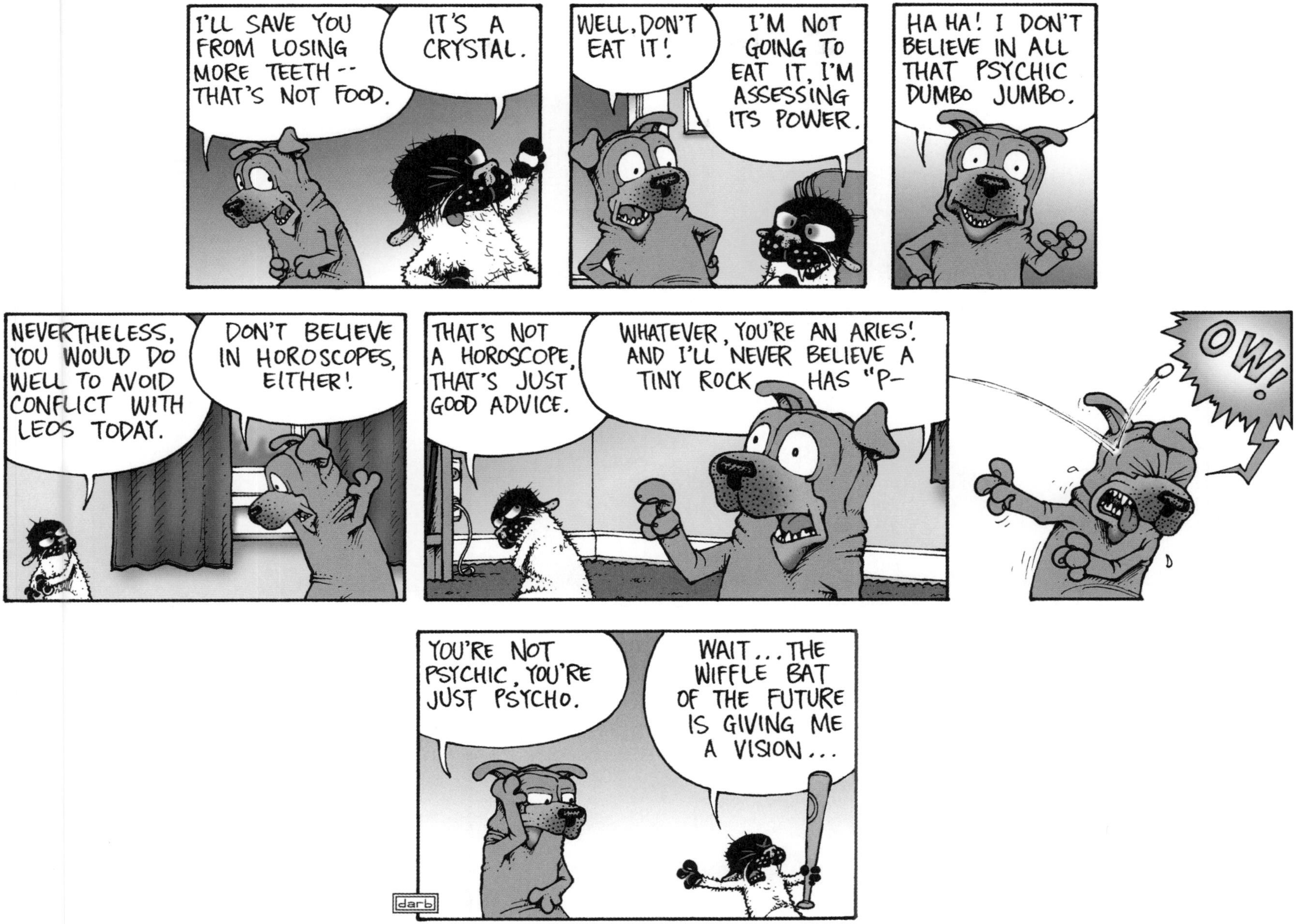
I'LL SAVE YOU FROM LOSING MORE TEETH -- THAT'S NOT FOOD.
IT'S A CRYSTAL.
WELL, DON'T EAT IT!
I'M NOT GOING TO EAT IT, I'M ASSESSING ITS POWER.
HA HA! I DON'T BELIEVE IN ALL THAT PSYCHIC DUMBO JUMBO.
NEVERTHELESS, YOU WOULD DO WELL TO AVOID CONFLICT WITH LEOS TODAY.
DON'T BELIEVE IN HOROSCOPES, EITHER!
THAT'S NOT A HOROSCOPE, THAT'S JUST GOOD ADVICE.
WHATEVER, YOU'RE AN ARIES! AND I'LL NEVER BELIEVE A TINY ROCK HAS "P-
OW!
YOU'RE NOT PSYCHIC, YOU'RE JUST PSYCHO.
WAIT... THE WIFFLE BAT OF THE FUTURE IS GIVING ME A VISION...
darb

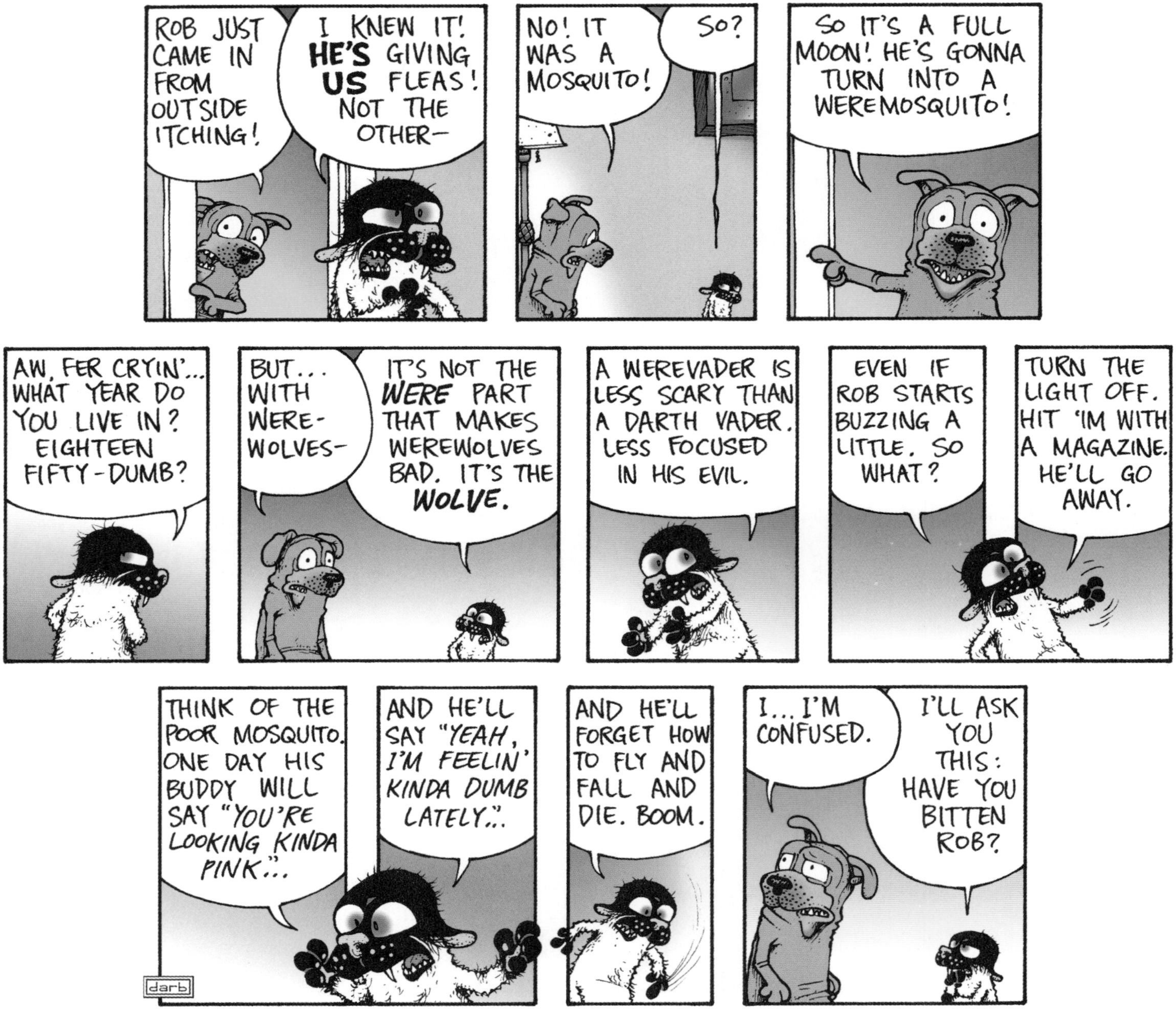

ROB JUST CAME IN FROM OUTSIDE ITCHING!
I KNEW IT! **HE'S** GIVING **US** FLEAS! NOT THE OTHER–
NO! IT WAS A MOSQUITO!
SO?
SO IT'S A FULL MOON! HE'S GONNA TURN INTO A WEREMOSQUITO!
AW, FER CRYIN'... WHAT YEAR DO YOU LIVE IN? EIGHTEEN FIFTY-DUMB?
BUT... WITH WERE-WOLVES–
IT'S NOT THE *WERE* PART THAT MAKES WEREWOLVES BAD. IT'S THE *WOLVE*.
A WEREVADER IS LESS SCARY THAN A DARTH VADER. LESS FOCUSED IN HIS EVIL.
EVEN IF ROB STARTS BUZZING A LITTLE. SO WHAT?
TURN THE LIGHT OFF. HIT 'IM WITH A MAGAZINE. HE'LL GO AWAY.
THINK OF THE POOR MOSQUITO. ONE DAY HIS BUDDY WILL SAY "*YOU'RE LOOKING KINDA PINK*."...
AND HE'LL SAY "*YEAH, I'M FEELIN' KINDA DUMB LATELY*."...
AND HE'LL FORGET HOW TO FLY AND FALL AND DIE. BOOM.
I... I'M CONFUSED.
I'LL ASK YOU THIS: HAVE YOU BITTEN ROB?
darb

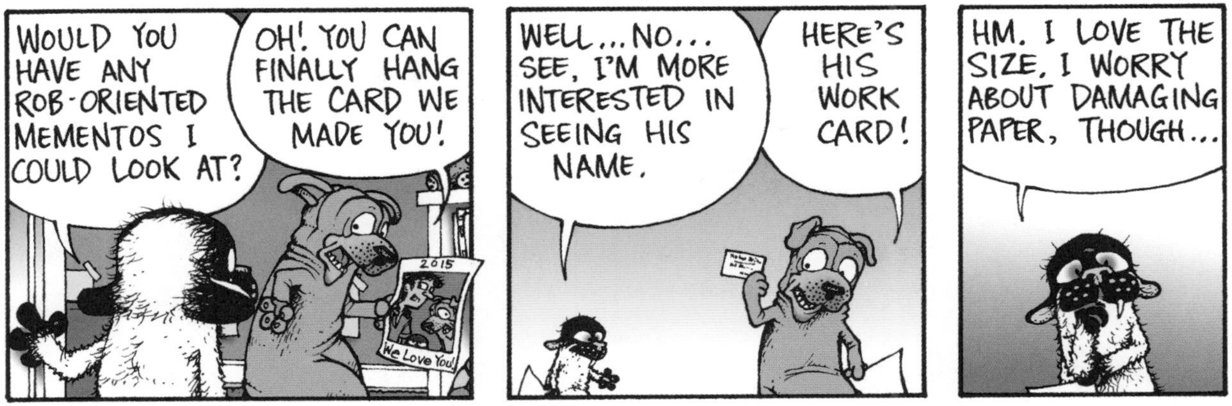
WOULD YOU HAVE ANY ROB-ORIENTED MEMENTOS I COULD LOOK AT?
OH! YOU CAN FINALLY HANG THE CARD WE MADE YOU!
2015
We Love You!
WELL... NO... SEE, I'M MORE INTERESTED IN SEEING HIS NAME.
HERE'S HIS WORK CARD!
HM. I LOVE THE SIZE. I WORRY ABOUT DAMAGING PAPER, THOUGH...

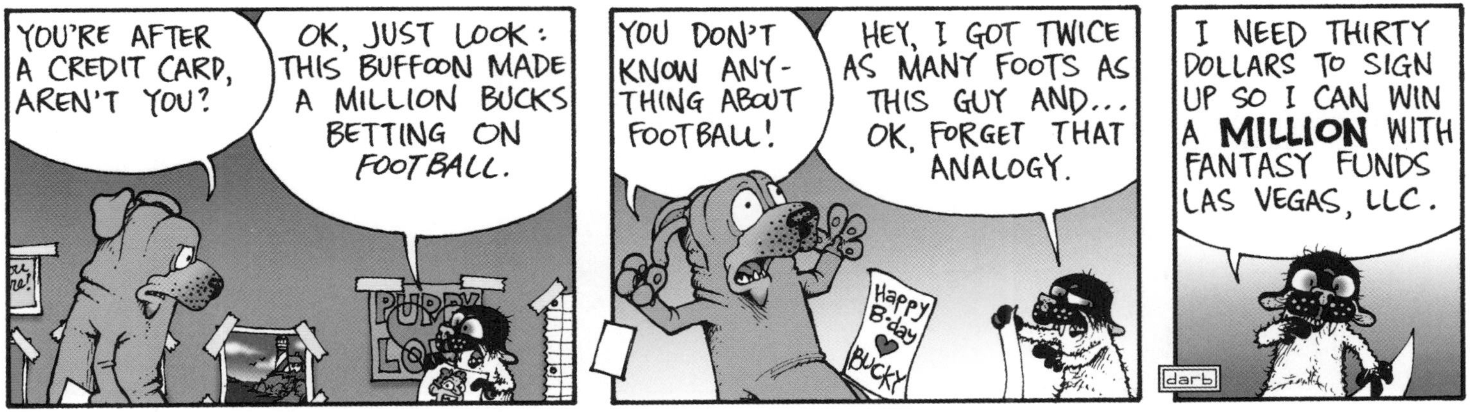
YOU'RE AFTER A CREDIT CARD, AREN'T YOU?
OK, JUST LOOK: THIS BUFFOON MADE A MILLION BUCKS BETTING ON *FOOTBALL.*
YOU DON'T KNOW ANYTHING ABOUT FOOTBALL!
HEY, I GOT TWICE AS MANY FOOTS AS THIS GUY AND... OK, FORGET THAT ANALOGY.
Happy B-day ♥ BUCKY
I NEED THIRTY DOLLARS TO SIGN UP SO I CAN WIN A **MILLION** WITH FANTASY FUNDS LAS VEGAS, LLC.
darb

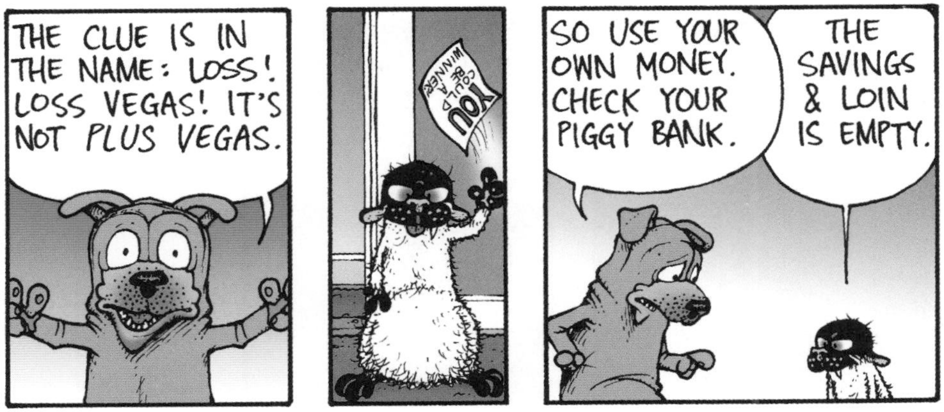
THE CLUE IS IN THE NAME: LOSS! LOSS VEGAS! IT'S NOT *PLUS* VEGAS.
YOU COULD BE A WINNER
SO USE YOUR OWN MONEY. CHECK YOUR PIGGY BANK.
THE SAVINGS & LOIN IS EMPTY.

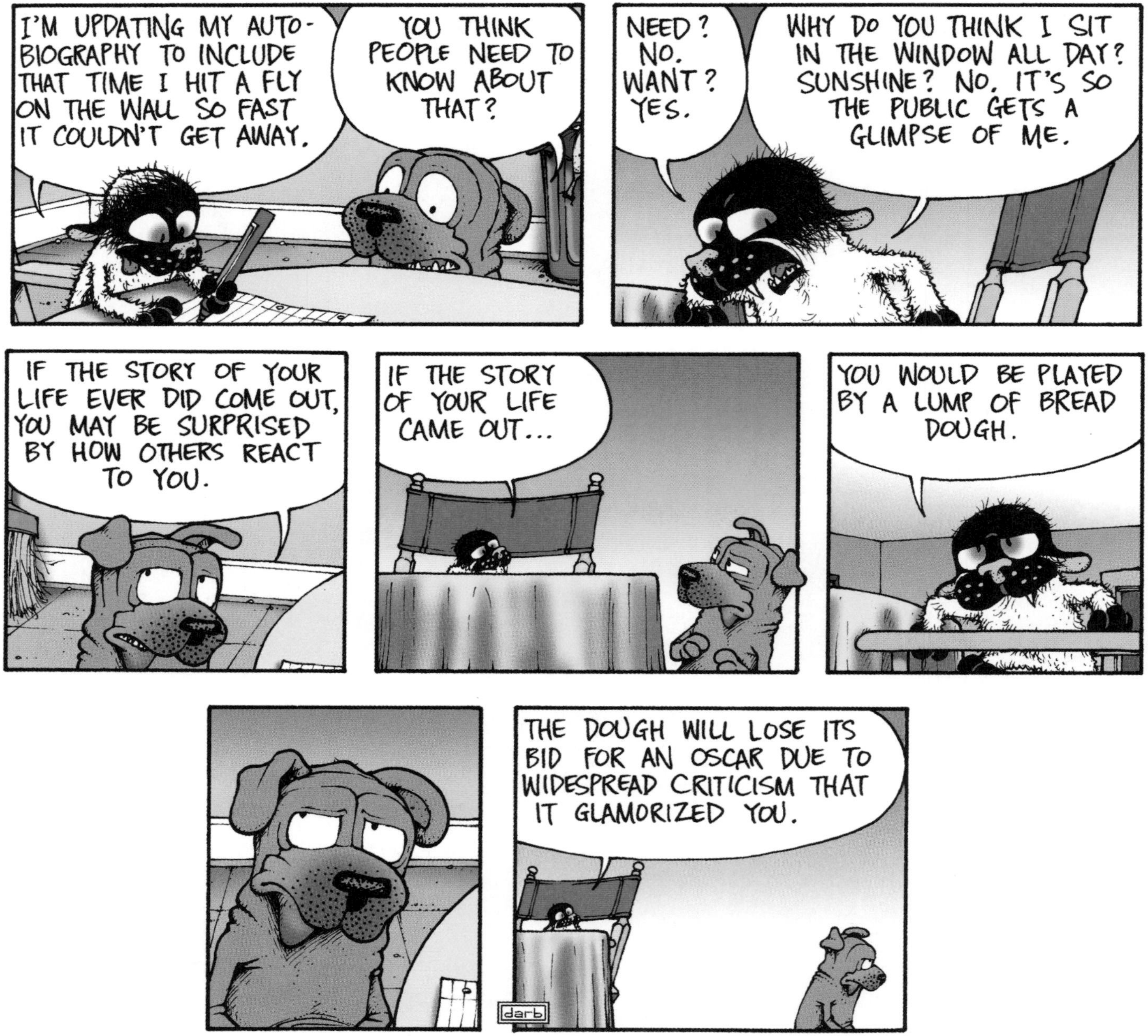
I'M UPDATING MY AUTO-BIOGRAPHY TO INCLUDE THAT TIME I HIT A FLY ON THE WALL SO FAST IT COULDN'T GET AWAY.
YOU THINK PEOPLE NEED TO KNOW ABOUT THAT?
NEED? NO. WANT? YES.
WHY DO YOU THINK I SIT IN THE WINDOW ALL DAY? SUNSHINE? NO. IT'S SO THE PUBLIC GETS A GLIMPSE OF ME.
IF THE STORY OF YOUR LIFE EVER DID COME OUT, YOU MAY BE SURPRISED BY HOW OTHERS REACT TO YOU.
IF THE STORY OF YOUR LIFE CAME OUT...
YOU WOULD BE PLAYED BY A LUMP OF BREAD DOUGH.
THE DOUGH WILL LOSE ITS BID FOR AN OSCAR DUE TO WIDESPREAD CRITICISM THAT IT GLAMORIZED YOU.
darb

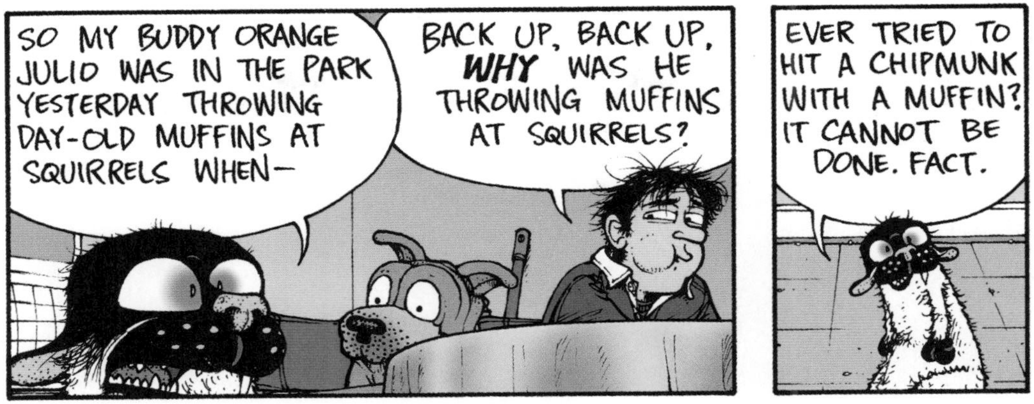
SO MY BUDDY ORANGE JULIO WAS IN THE PARK YESTERDAY THROWING DAY-OLD MUFFINS AT SQUIRRELS WHEN—
BACK UP, BACK UP, **WHY** WAS HE THROWING MUFFINS AT SQUIRRELS?
EVER TRIED TO HIT A CHIPMUNK WITH A MUFFIN? IT CANNOT BE DONE. FACT.

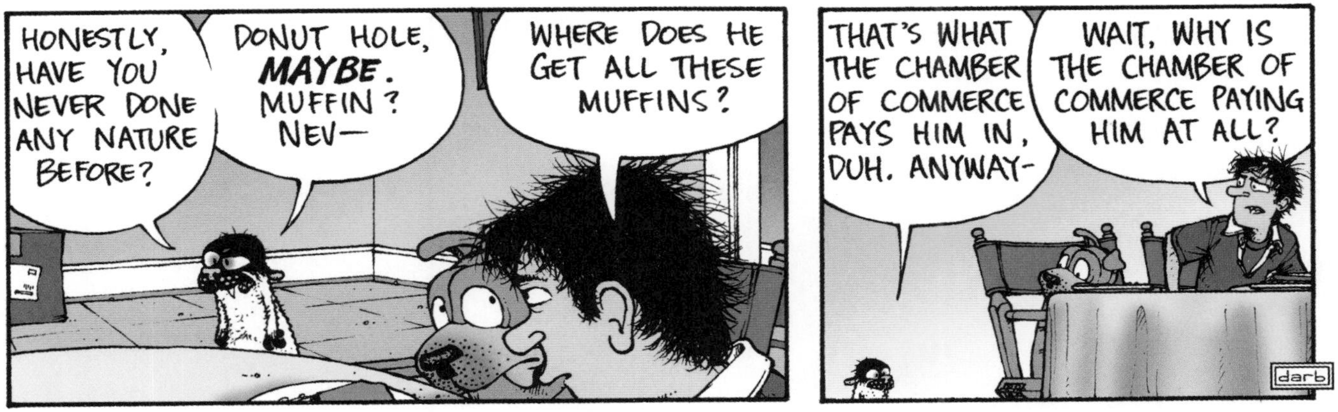
HONESTLY, HAVE YOU NEVER DONE ANY NATURE BEFORE?
DONUT HOLE, **MAYBE**. MUFFIN? NEV—
WHERE DOES HE GET ALL THESE MUFFINS?
THAT'S WHAT THE CHAMBER OF COMMERCE PAYS HIM IN, DUH. ANYWAY—
WAIT, WHY IS THE CHAMBER OF COMMERCE PAYING HIM AT ALL?
darb

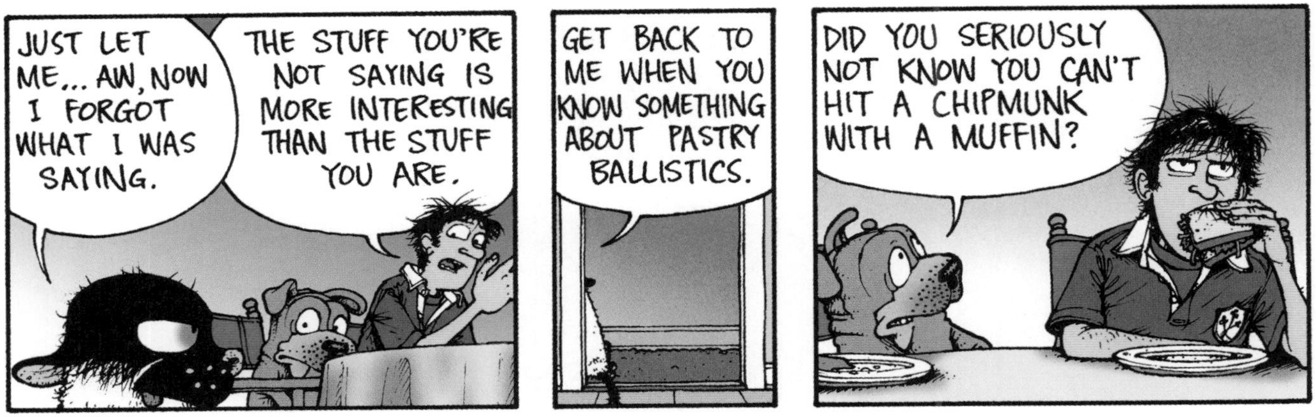
JUST LET ME... AW, NOW I FORGOT WHAT I WAS SAYING.
THE STUFF YOU'RE NOT SAYING IS MORE INTERESTING THAN THE STUFF YOU ARE.
GET BACK TO ME WHEN YOU KNOW SOMETHING ABOUT PASTRY BALLISTICS.
DID YOU SERIOUSLY NOT KNOW YOU CAN'T HIT A CHIPMUNK WITH A MUFFIN?

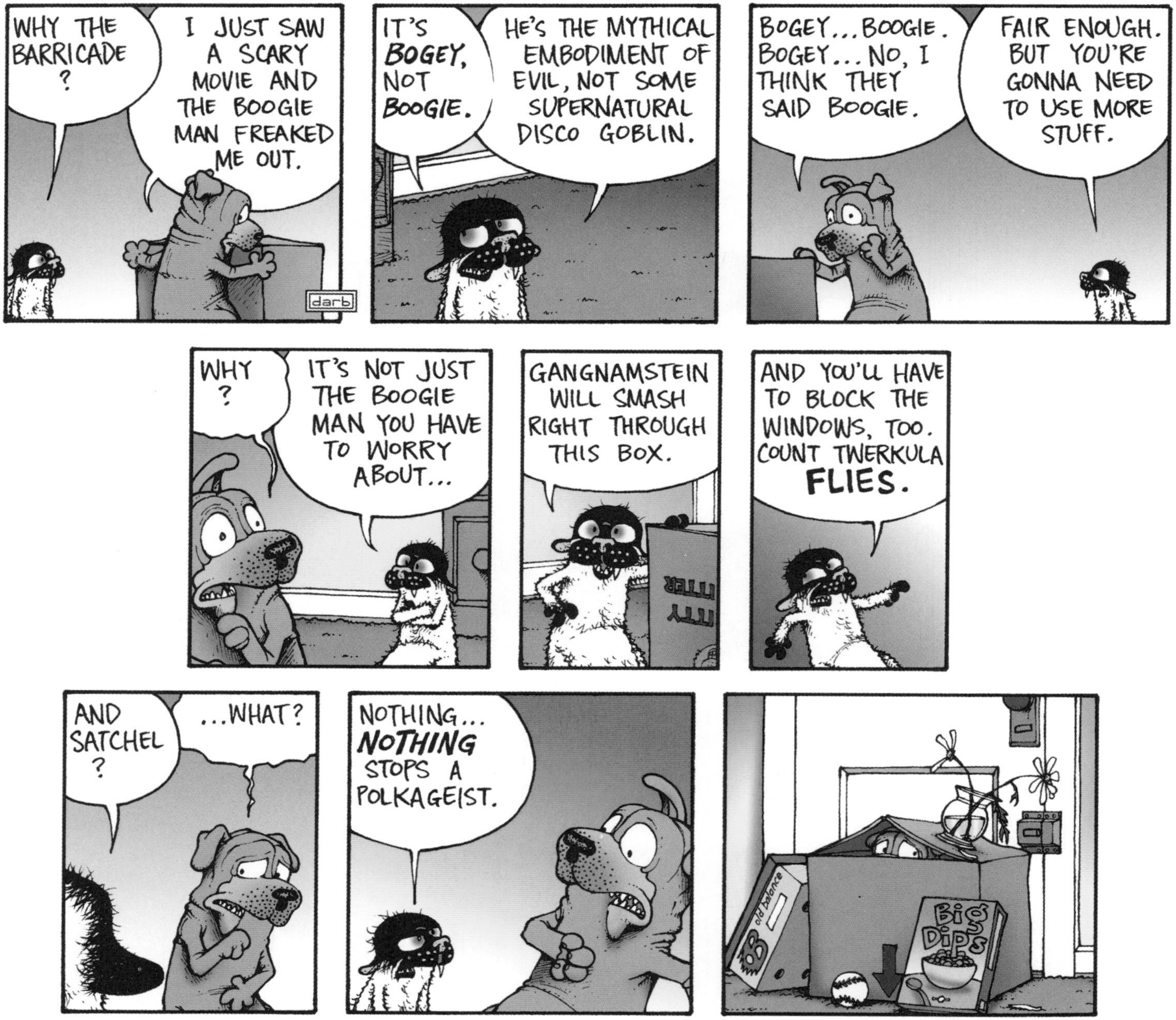
WHY THE BARRICADE?
I JUST SAW A SCARY MOVIE AND THE BOOGIE MAN FREAKED ME OUT.
darb
IT'S *BOGEY*, NOT *BOOGIE*.
HE'S THE MYTHICAL EMBODIMENT OF EVIL, NOT SOME SUPERNATURAL DISCO GOBLIN.
BOGEY... BOOGIE. BOGEY... NO, I THINK THEY SAID BOOGIE.
FAIR ENOUGH. BUT YOU'RE GONNA NEED TO USE MORE STUFF.
WHY?
IT'S NOT JUST THE BOOGIE MAN YOU HAVE TO WORRY ABOUT...
GANGNAMSTEIN WILL SMASH RIGHT THROUGH THIS BOX.
AND YOU'LL HAVE TO BLOCK THE WINDOWS, TOO. COUNT TWERKULA **FLIES**.
AND SATCHEL?
...WHAT?
NOTHING... ***NOTHING*** STOPS A POLKAGEIST.
old balance
BIG DIPS

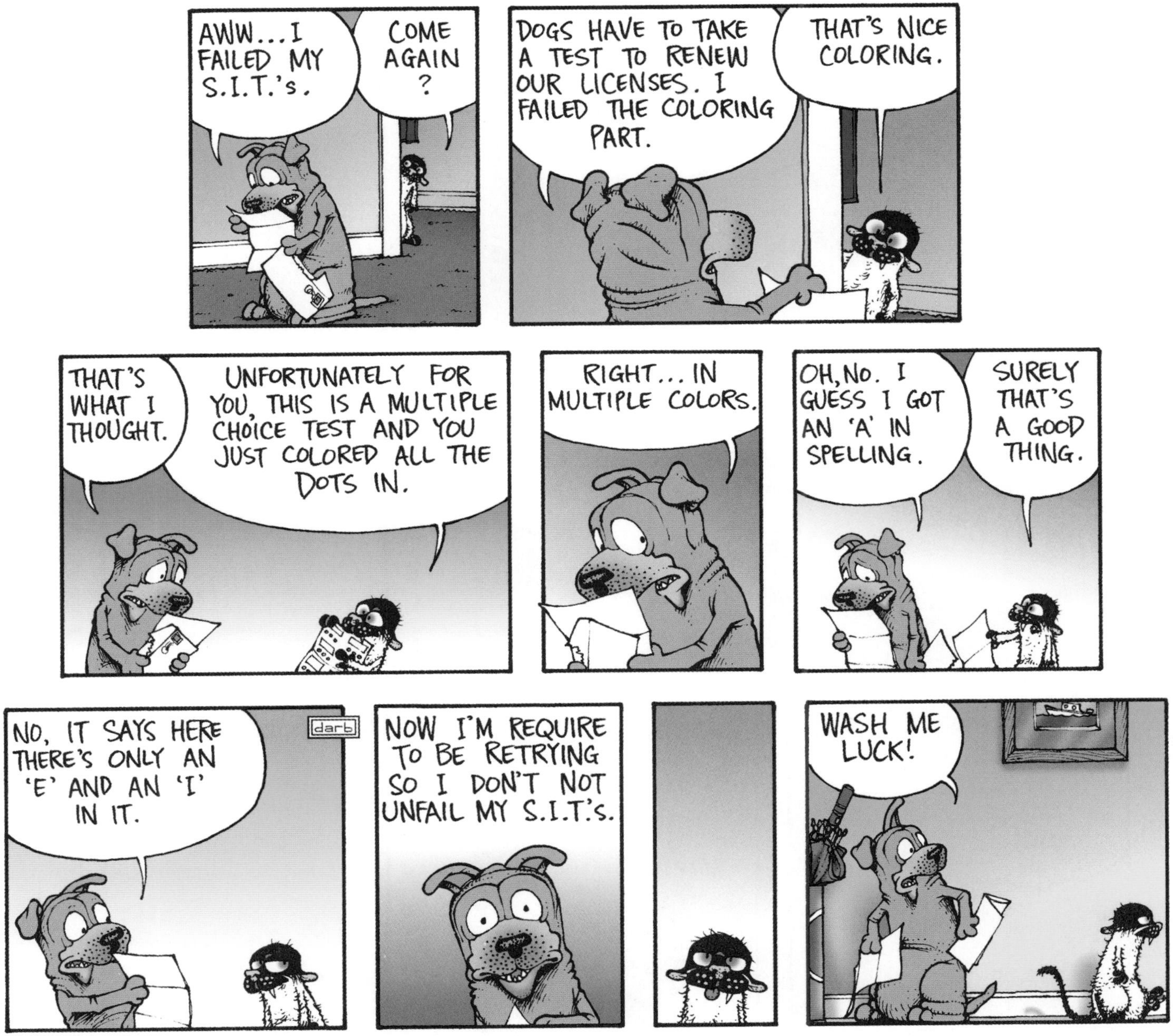
AWW... I FAILED MY S.I.T.'s.
COME AGAIN ?
DOGS HAVE TO TAKE A TEST TO RENEW OUR LICENSES. I FAILED THE COLORING PART.
THAT'S NICE COLORING.
THAT'S WHAT I THOUGHT.
UNFORTUNATELY FOR YOU, THIS IS A MULTIPLE CHOICE TEST AND YOU JUST COLORED ALL THE DOTS IN.
RIGHT... IN MULTIPLE COLORS.
OH, NO. I GUESS I GOT AN 'A' IN SPELLING.
SURELY THAT'S A GOOD THING.
NO, IT SAYS HERE THERE'S ONLY AN 'E' AND AN 'I' IN IT.
darb
NOW I'M REQUIRE TO BE RETRYING SO I DON'T NOT UNFAIL MY S.I.T.'s.
WASH ME LUCK!

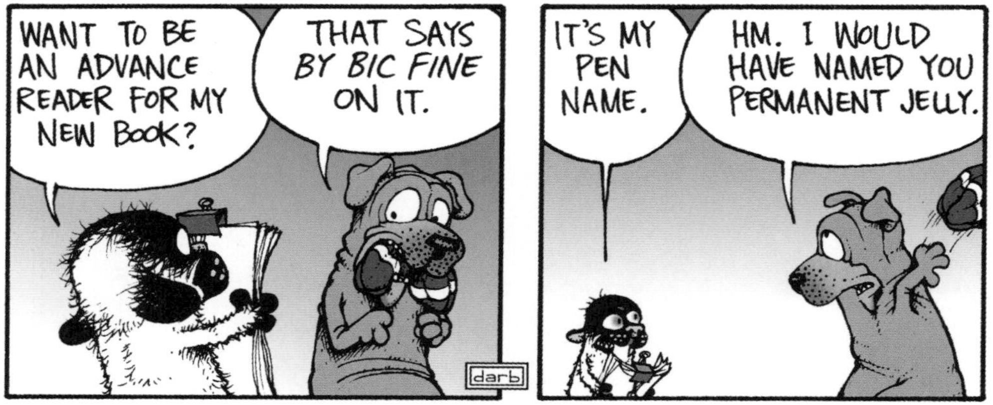
WANT TO BE AN ADVANCE READER FOR MY NEW BOOK?
THAT SAYS *BY BIC FINE* ON IT.
darb
IT'S MY PEN NAME.
HM. I WOULD HAVE NAMED YOU PERMANENT JELLY.

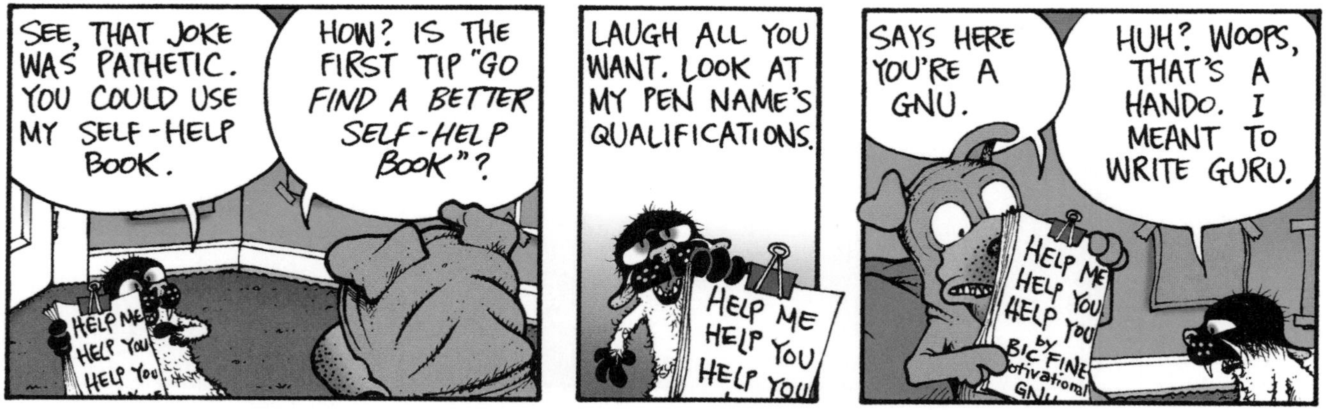
SEE, THAT JOKE WAS PATHETIC. YOU COULD USE MY SELF-HELP BOOK.
HOW? IS THE FIRST TIP "*GO FIND A BETTER SELF-HELP BOOK*"?
HELP ME HELP YOU HELP YOU
LAUGH ALL YOU WANT. LOOK AT MY PEN NAME'S QUALIFICATIONS.
HELP ME HELP YOU HELP YOU
SAYS HERE YOU'RE A GNU.
HUH? WOOPS, THAT'S A HANDO. I MEANT TO WRITE GURU.
HELP ME HELP YOU HELP YOU by BIC FINE

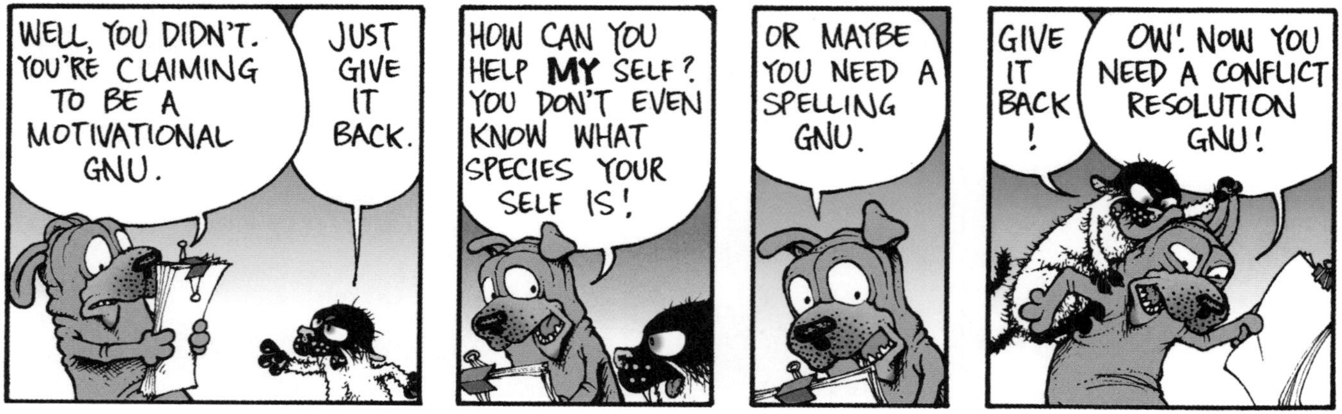
WELL, YOU DIDN'T. YOU'RE CLAIMING TO BE A MOTIVATIONAL GNU.
JUST GIVE IT BACK.
HOW CAN YOU HELP **MY** SELF? YOU DON'T EVEN KNOW WHAT SPECIES YOUR SELF IS!
OR MAYBE YOU NEED A SPELLING GNU.
GIVE IT BACK!
OW! NOW YOU NEED A CONFLICT RESOLUTION GNU!

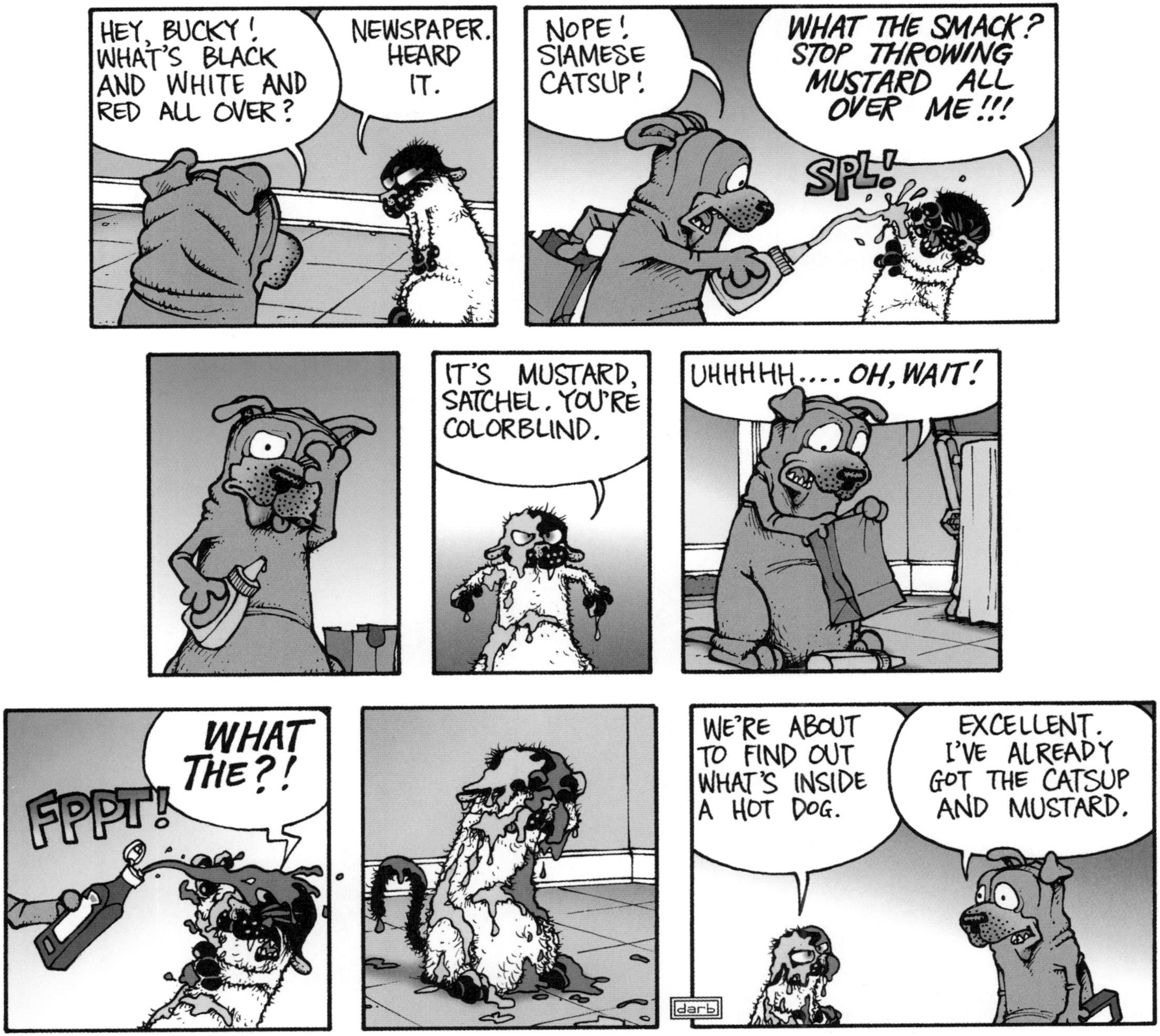
HEY, BUCKY! WHAT'S BLACK AND WHITE AND RED ALL OVER?
NEWSPAPER. HEARD IT.
NOPE! SIAMESE CATSUP!
SPL!
WHAT THE SMACK? STOP THROWING MUSTARD ALL OVER ME!!!
IT'S MUSTARD, SATCHEL. YOU'RE COLORBLIND.
UHHHHH.... OH, WAIT!
FPPT!
WHAT THE?!
WE'RE ABOUT TO FIND OUT WHAT'S INSIDE A HOT DOG.
EXCELLENT. I'VE ALREADY GOT THE CATSUP AND MUSTARD.
darb

Panel 1: CAN I ASK YOUR ADVICE?

NOPE.

Panel 2: WAIT, IS IT ABOUT YOUR SHAPE? I JUST HEARD ABOUT A VET WHO'S EXPERIMENTING WITH LABROSUCTION.

Panel 3: NO, SEE, I'M WRITING A RECOMMENDATION...DID YOU JUST CALL ME FAT?

WHERE?

Panel 4: WHERE WHAT?

RECOMMEN-DATION?

Panel 5: HUH? OH, RIGHT. A PUPPY I KNOW IS APPLYING TO MY OLD OBEDIENCE SCHOOL...

Panel 6: SO I WROTE: *SHE KNEW HER NAME AT NINE WEEKS.* IS THAT IMPRESSIVE?

LEMME PUT IT THIS WAY: THAT'S LIKE BRINGING PARMESAN TO A MUSK GLAND FIGHT.

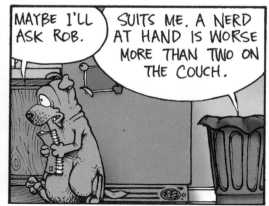

Panel 7: UH...I DON'T ALWAYS KNOW WHAT YOU'RE SAYING.

WOW, IF THAT ISN'T THE MANTA CALLING THE BASKING PELAGIC...

Panel 9: MAYBE I'LL ASK ROB.

SUITS ME. A NERD AT HAND IS WORSE MORE THAN TWO ON THE COUCH.

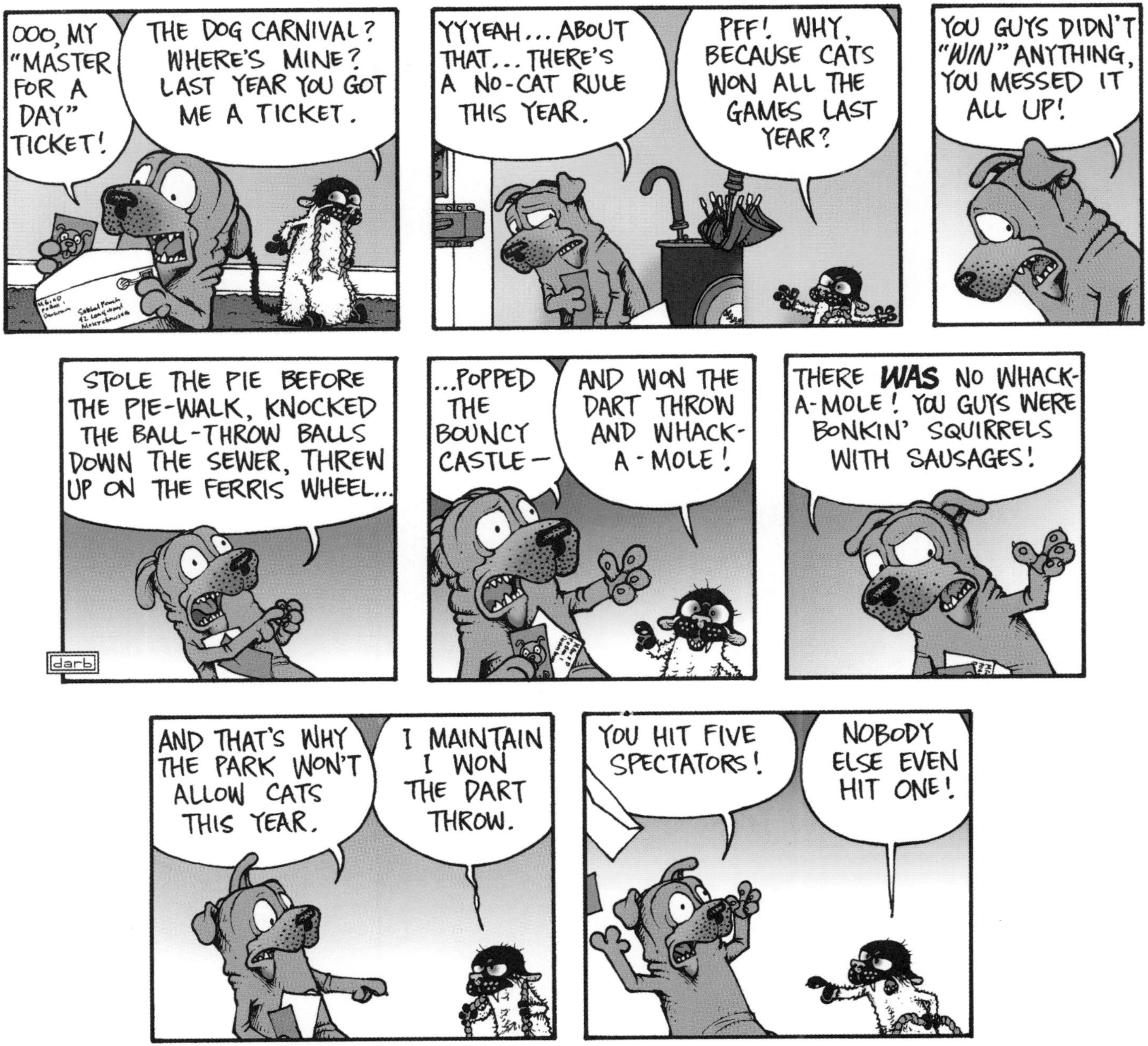
OOO, MY "MASTER FOR A DAY" TICKET!
THE DOG CARNIVAL? WHERE'S MINE? LAST YEAR YOU GOT ME A TICKET.
YYYEAH... ABOUT THAT... THERE'S A NO-CAT RULE THIS YEAR.
PFF! WHY, BECAUSE CATS WON ALL THE GAMES LAST YEAR?
YOU GUYS DIDN'T "WIN" ANYTHING, YOU MESSED IT ALL UP!
STOLE THE PIE BEFORE THE PIE-WALK, KNOCKED THE BALL-THROW BALLS DOWN THE SEWER, THREW UP ON THE FERRIS WHEEL...
darb
...POPPED THE BOUNCY CASTLE—
AND WON THE DART THROW AND WHACK-A-MOLE!
THERE WAS NO WHACK-A-MOLE! YOU GUYS WERE BONKIN' SQUIRRELS WITH SAUSAGES!
AND THAT'S WHY THE PARK WON'T ALLOW CATS THIS YEAR.
I MAINTAIN I WON THE DART THROW.
YOU HIT FIVE SPECTATORS!
NOBODY ELSE EVEN HIT ONE!

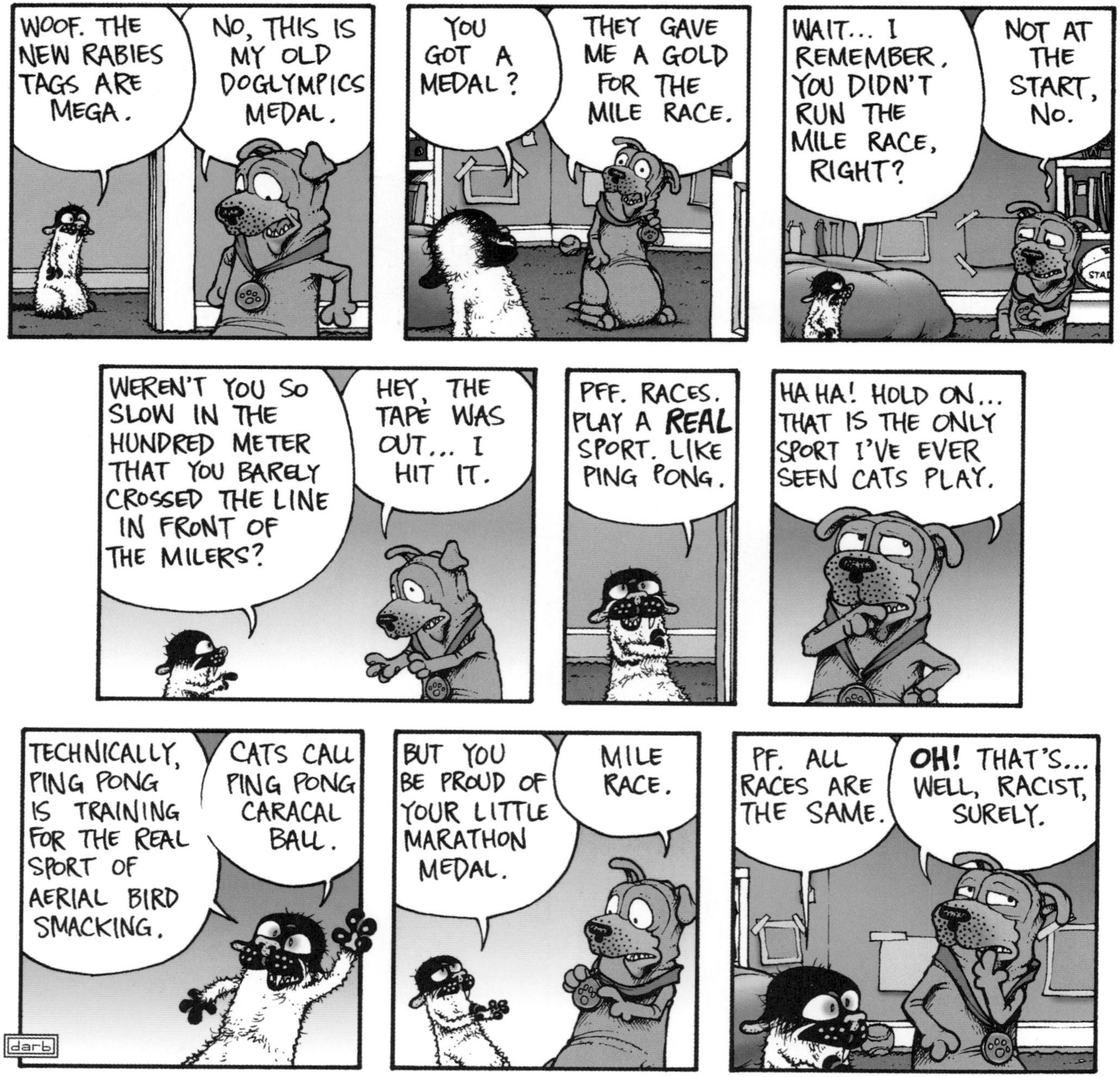
WOOF. THE NEW RABIES TAGS ARE MEGA.
NO, THIS IS MY OLD DOGLYMPICS MEDAL.
YOU GOT A MEDAL?
THEY GAVE ME A GOLD FOR THE MILE RACE.
WAIT... I REMEMBER, YOU DIDN'T RUN THE MILE RACE, RIGHT?
NOT AT THE START, NO.
WEREN'T YOU SO SLOW IN THE HUNDRED METER THAT YOU BARELY CROSSED THE LINE IN FRONT OF THE MILERS?
HEY, THE TAPE WAS OUT... I HIT IT.
PFF. RACES. PLAY A **REAL** SPORT. LIKE PING PONG.
HA HA! HOLD ON... THAT IS THE ONLY SPORT I'VE EVER SEEN CATS PLAY.
TECHNICALLY, PING PONG IS TRAINING FOR THE REAL SPORT OF AERIAL BIRD SMACKING.
CATS CALL PING PONG CARACAL BALL.
darb
BUT YOU BE PROUD OF YOUR LITTLE MARATHON MEDAL.
MILE RACE.
PF. ALL RACES ARE THE SAME.
OH! THAT'S... WELL, RACIST, SURELY.

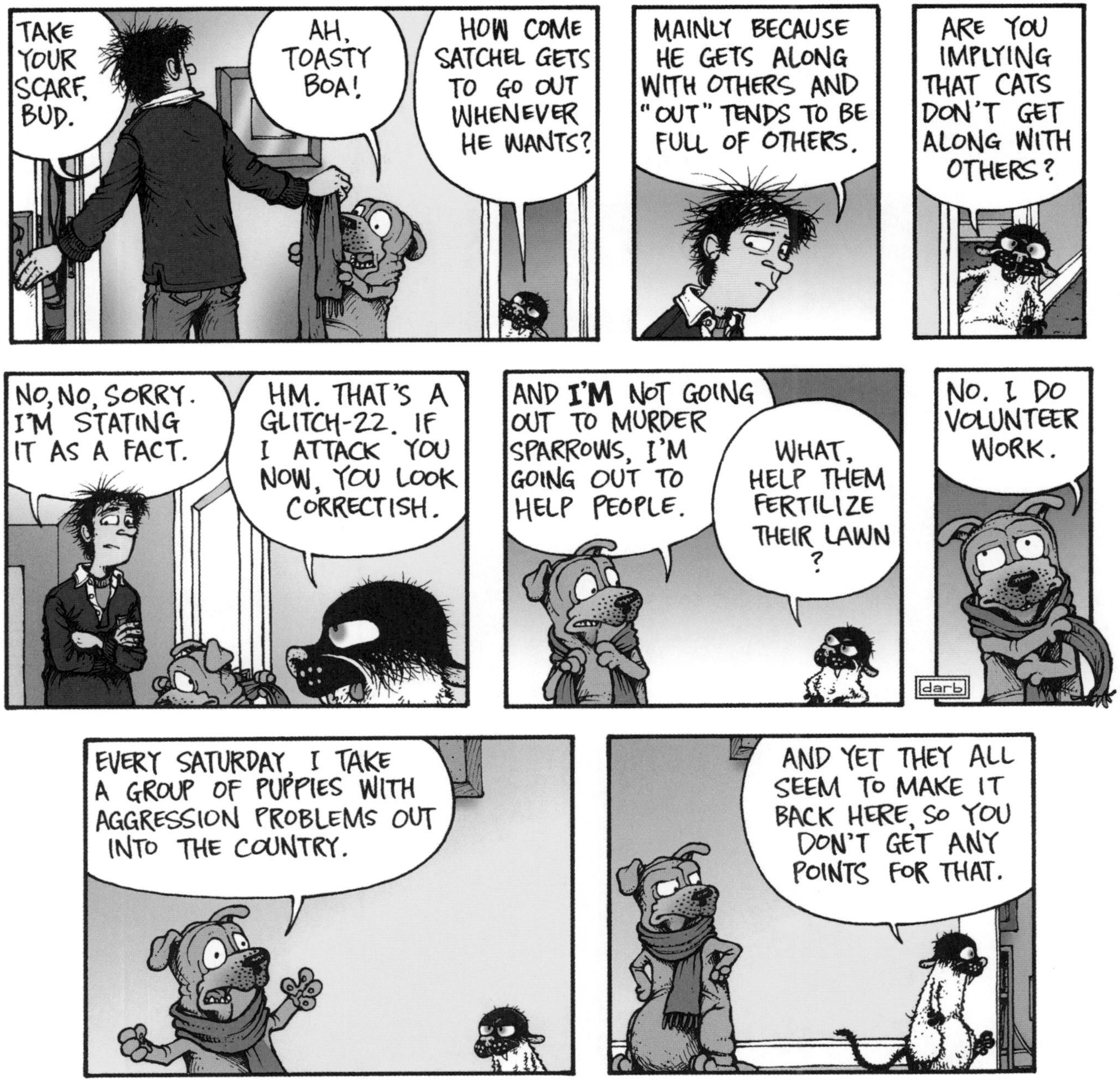
TAKE YOUR SCARF, BUD.
AH, TOASTY BOA!
HOW COME SATCHEL GETS TO GO OUT WHENEVER HE WANTS?
MAINLY BECAUSE HE GETS ALONG WITH OTHERS AND "OUT" TENDS TO BE FULL OF OTHERS.
ARE YOU IMPLYING THAT CATS DON'T GET ALONG WITH OTHERS?
NO, NO, SORRY. I'M STATING IT AS A FACT.
HM. THAT'S A GLITCH-22. IF I ATTACK YOU NOW, YOU LOOK CORRECTISH.
AND **I'M** NOT GOING OUT TO MURDER SPARROWS, I'M GOING OUT TO HELP PEOPLE.
WHAT, HELP THEM FERTILIZE THEIR LAWN?
NO. I DO VOLUNTEER WORK.
darb
EVERY SATURDAY, I TAKE A GROUP OF PUPPIES WITH AGGRESSION PROBLEMS OUT INTO THE COUNTRY.
AND YET THEY ALL SEEM TO MAKE IT BACK HERE, SO YOU DON'T GET ANY POINTS FOR THAT.

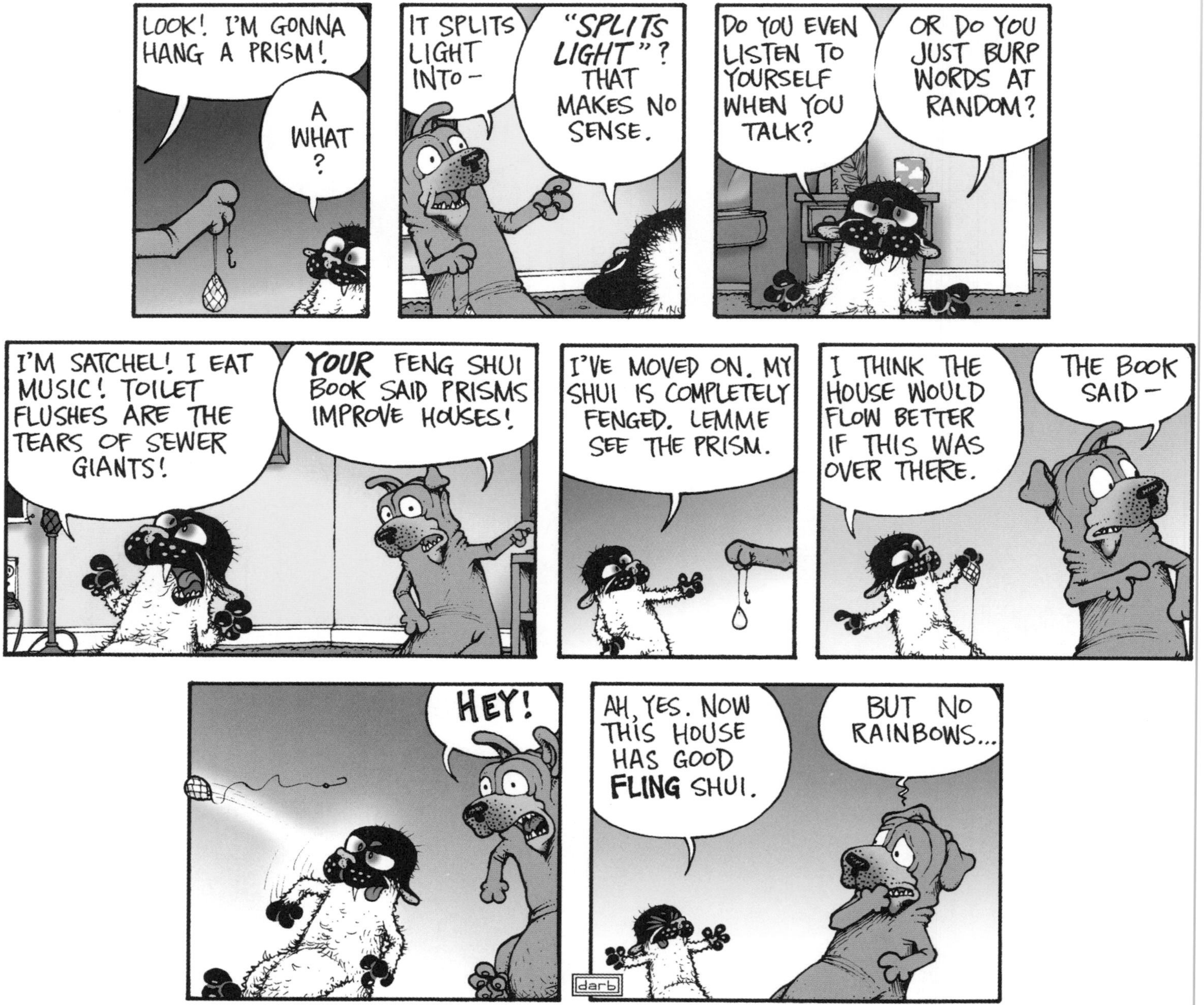
LOOK! I'M GONNA HANG A PRISM!
A WHAT?
IT SPLITS LIGHT INTO–
"SPLITS LIGHT"? THAT MAKES NO SENSE.
DO YOU EVEN LISTEN TO YOURSELF WHEN YOU TALK?
OR DO YOU JUST BURP WORDS AT RANDOM?
I'M SATCHEL! I EAT MUSIC! TOILET FLUSHES ARE THE TEARS OF SEWER GIANTS!
YOUR FENG SHUI BOOK SAID PRISMS IMPROVE HOUSES!
I'VE MOVED ON. MY SHUI IS COMPLETELY FENGED. LEMME SEE THE PRISM.
I THINK THE HOUSE WOULD FLOW BETTER IF THIS WAS OVER THERE.
THE BOOK SAID–
HEY!
AH, YES. NOW THIS HOUSE HAS GOOD FLING SHUI.
BUT NO RAINBOWS...
darb

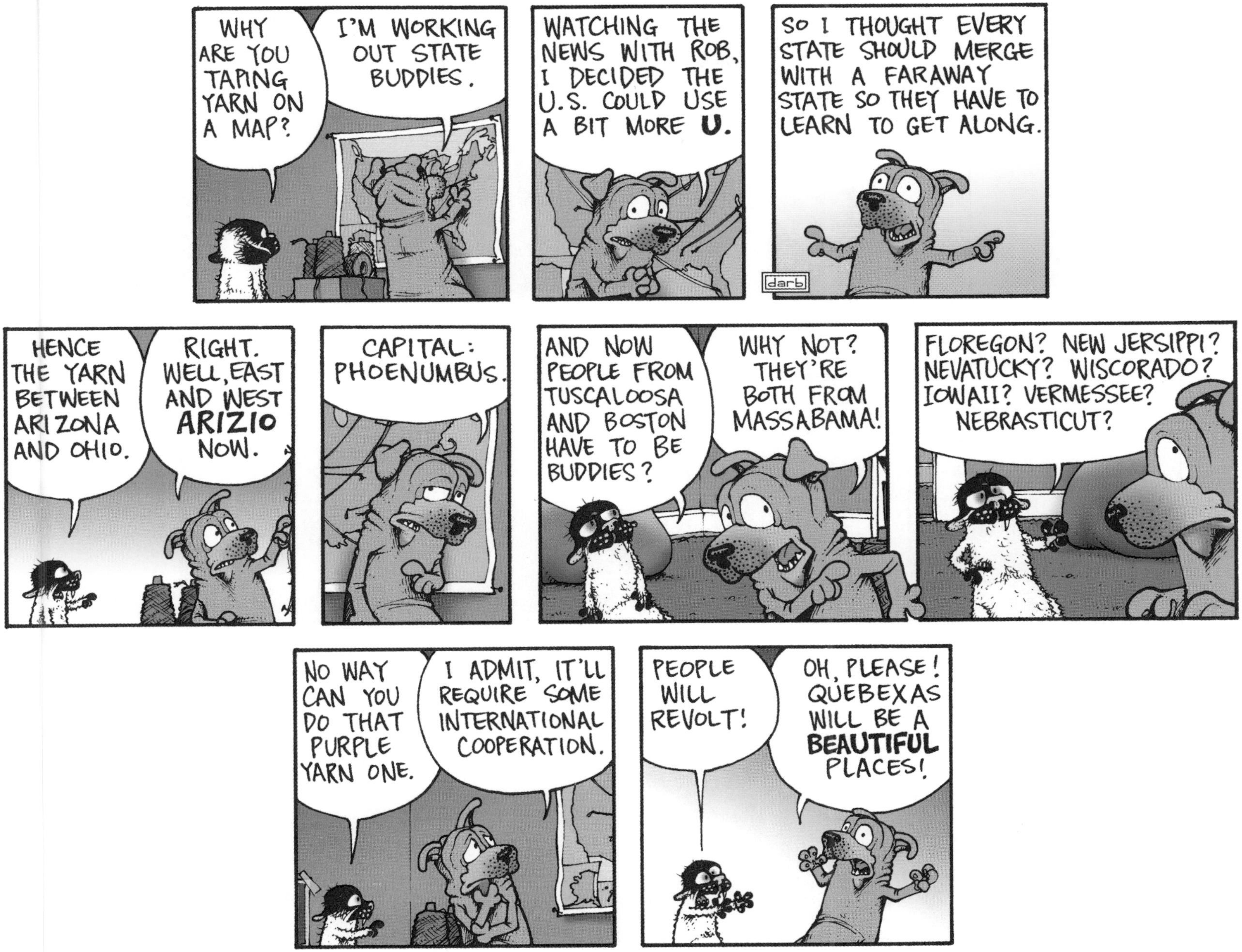
WHY ARE YOU TAPING YARN ON A MAP?
I'M WORKING OUT STATE BUDDIES.
WATCHING THE NEWS WITH ROB, I DECIDED THE U.S. COULD USE A BIT MORE U.
SO I THOUGHT EVERY STATE SHOULD MERGE WITH A FARAWAY STATE SO THEY HAVE TO LEARN TO GET ALONG.
darb
HENCE THE YARN BETWEEN ARIZONA AND OHIO.
RIGHT. WELL, EAST AND WEST ARIZIO NOW.
CAPITAL: PHOENUMBUS.
AND NOW PEOPLE FROM TUSCALOOSA AND BOSTON HAVE TO BE BUDDIES?
WHY NOT? THEY'RE BOTH FROM MASSABAMA!
FLOREGON? NEW JERSIPPI? NEVATUCKY? WISCORADO? IOWAII? VERMESSEE? NEBRASTICUT?
NO WAY CAN YOU DO THAT PURPLE YARN ONE.
I ADMIT, IT'LL REQUIRE SOME INTERNATIONAL COOPERATION.
PEOPLE WILL REVOLT!
OH, PLEASE! QUEBEXAS WILL BE A BEAUTIFUL PLACES!

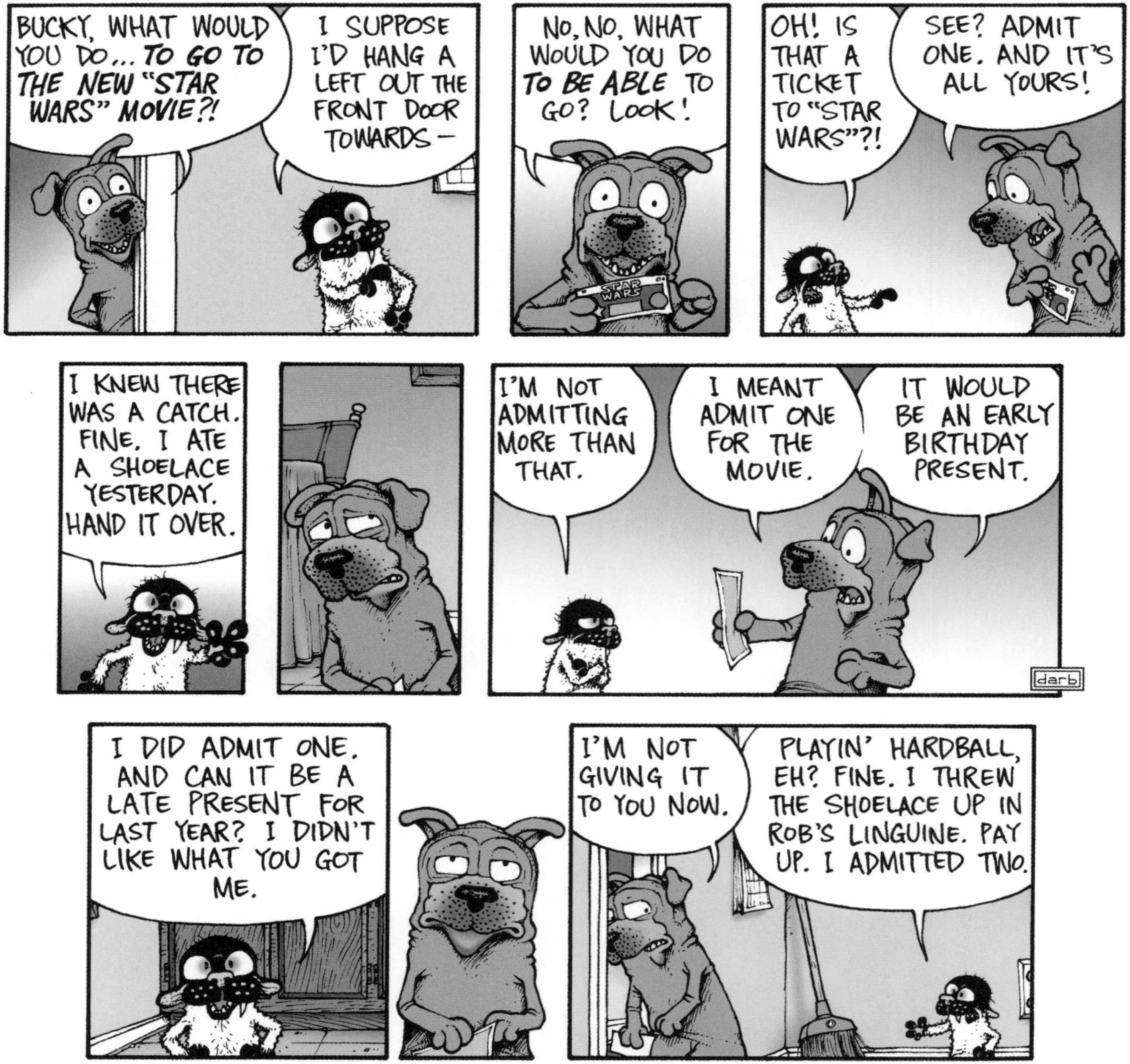
BUCKY, WHAT WOULD YOU DO... TO GO TO THE NEW "STAR WARS" MOVIE?!
I SUPPOSE I'D HANG A LEFT OUT THE FRONT DOOR TOWARDS—
NO, NO, WHAT WOULD YOU DO TO BE ABLE TO GO? LOOK!
STAR WARS
OH! IS THAT A TICKET TO "STAR WARS"?!
SEE? ADMIT ONE. AND IT'S ALL YOURS!
I KNEW THERE WAS A CATCH. FINE. I ATE A SHOELACE YESTERDAY. HAND IT OVER.
I'M NOT ADMITTING MORE THAN THAT.
I MEANT ADMIT ONE FOR THE MOVIE.
IT WOULD BE AN EARLY BIRTHDAY PRESENT.
darb
I DID ADMIT ONE. AND CAN IT BE A LATE PRESENT FOR LAST YEAR? I DIDN'T LIKE WHAT YOU GOT ME.
I'M NOT GIVING IT TO YOU NOW.
PLAYIN' HARDBALL, EH? FINE. I THREW THE SHOELACE UP IN ROB'S LINGUINE. PAY UP. I ADMITTED TWO.

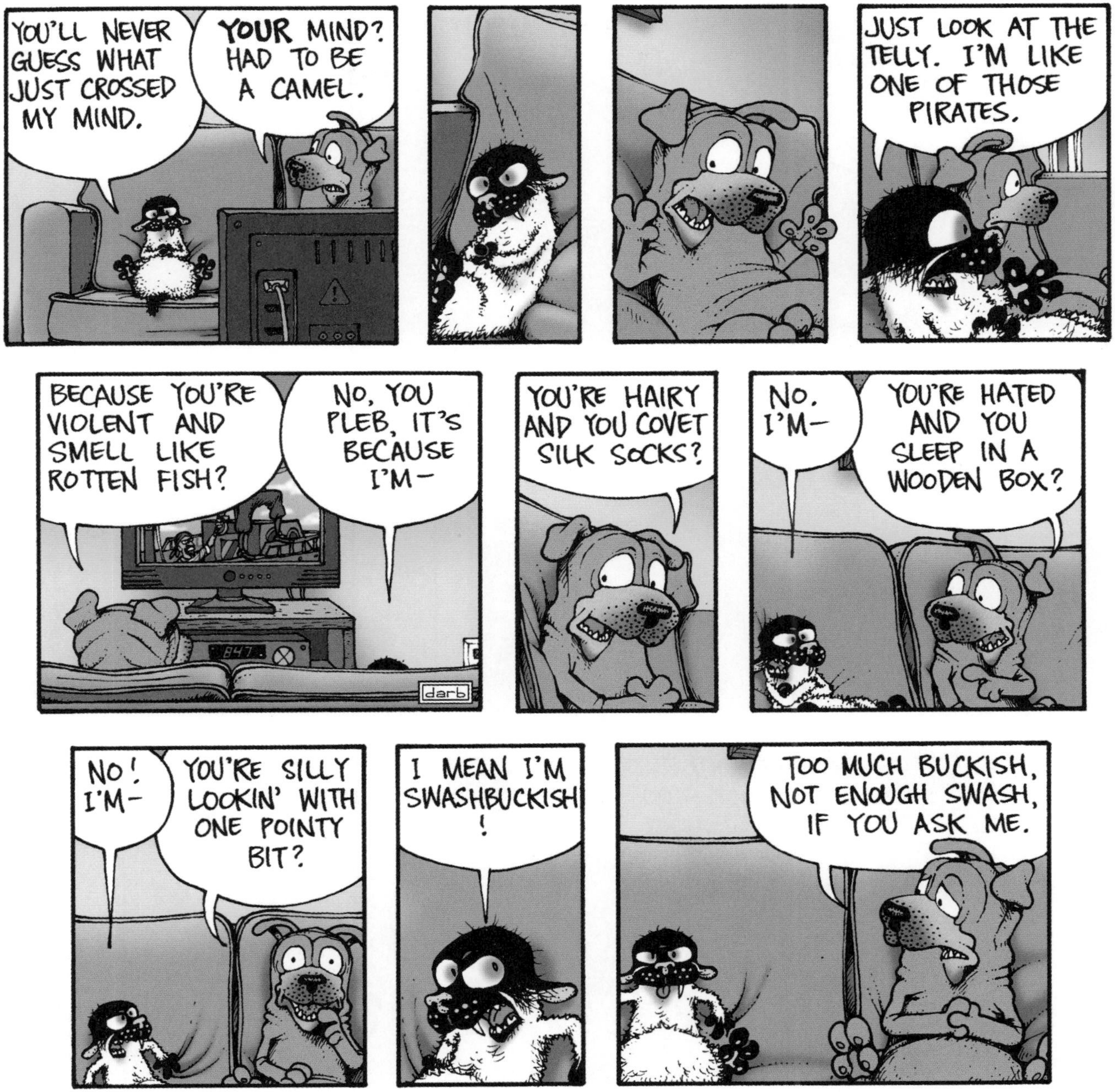
YOU'LL NEVER GUESS WHAT JUST CROSSED MY MIND.
YOUR MIND? HAD TO BE A CAMEL.
JUST LOOK AT THE TELLY. I'M LIKE ONE OF THOSE PIRATES.
BECAUSE YOU'RE VIOLENT AND SMELL LIKE ROTTEN FISH?
NO, YOU PLEB, IT'S BECAUSE I'M—
darb
YOU'RE HAIRY AND YOU COVET SILK SOCKS?
NO. I'M—
YOU'RE HATED AND YOU SLEEP IN A WOODEN BOX?
NO! I'M—
YOU'RE SILLY LOOKIN' WITH ONE POINTY BIT?
I MEAN I'M SWASHBUCKISH!
TOO MUCH BUCKISH, NOT ENOUGH SWASH, IF YOU ASK ME.

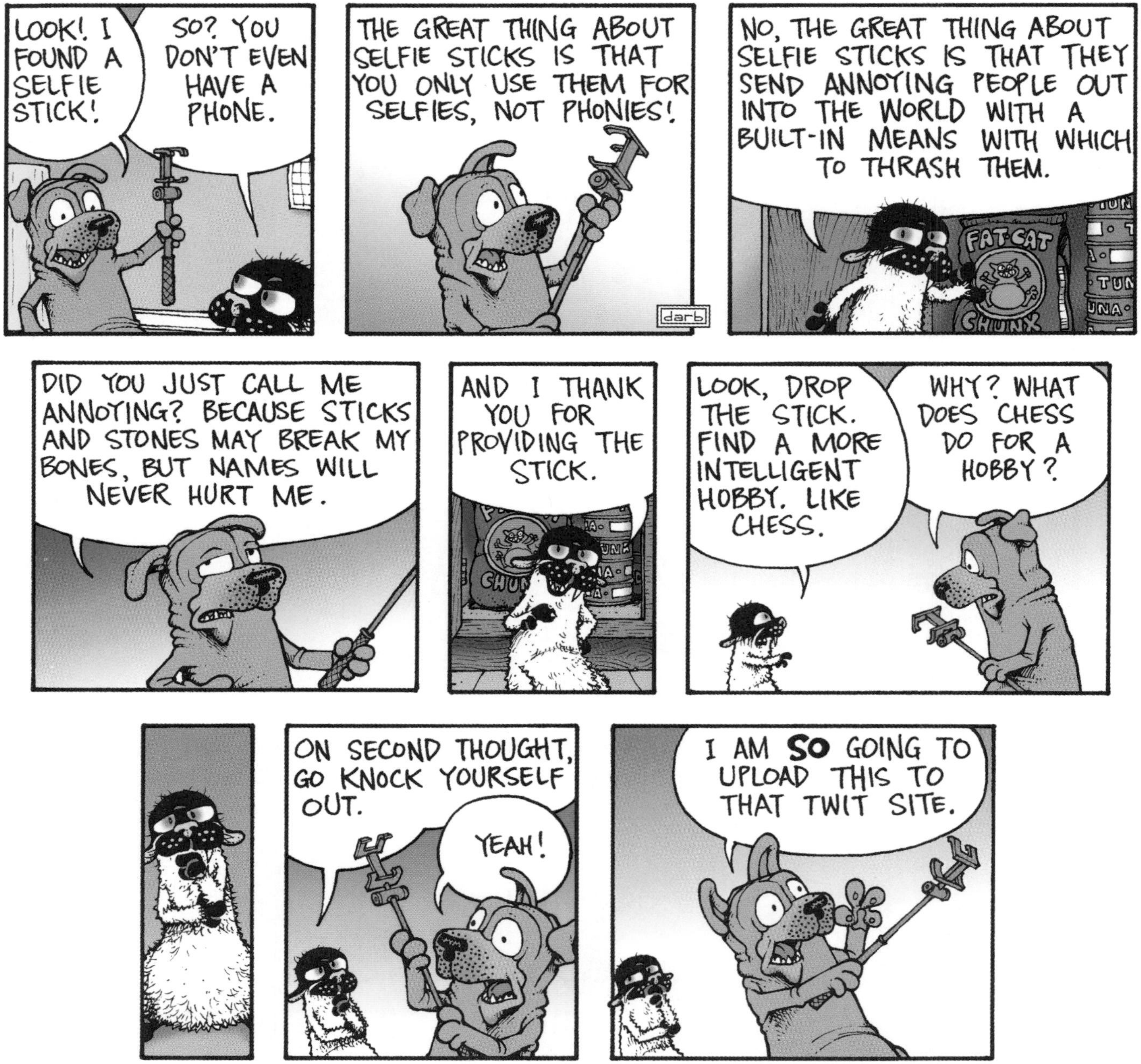
LOOK! I FOUND A SELFIE STICK!
SO? YOU DON'T EVEN HAVE A PHONE.
THE GREAT THING ABOUT SELFIE STICKS IS THAT YOU ONLY USE THEM FOR SELFIES, NOT PHONIES!
darb
NO, THE GREAT THING ABOUT SELFIE STICKS IS THAT THEY SEND ANNOYING PEOPLE OUT INTO THE WORLD WITH A BUILT-IN MEANS WITH WHICH TO THRASH THEM.
FAT CAT
CHUNX
DID YOU JUST CALL ME ANNOYING? BECAUSE STICKS AND STONES MAY BREAK MY BONES, BUT NAMES WILL NEVER HURT ME.
AND I THANK YOU FOR PROVIDING THE STICK.
LOOK, DROP THE STICK. FIND A MORE INTELLIGENT HOBBY. LIKE CHESS.
WHY? WHAT DOES CHESS DO FOR A HOBBY?
ON SECOND THOUGHT, GO KNOCK YOURSELF OUT.
YEAH!
I AM **SO** GOING TO UPLOAD THIS TO THAT TWIT SITE.

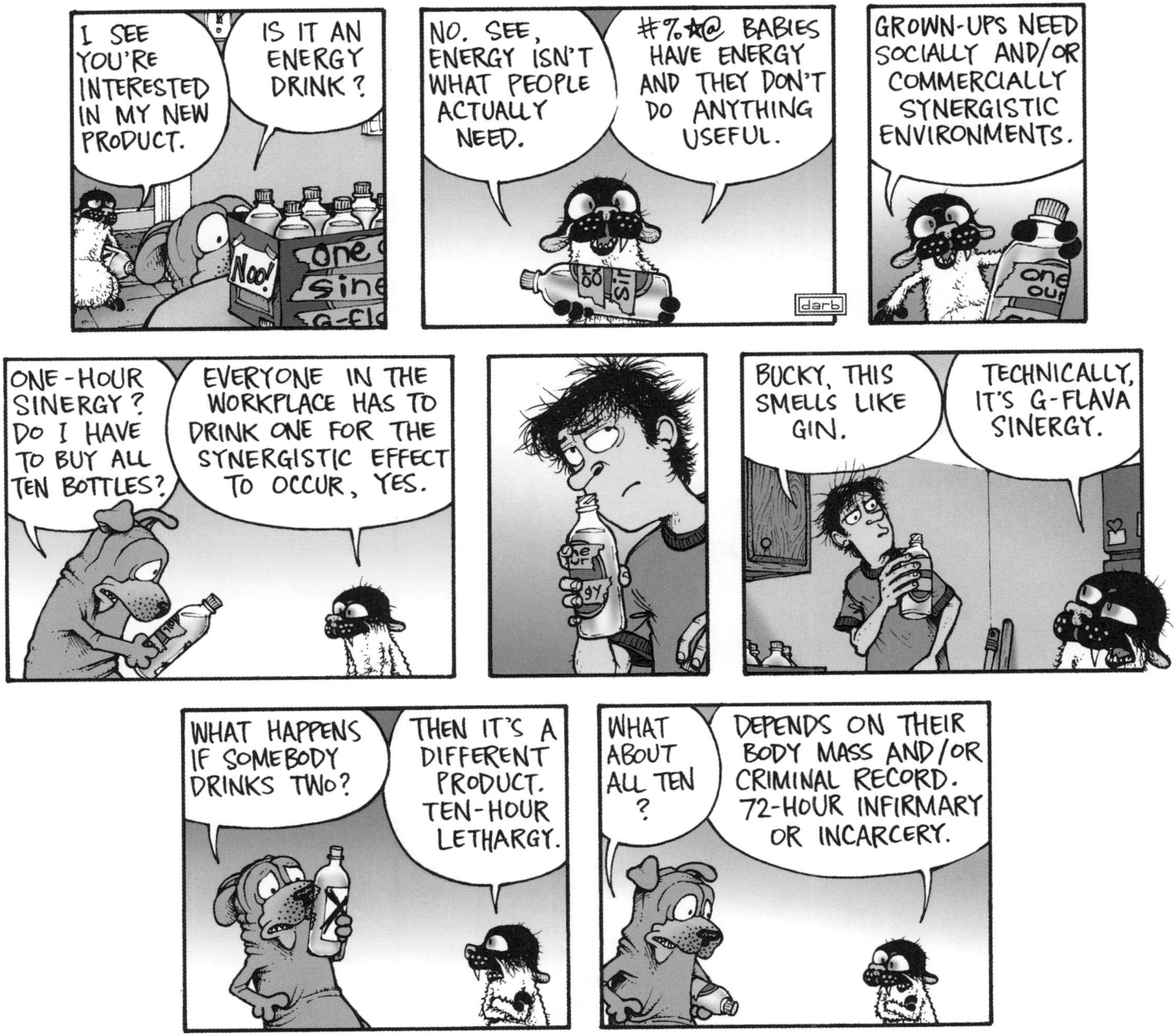

I SEE YOU'RE INTERESTED IN MY NEW PRODUCT.
IS IT AN ENERGY DRINK?
Noo!
NO. SEE, ENERGY ISN'T WHAT PEOPLE ACTUALLY NEED.
#%☆@ BABIES HAVE ENERGY AND THEY DON'T DO ANYTHING USEFUL.
darb
GROWN-UPS NEED SOCIALLY AND/OR COMMERCIALLY SYNERGISTIC ENVIRONMENTS.
ONE-HOUR SINERGY? DO I HAVE TO BUY ALL TEN BOTTLES?
EVERYONE IN THE WORKPLACE HAS TO DRINK ONE FOR THE SYNERGISTIC EFFECT TO OCCUR, YES.
BUCKY, THIS SMELLS LIKE GIN.
TECHNICALLY, IT'S G-FLAVA SINERGY.
WHAT HAPPENS IF SOMEBODY DRINKS TWO?
THEN IT'S A DIFFERENT PRODUCT. TEN-HOUR LETHARGY.
WHAT ABOUT ALL TEN?
DEPENDS ON THEIR BODY MASS AND/OR CRIMINAL RECORD. 72-HOUR INFIRMARY OR INCARCERY.

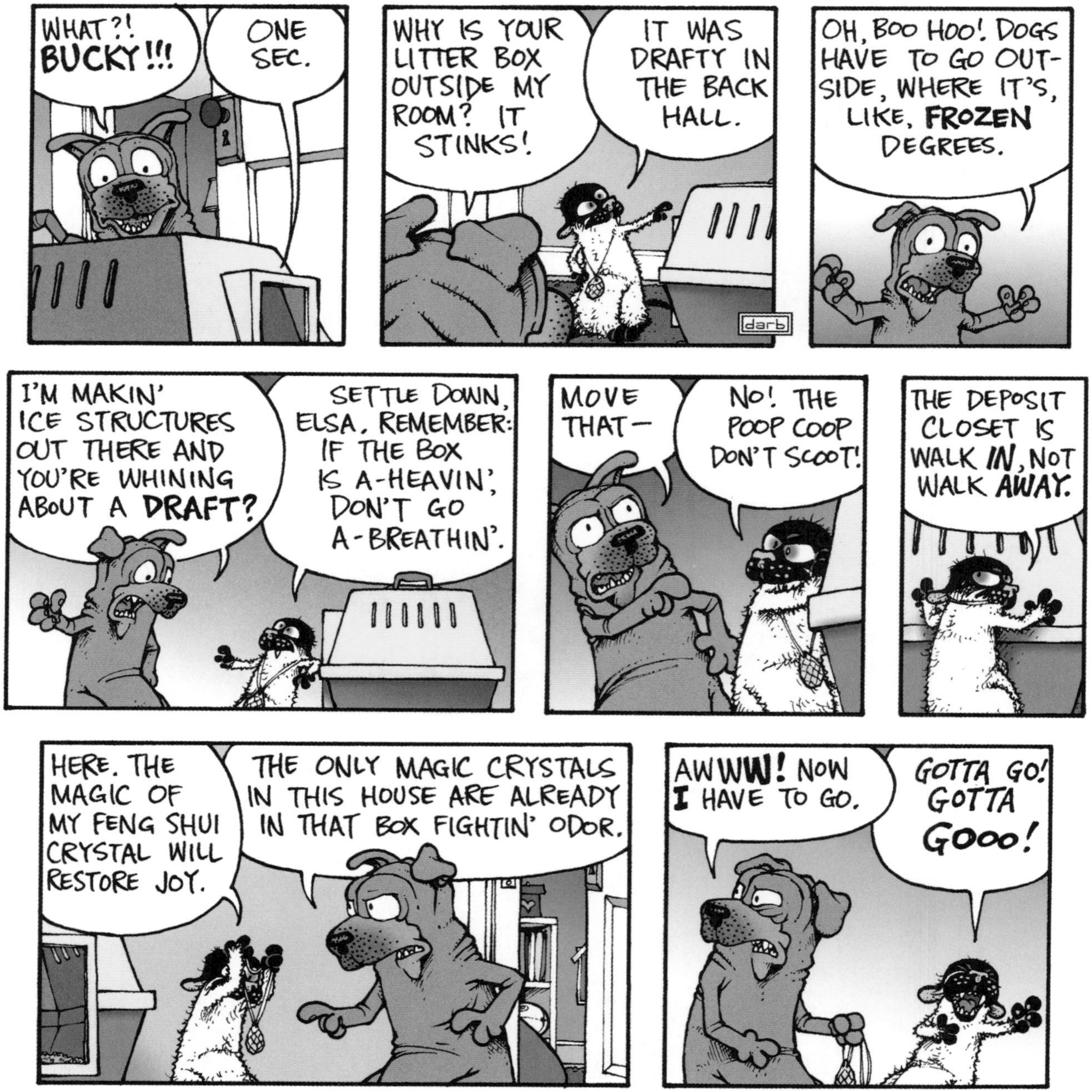
WHAT?! BUCKY!!!
ONE SEC.
WHY IS YOUR LITTER BOX OUTSIDE MY ROOM? IT STINKS!
IT WAS DRAFTY IN THE BACK HALL.
darb
OH, BOO HOO! DOGS HAVE TO GO OUTSIDE, WHERE IT'S, LIKE, FROZEN DEGREES.
I'M MAKIN' ICE STRUCTURES OUT THERE AND YOU'RE WHINING ABOUT A DRAFT?
SETTLE DOWN, ELSA, REMEMBER: IF THE BOX IS A-HEAVIN', DON'T GO A-BREATHIN'.
MOVE THAT—
NO! THE POOP COOP DON'T SCOOT!
THE DEPOSIT CLOSET IS WALK IN, NOT WALK AWAY.
HERE. THE MAGIC OF MY FENG SHUI CRYSTAL WILL RESTORE JOY.
THE ONLY MAGIC CRYSTALS IN THIS HOUSE ARE ALREADY IN THAT BOX FIGHTIN' ODOR.
AWWW! NOW I HAVE TO GO.
GOTTA GO! GOTTA GOOO!

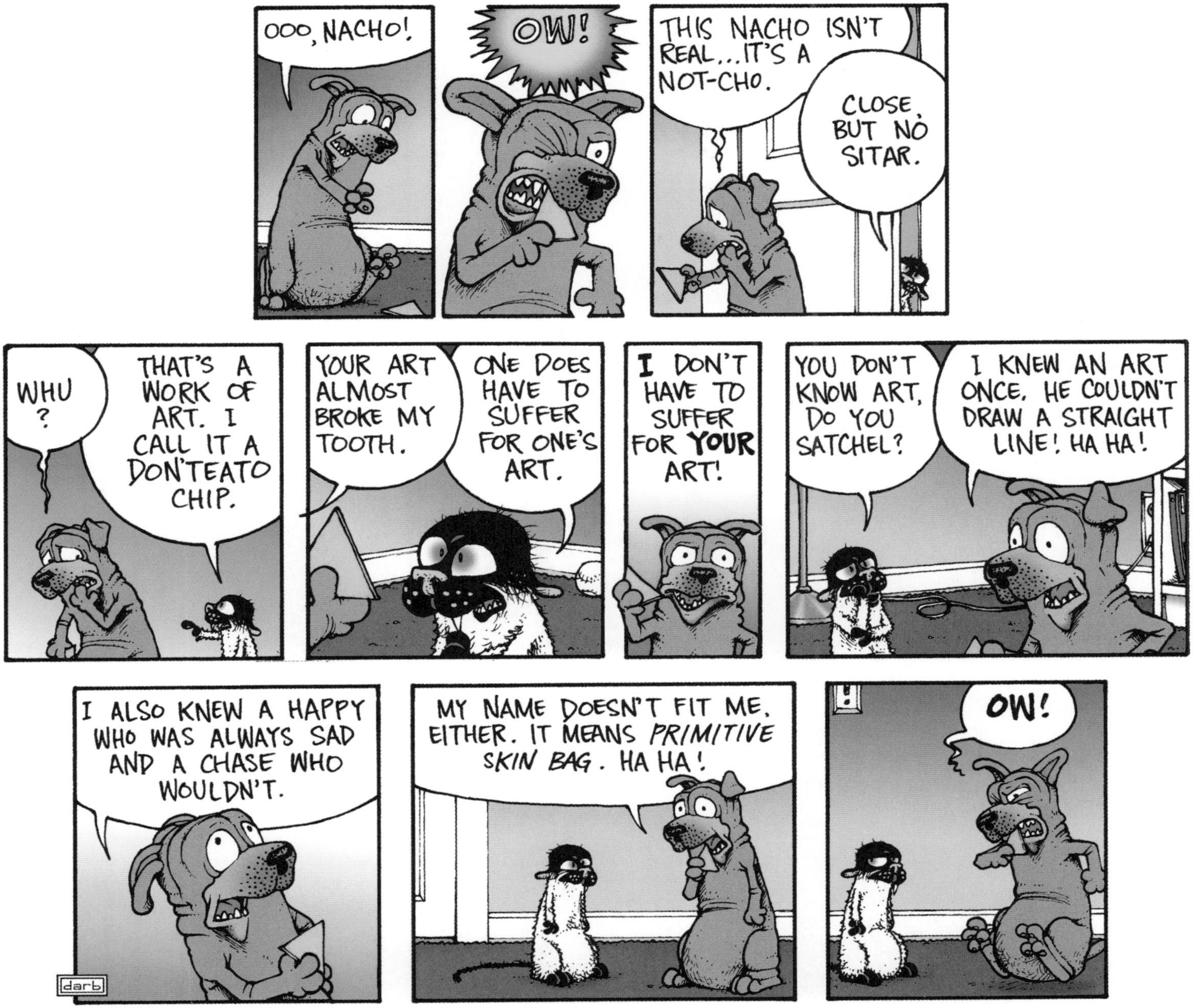
OOO, NACHO!
OW!
THIS NACHO ISN'T REAL...IT'S A NOT-CHO.
CLOSE, BUT NO SITAR.
WHU ?
THAT'S A WORK OF ART. I CALL IT A DON'TEATO CHIP.
YOUR ART ALMOST BROKE MY TOOTH.
ONE DOES HAVE TO SUFFER FOR ONE'S ART.
I DON'T HAVE TO SUFFER FOR YOUR ART!
YOU DON'T KNOW ART, DO YOU SATCHEL?
I KNEW AN ART ONCE. HE COULDN'T DRAW A STRAIGHT LINE! HA HA!
I ALSO KNEW A HAPPY WHO WAS ALWAYS SAD AND A CHASE WHO WOULDN'T.
darb
MY NAME DOESN'T FIT ME, EITHER. IT MEANS PRIMITIVE SKIN BAG. HA HA!
OW!

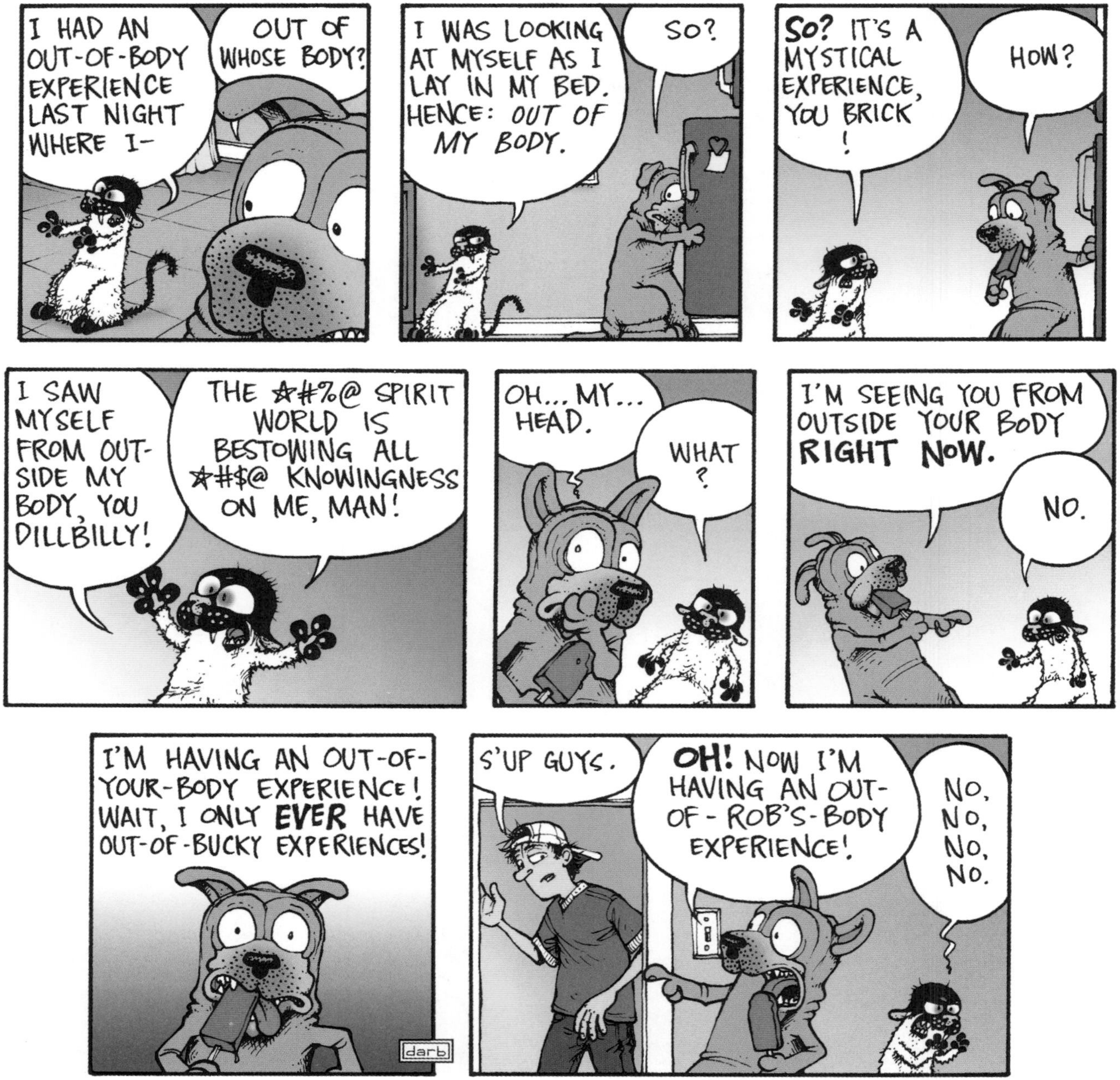
I HAD AN OUT-OF-BODY EXPERIENCE LAST NIGHT WHERE I-
OUT OF WHOSE BODY?
I WAS LOOKING AT MYSELF AS I LAY IN MY BED. HENCE: OUT OF MY BODY.
SO?
SO? IT'S A MYSTICAL EXPERIENCE, YOU BRICK!
HOW?
I SAW MYSELF FROM OUTSIDE MY BODY, YOU DILLBILLY!
THE ☆#%@ SPIRIT WORLD IS BESTOWING ALL ☆#$@ KNOWINGNESS ON ME, MAN!
OH... MY... HEAD.
WHAT?
I'M SEEING YOU FROM OUTSIDE YOUR BODY RIGHT NOW.
NO.
I'M HAVING AN OUT-OF-YOUR-BODY EXPERIENCE! WAIT, I ONLY EVER HAVE OUT-OF-BUCKY EXPERIENCES!
darb
S'UP GUYS.
OH! NOW I'M HAVING AN OUT-OF-ROB'S-BODY EXPERIENCE!
NO, NO, NO, NO.

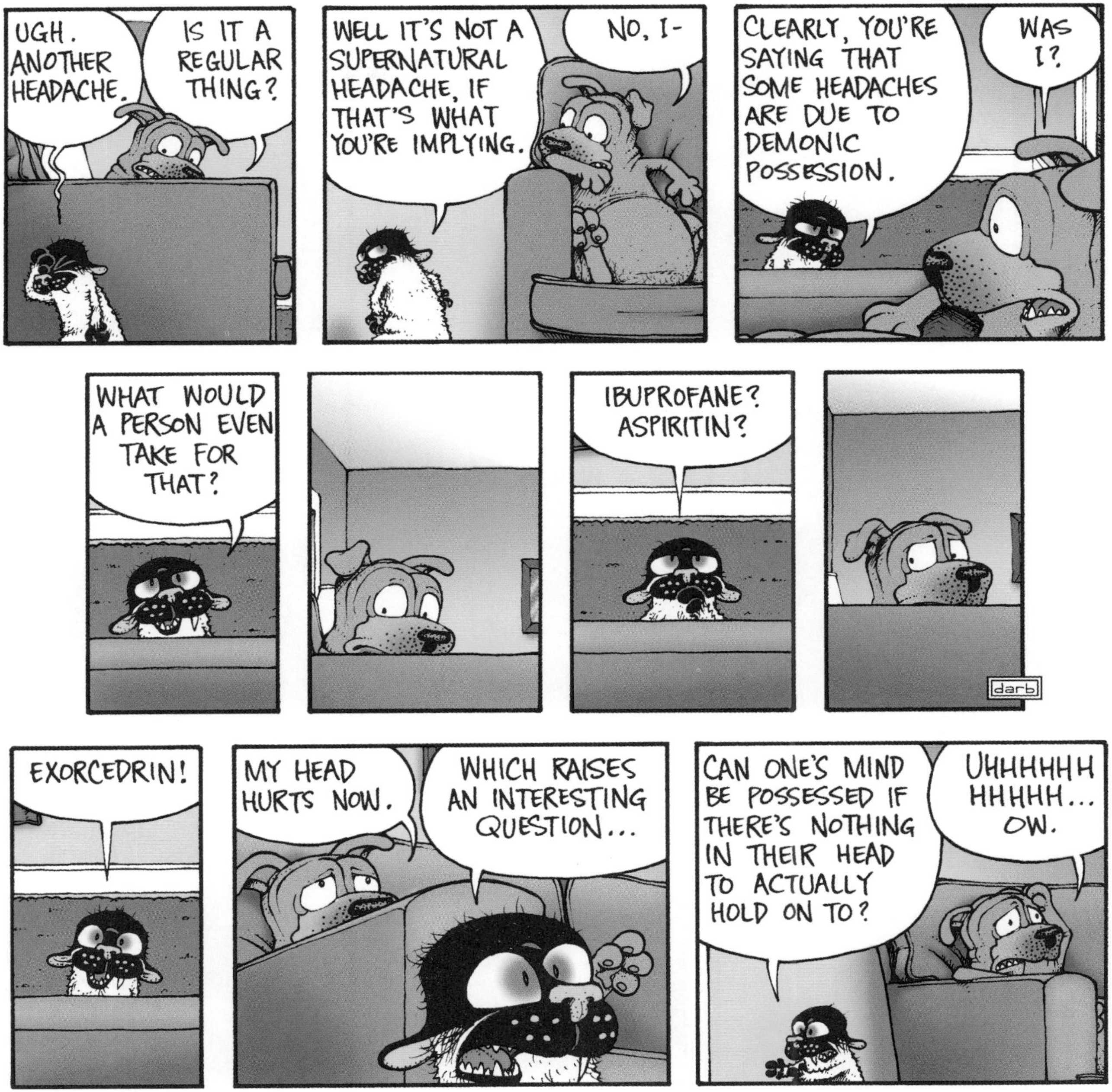
UGH. ANOTHER HEADACHE.
IS IT A REGULAR THING?
WELL IT'S NOT A SUPERNATURAL HEADACHE, IF THAT'S WHAT YOU'RE IMPLYING.
NO, I-
CLEARLY, YOU'RE SAYING THAT SOME HEADACHES ARE DUE TO DEMONIC POSSESSION.
WAS I?
WHAT WOULD A PERSON EVEN TAKE FOR THAT?
IBUPROFANE? ASPIRITIN?
darb
EXORCEDRIN!
MY HEAD HURTS NOW.
WHICH RAISES AN INTERESTING QUESTION...
CAN ONE'S MIND BE POSSESSED IF THERE'S NOTHING IN THEIR HEAD TO ACTUALLY HOLD ON TO?
UHHHHHH HHHHH... OW.

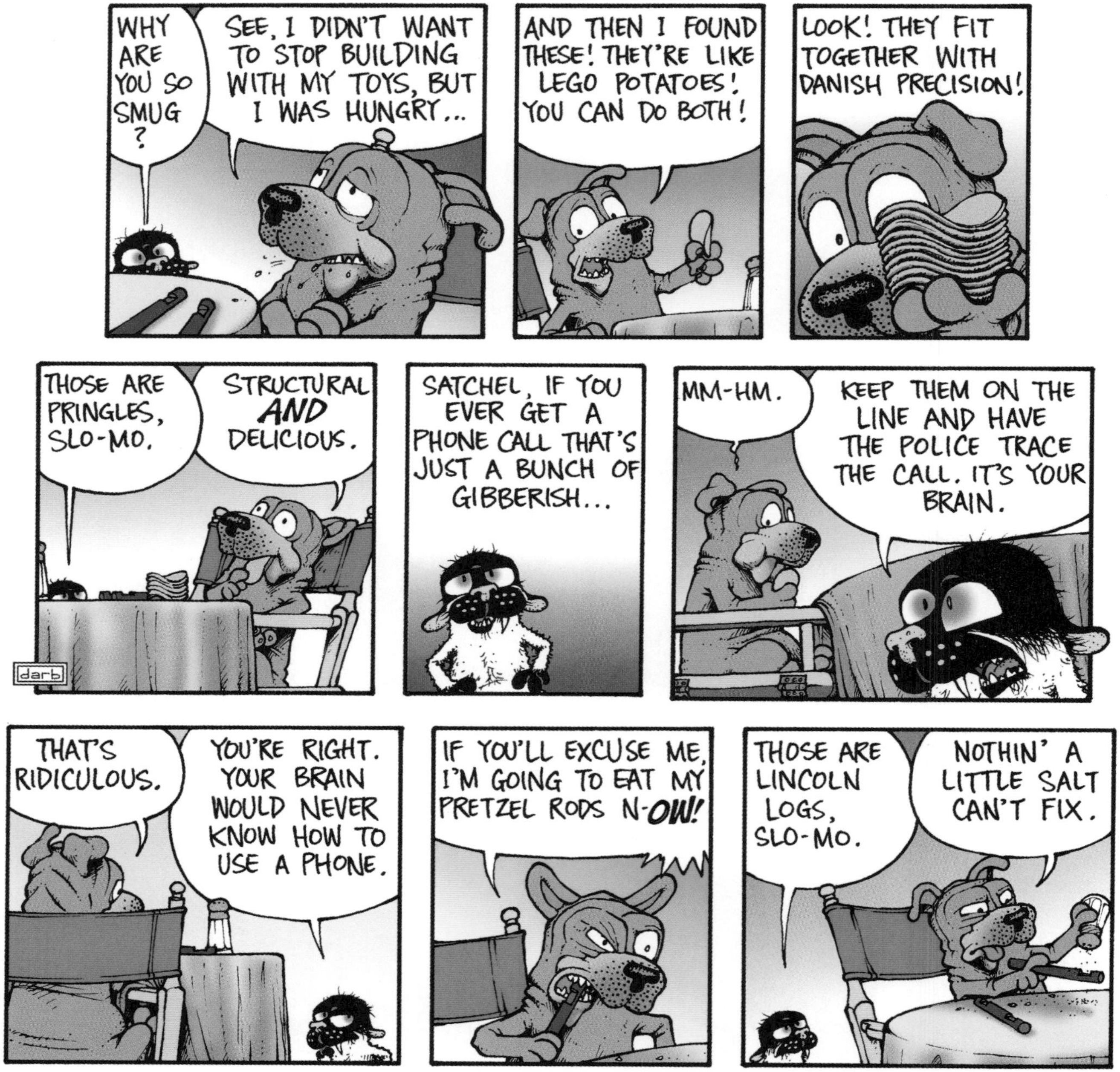
WHY ARE YOU SO SMUG?
SEE, I DIDN'T WANT TO STOP BUILDING WITH MY TOYS, BUT I WAS HUNGRY...
AND THEN I FOUND THESE! THEY'RE LIKE LEGO POTATOES! YOU CAN DO BOTH!
LOOK! THEY FIT TOGETHER WITH DANISH PRECISION!
THOSE ARE PRINGLES, SLO-MO.
STRUCTURAL *AND* DELICIOUS.
darb
SATCHEL, IF YOU EVER GET A PHONE CALL THAT'S JUST A BUNCH OF GIBBERISH...
MM-HM.
KEEP THEM ON THE LINE AND HAVE THE POLICE TRACE THE CALL. IT'S YOUR BRAIN.
THAT'S RIDICULOUS.
YOU'RE RIGHT. YOUR BRAIN WOULD NEVER KNOW HOW TO USE A PHONE.
IF YOU'LL EXCUSE ME, I'M GOING TO EAT MY PRETZEL RODS N-*OW!*
THOSE ARE LINCOLN LOGS, SLO-MO.
NOTHIN' A LITTLE SALT CAN'T FIX.

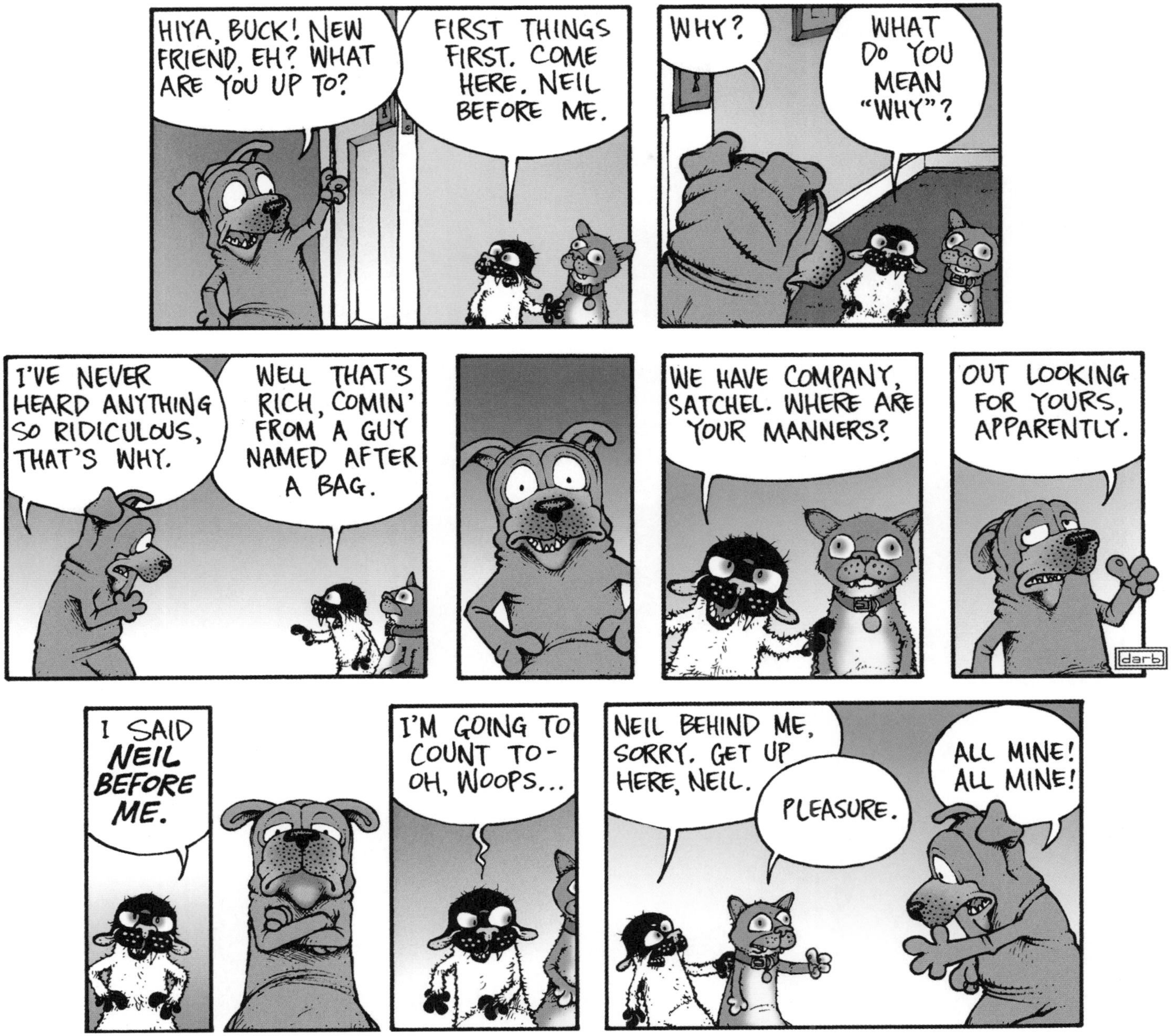
HIYA, BUCK! NEW FRIEND, EH? WHAT ARE YOU UP TO?
FIRST THINGS FIRST. COME HERE. NEIL BEFORE ME.
WHY?
WHAT DO YOU MEAN "WHY"?
I'VE NEVER HEARD ANYTHING SO RIDICULOUS, THAT'S WHY.
WELL THAT'S RICH, COMIN' FROM A GUY NAMED AFTER A BAG.
WE HAVE COMPANY, SATCHEL. WHERE ARE YOUR MANNERS?
OUT LOOKING FOR YOURS, APPARENTLY.
darb
I SAID NEIL BEFORE ME.
I'M GOING TO COUNT TO- OH, WOOPS...
NEIL BEHIND ME, SORRY. GET UP HERE, NEIL.
PLEASURE.
ALL MINE! ALL MINE!

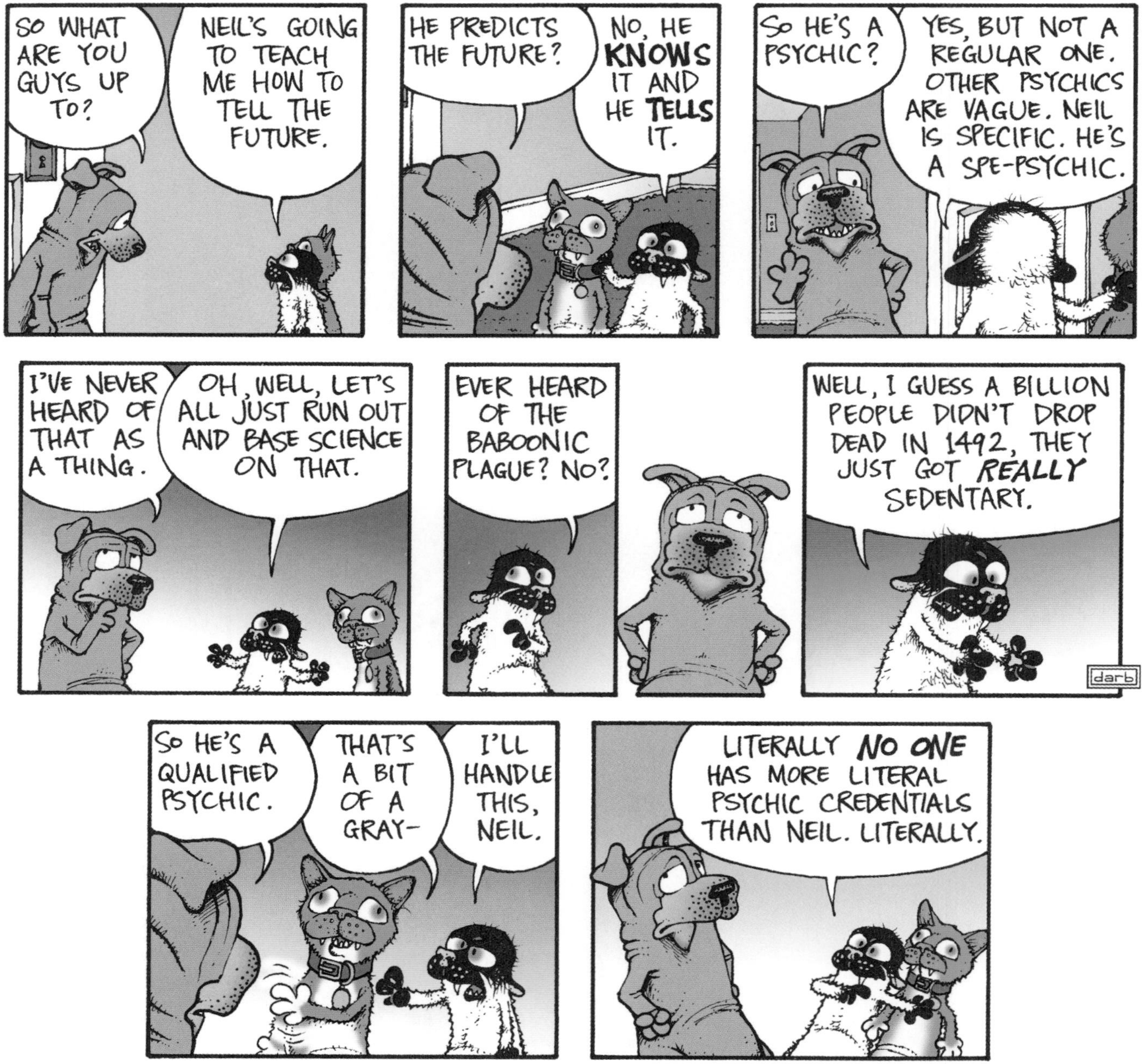
SO WHAT ARE YOU GUYS UP TO?
NEIL'S GOING TO TEACH ME HOW TO TELL THE FUTURE.
HE PREDICTS THE FUTURE?
NO, HE **KNOWS** IT AND HE **TELLS** IT.
SO HE'S A PSYCHIC?
YES, BUT NOT A REGULAR ONE. OTHER PSYCHICS ARE VAGUE. NEIL IS SPECIFIC. HE'S A SPE-PSYCHIC.
I'VE NEVER HEARD OF THAT AS A THING.
OH, WELL, LET'S ALL JUST RUN OUT AND BASE SCIENCE ON THAT.
EVER HEARD OF THE BABOONIC PLAGUE? NO?
WELL, I GUESS A BILLION PEOPLE DIDN'T DROP DEAD IN 1492, THEY JUST GOT ***REALLY*** SEDENTARY.
darb
SO HE'S A QUALIFIED PSYCHIC.
THAT'S A BIT OF A GRAY-
I'LL HANDLE THIS, NEIL.
LITERALLY ***NO ONE*** HAS MORE LITERAL PSYCHIC CREDENTIALS THAN NEIL. LITERALLY.

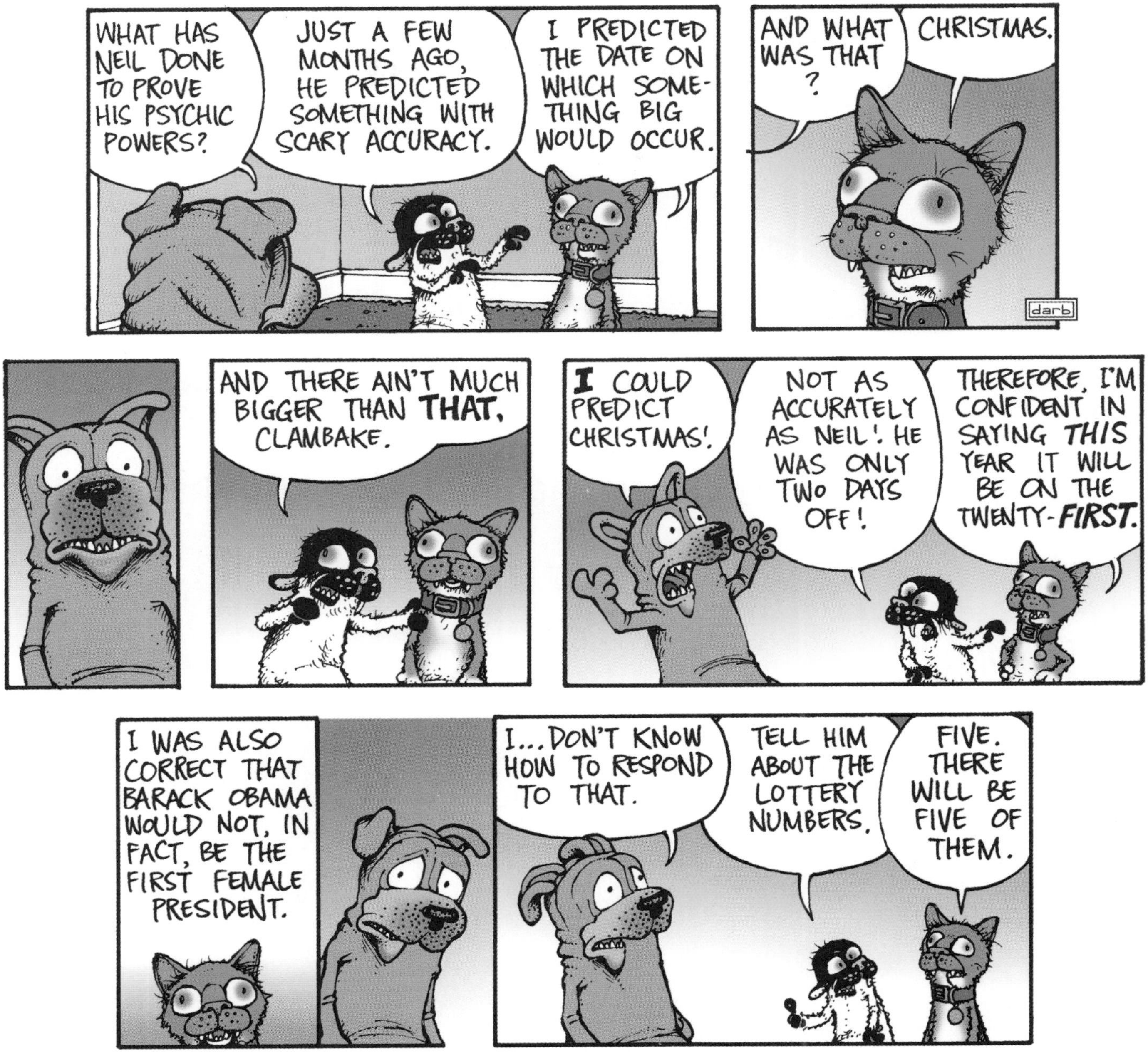
WHAT HAS NEIL DONE TO PROVE HIS PSYCHIC POWERS?
JUST A FEW MONTHS AGO, HE PREDICTED SOMETHING WITH SCARY ACCURACY.
I PREDICTED THE DATE ON WHICH SOMETHING BIG WOULD OCCUR.
AND WHAT WAS THAT?
CHRISTMAS.
darb
AND THERE AIN'T MUCH BIGGER THAN **THAT**, CLAMBAKE.
I COULD PREDICT CHRISTMAS!
NOT AS ACCURATELY AS NEIL! HE WAS ONLY TWO DAYS OFF!
THEREFORE, I'M CONFIDENT IN SAYING ***THIS*** YEAR IT WILL BE ON THE TWENTY-***FIRST***.
I WAS ALSO CORRECT THAT BARACK OBAMA WOULD NOT, IN FACT, BE THE FIRST FEMALE PRESIDENT.
I...DON'T KNOW HOW TO RESPOND TO THAT.
TELL HIM ABOUT THE LOTTERY NUMBERS.
FIVE. THERE WILL BE FIVE OF THEM.

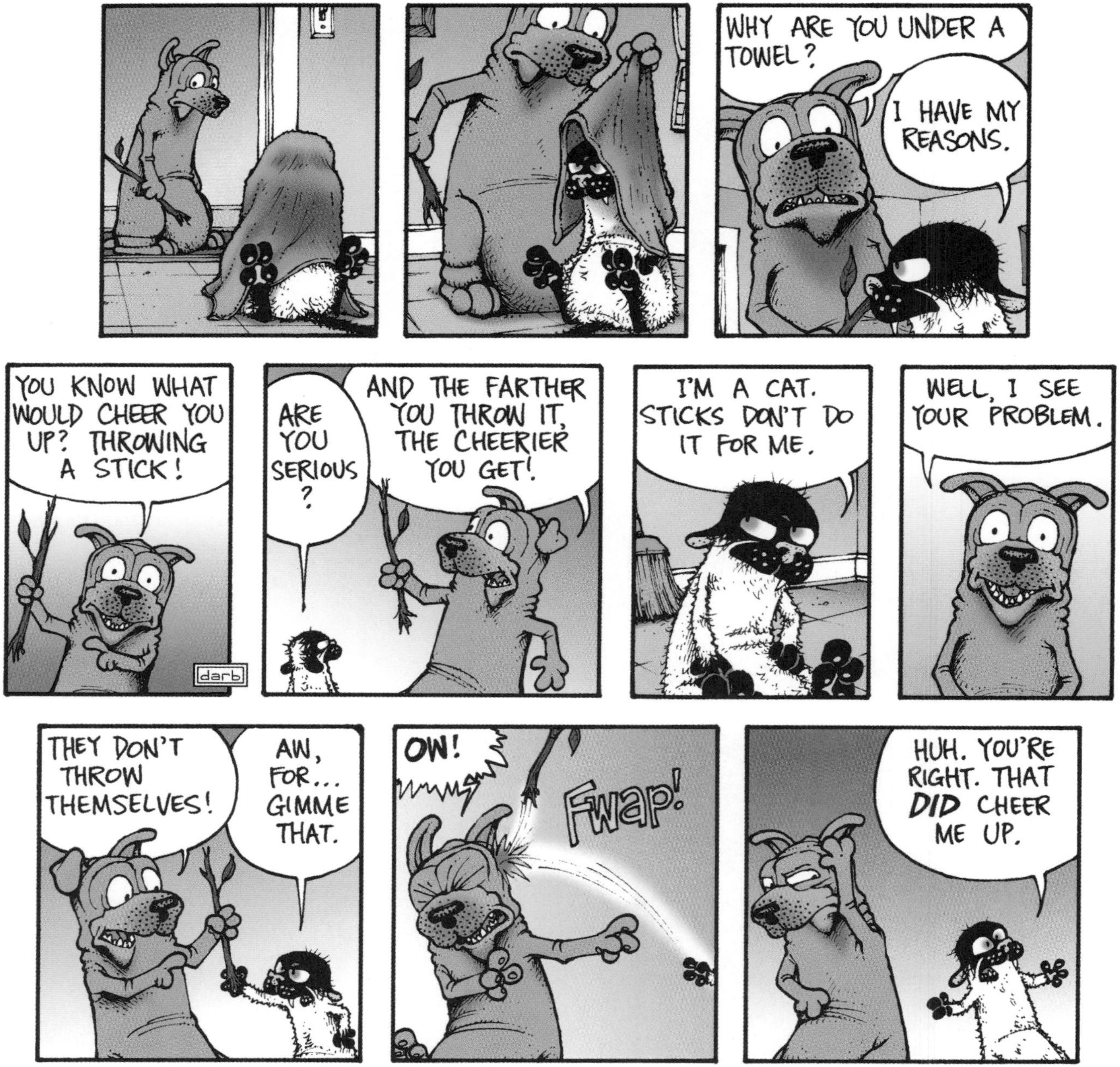
WHY ARE YOU UNDER A TOWEL?
I HAVE MY REASONS.
YOU KNOW WHAT WOULD CHEER YOU UP? THROWING A STICK!
darb
ARE YOU SERIOUS?
AND THE FARTHER YOU THROW IT, THE CHEERIER YOU GET!
I'M A CAT. STICKS DON'T DO IT FOR ME.
WELL, I SEE YOUR PROBLEM.
THEY DON'T THROW THEMSELVES!
AW, FOR... GIMME THAT.
OW!
Fwap!
HUH. YOU'RE RIGHT. THAT DID CHEER ME UP.

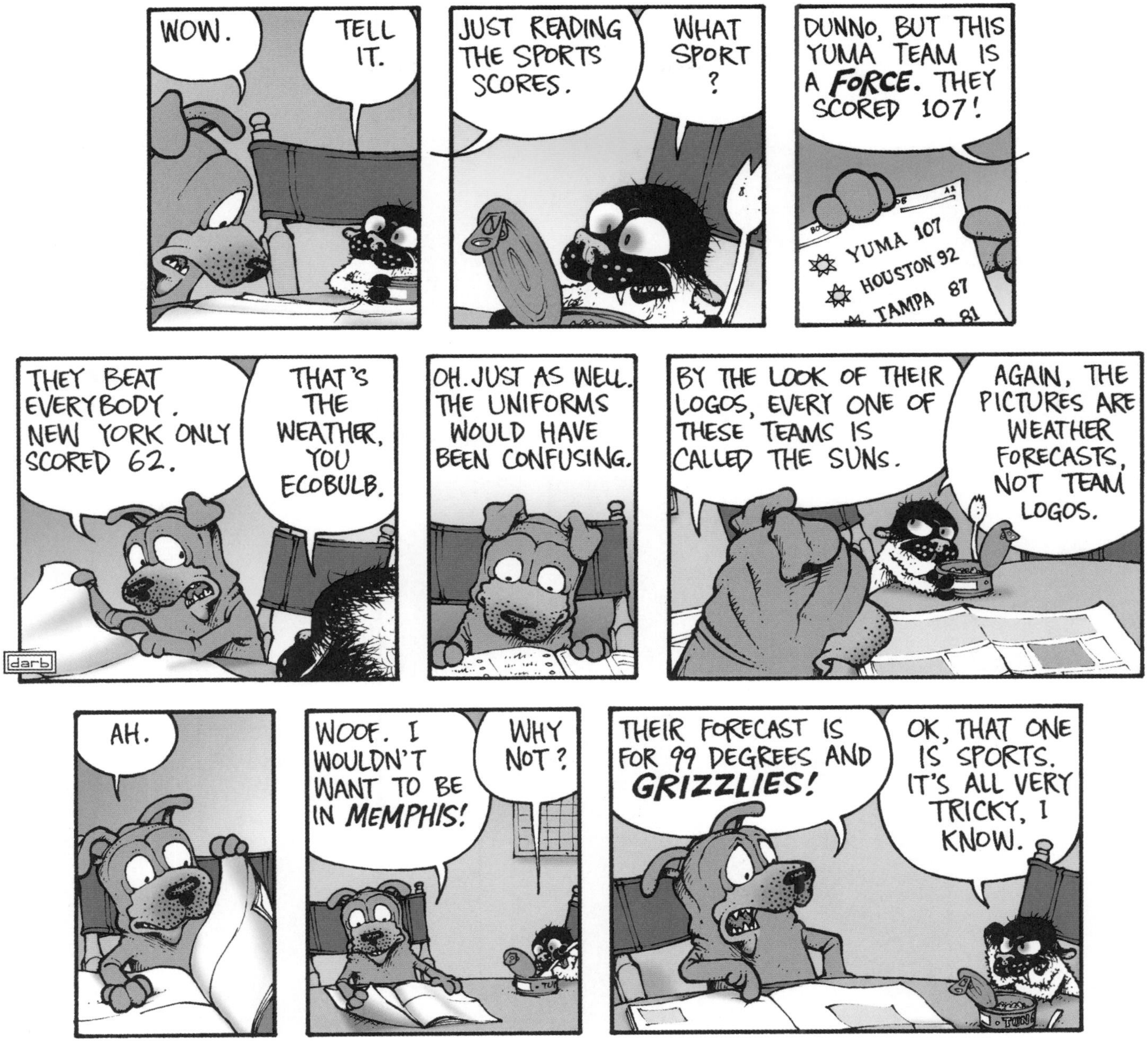
WOW.
TELL IT.
JUST READING THE SPORTS SCORES.
WHAT SPORT ?
DUNNO, BUT THIS YUMA TEAM IS A FORCE. THEY SCORED 107!
YUMA 107
HOUSTON 92
TAMPA 87
THEY BEAT EVERYBODY. NEW YORK ONLY SCORED 62.
THAT'S THE WEATHER, YOU ECOBULB.
darb
OH. JUST AS WELL. THE UNIFORMS WOULD HAVE BEEN CONFUSING.
BY THE LOOK OF THEIR LOGOS, EVERY ONE OF THESE TEAMS IS CALLED THE SUNS.
AGAIN, THE PICTURES ARE WEATHER FORECASTS, NOT TEAM LOGOS.
AH.
WOOF. I WOULDN'T WANT TO BE IN MEMPHIS!
WHY NOT ?
THEIR FORECAST IS FOR 99 DEGREES AND GRIZZLIES!
OK, THAT ONE IS SPORTS. IT'S ALL VERY TRICKY, I KNOW.

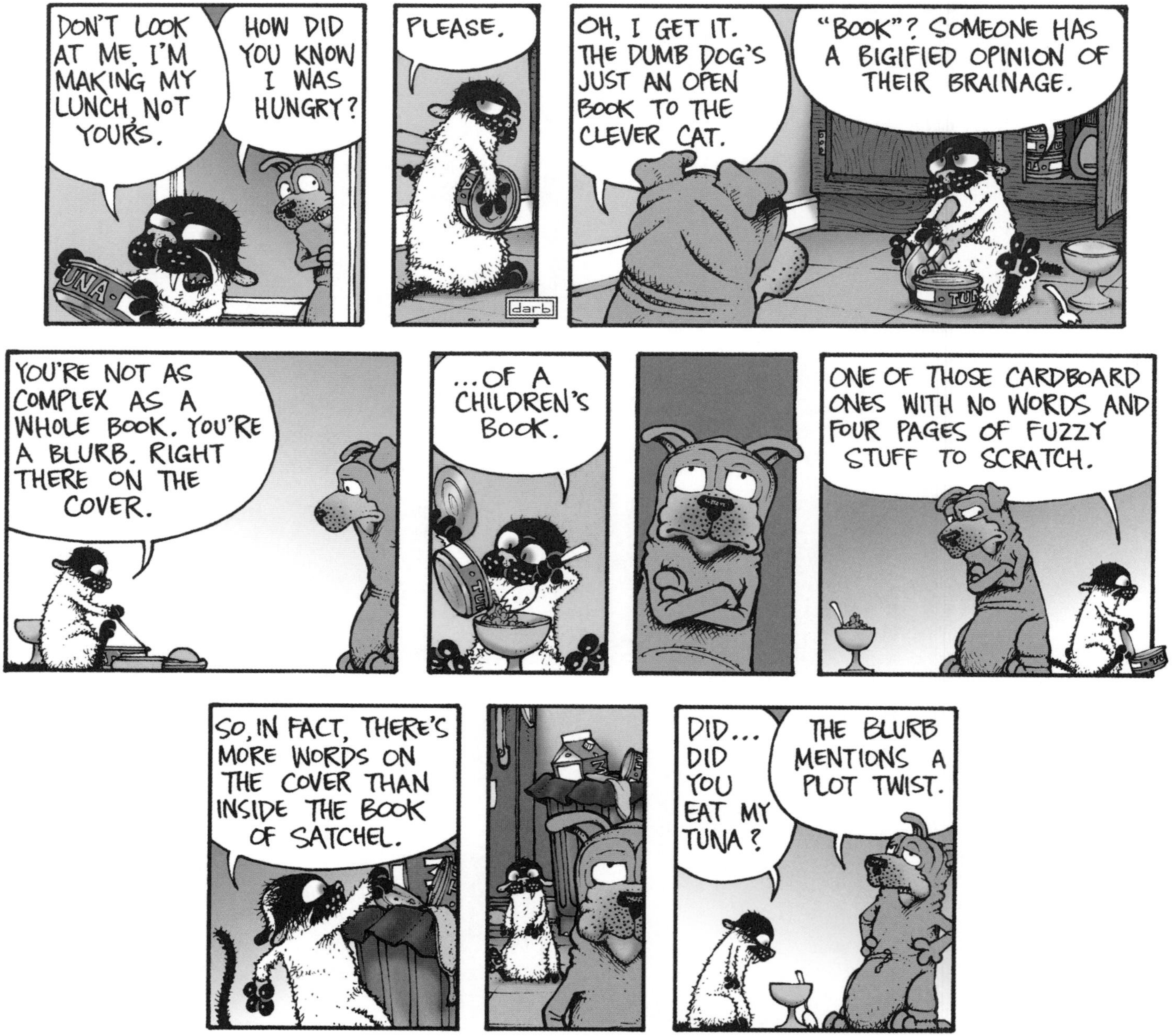
DON'T LOOK AT ME. I'M MAKING MY LUNCH, NOT YOURS.
HOW DID YOU KNOW I WAS HUNGRY?
PLEASE.
darb
OH, I GET IT. THE DUMB DOG'S JUST AN OPEN BOOK TO THE CLEVER CAT.
"BOOK"? SOMEONE HAS A BIGIFIED OPINION OF THEIR BRAINAGE.
YOU'RE NOT AS COMPLEX AS A WHOLE BOOK. YOU'RE A BLURB. RIGHT THERE ON THE COVER.
...OF A CHILDREN'S BOOK.
ONE OF THOSE CARDBOARD ONES WITH NO WORDS AND FOUR PAGES OF FUZZY STUFF TO SCRATCH.
SO, IN FACT, THERE'S MORE WORDS ON THE COVER THAN INSIDE THE BOOK OF SATCHEL.
DID... DID YOU EAT MY TUNA?
THE BLURB MENTIONS A PLOT TWIST.

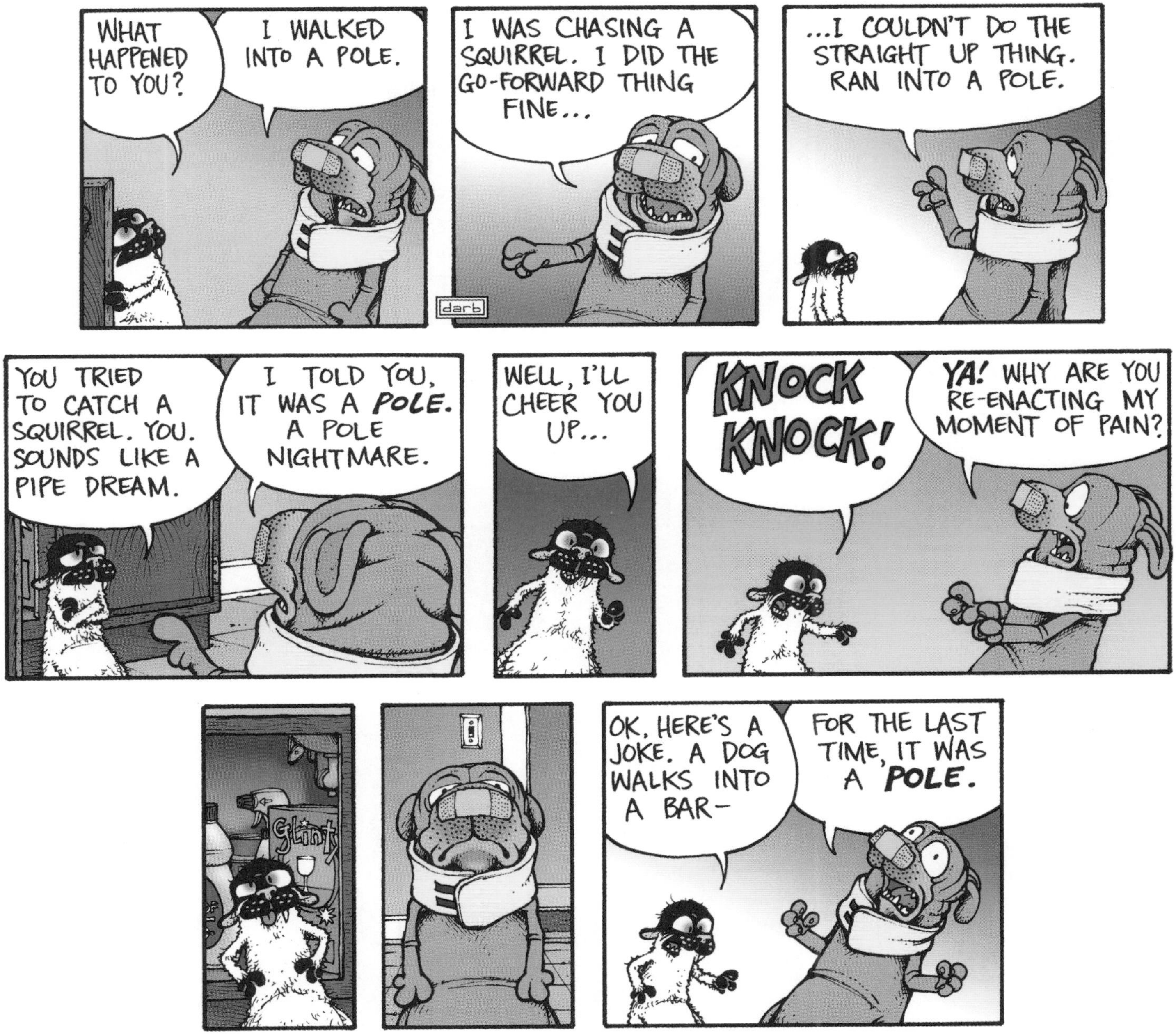
WHAT HAPPENED TO YOU?
I WALKED INTO A POLE.
I WAS CHASING A SQUIRREL. I DID THE GO-FORWARD THING FINE...
darb
...I COULDN'T DO THE STRAIGHT UP THING. RAN INTO A POLE.
YOU TRIED TO CATCH A SQUIRREL. YOU. SOUNDS LIKE A PIPE DREAM.
I TOLD YOU, IT WAS A POLE. A POLE NIGHTMARE.
WELL, I'LL CHEER YOU UP...
KNOCK KNOCK!
YA! WHY ARE YOU RE-ENACTING MY MOMENT OF PAIN?
Glint
OK, HERE'S A JOKE. A DOG WALKS INTO A BAR–
FOR THE LAST TIME, IT WAS A POLE.

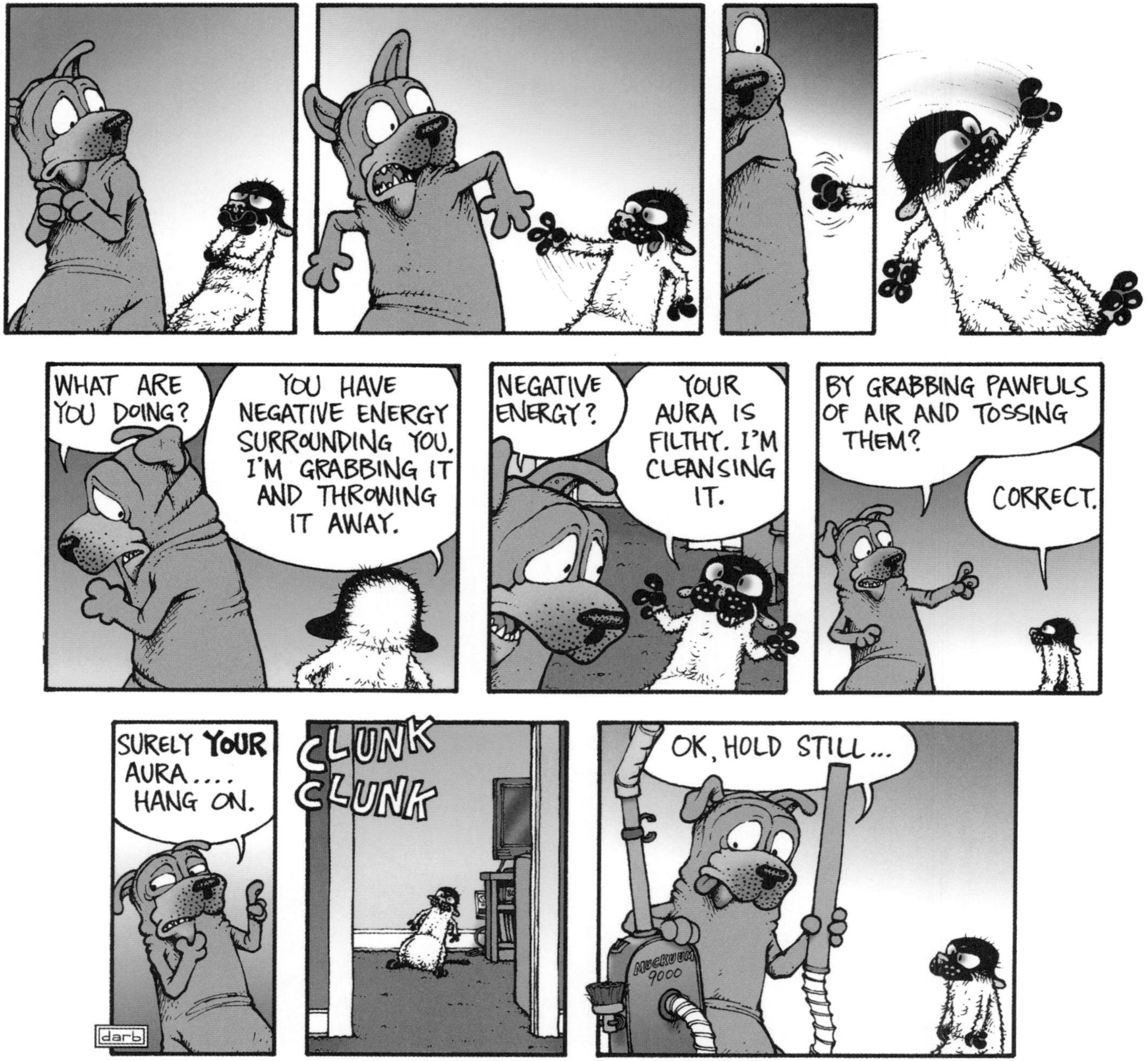
WHAT ARE YOU DOING?
YOU HAVE NEGATIVE ENERGY SURROUNDING YOU. I'M GRABBING IT AND THROWING IT AWAY.
NEGATIVE ENERGY?
YOUR AURA IS FILTHY. I'M CLEANSING IT.
BY GRABBING PAWFULS OF AIR AND TOSSING THEM?
CORRECT.
SURELY YOUR AURA.... HANG ON.
darb
CLUNK CLUNK
OK, HOLD STILL...
MUCKUUM 9000

COULD YOU WRITE ME A RECOMMENDATION?
STOP EATING GARBAGE. THERE. WRITE IT DOWN YOURSELF.
NO, SEE, IT'S FOR THE PAN-SPECIES CLUB-
PAN SPECIES? WHAT'S THAT?
IT'S WHERE ANIMALS LIKE CHIPMUNKS, RACCOONS-
HUH. I'VE ALWAYS THOUGHT OF CHIPMUNKS AS MORE OF AN OVEN SPECIES.
PAN GETS 'EM TOO CHEWY.
darb
PAN-SPECIES REFERS TO-
VERY FEW SPECIES DO WELL IN PANS.
MOST ARE EITHER TOO BIG OR TOO SMALL. FACT.
AS FAR AS CHIPMUNKS GO, MY OLD BUDDY ALLEY LOU USED TO SAY SMALLER THAN TOAST, YOU MUST ROAST.
THIS DOESN'T HELP ME.
RULE OF PAW: WHEN IN DOUBT, EAT IT RAW!

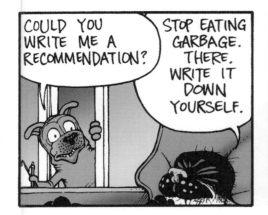

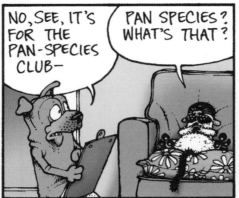

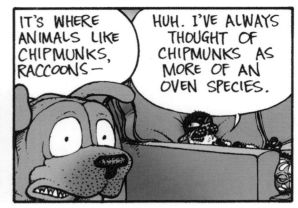

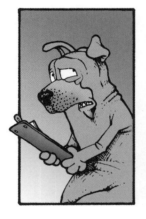

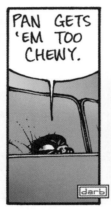

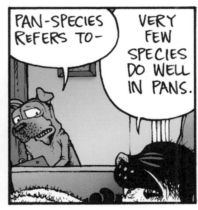

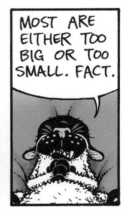

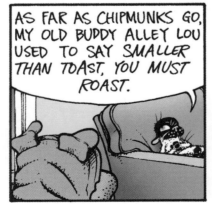

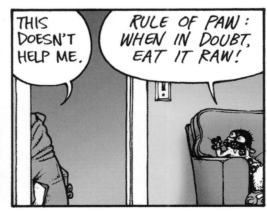

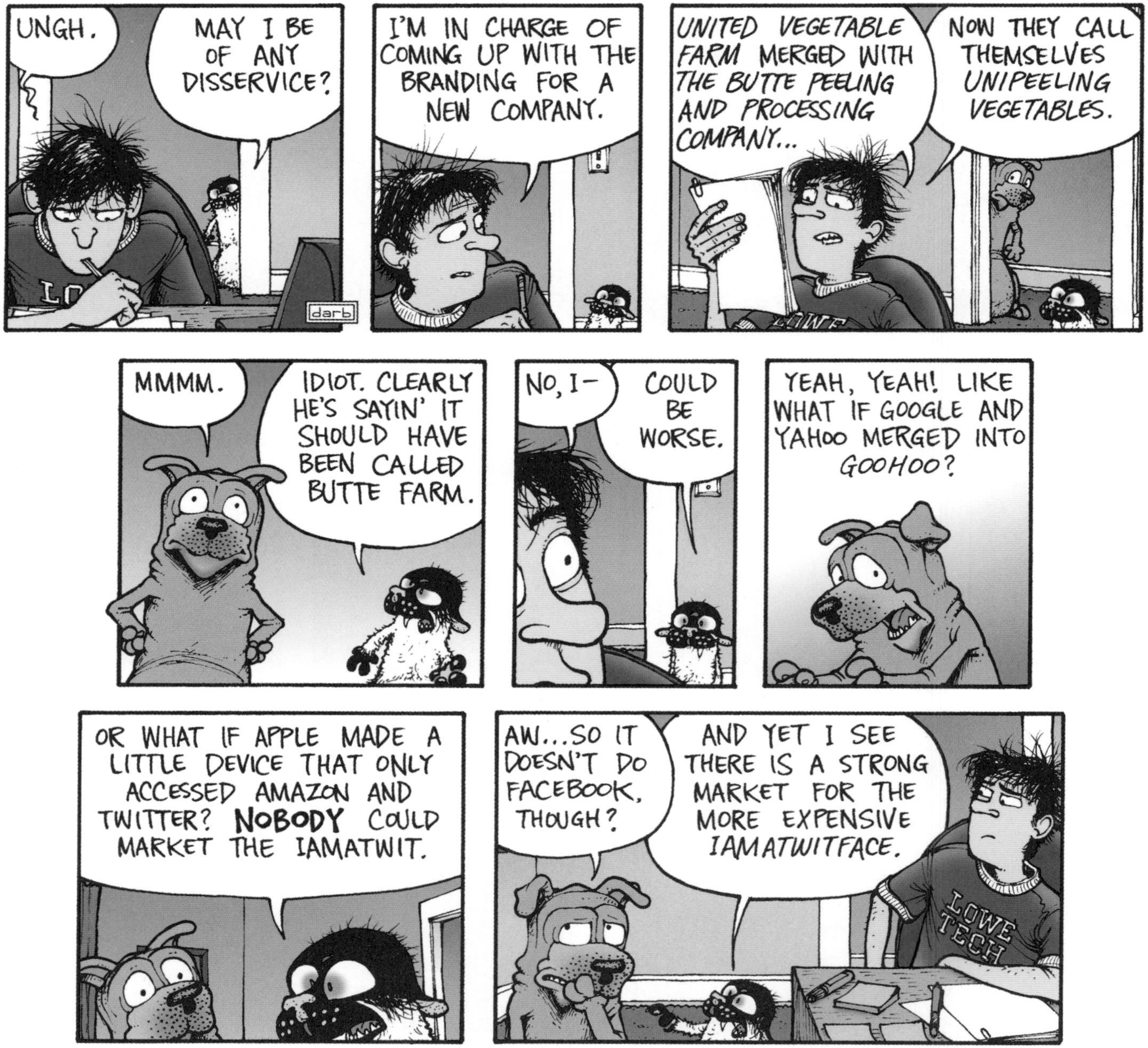
UNGH.
MAY I BE OF ANY DISSERVICE?
darb
I'M IN CHARGE OF COMING UP WITH THE BRANDING FOR A NEW COMPANY.
UNITED VEGETABLE FARM MERGED WITH *THE BUTTE PEELING AND PROCESSING COMPANY...*
NOW THEY CALL THEMSELVES *UNIPEELING VEGETABLES.*
MMMM.
IDIOT. CLEARLY HE'S SAYIN' IT SHOULD HAVE BEEN CALLED BUTTE FARM.
NO, I—
COULD BE WORSE.
YEAH, YEAH! LIKE WHAT IF GOOGLE AND YAHOO MERGED INTO *GOOHOO?*
OR WHAT IF APPLE MADE A LITTLE DEVICE THAT ONLY ACCESSED AMAZON AND TWITTER? **NOBODY** COULD MARKET THE IAMATWIT.
AW...SO IT DOESN'T DO FACEBOOK, THOUGH?
AND YET I SEE THERE IS A STRONG MARKET FOR THE MORE EXPENSIVE *IAMATWITFACE.*
LOWE TECH

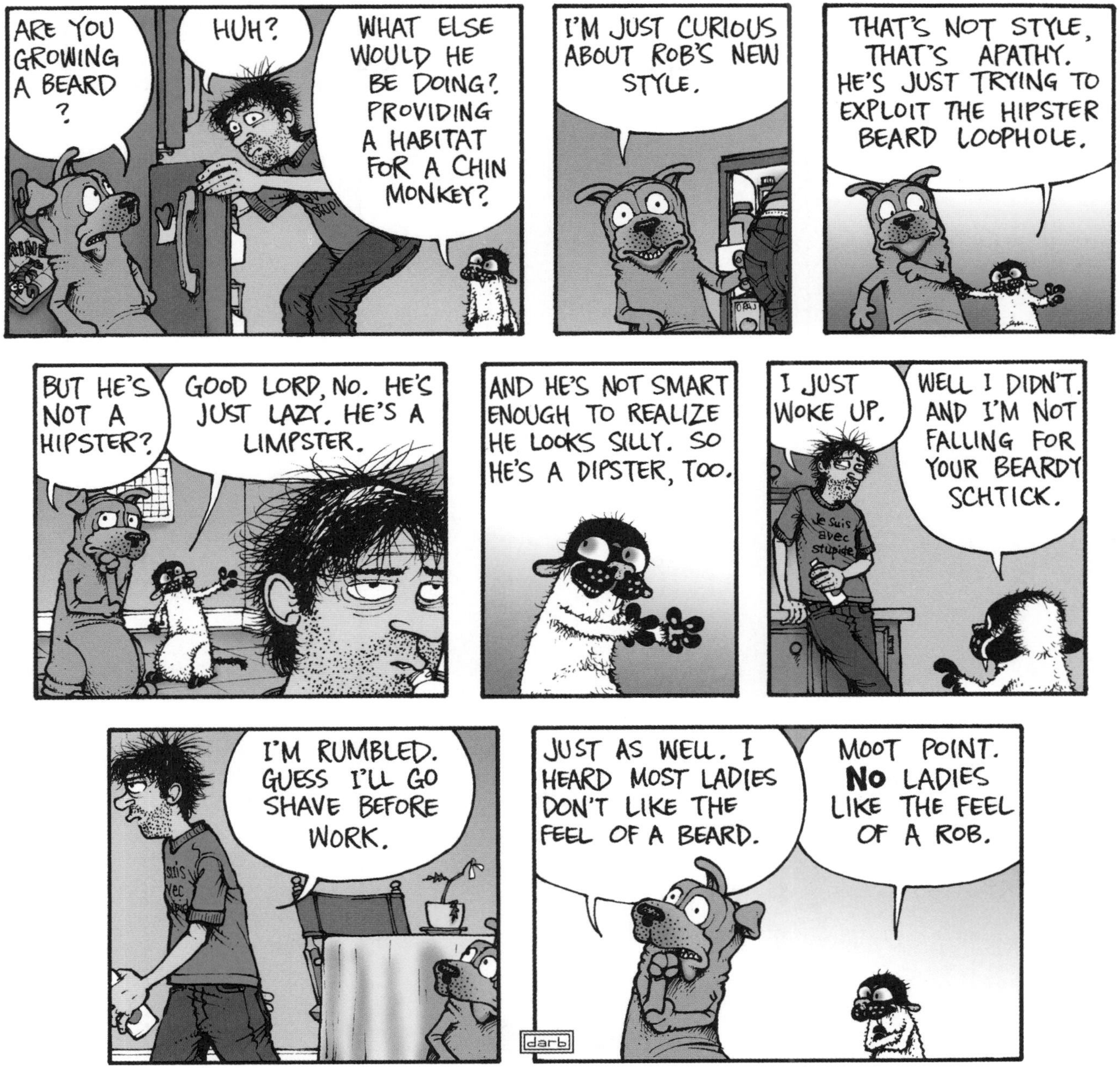
ARE YOU GROWING A BEARD?
HUH?
WHAT ELSE WOULD HE BE DOING? PROVIDING A HABITAT FOR A CHIN MONKEY?
I'M JUST CURIOUS ABOUT ROB'S NEW STYLE.
THAT'S NOT STYLE, THAT'S APATHY. HE'S JUST TRYING TO EXPLOIT THE HIPSTER BEARD LOOPHOLE.
BUT HE'S NOT A HIPSTER?
GOOD LORD, NO. HE'S JUST LAZY. HE'S A LIMPSTER.
AND HE'S NOT SMART ENOUGH TO REALIZE HE LOOKS SILLY. SO HE'S A DIPSTER, TOO.
I JUST WOKE UP.
WELL I DIDN'T. AND I'M NOT FALLING FOR YOUR BEARDY SCHTICK.
je suis avec stupide
I'M RUMBLED. GUESS I'LL GO SHAVE BEFORE WORK.
JUST AS WELL. I HEARD MOST LADIES DON'T LIKE THE FEEL OF A BEARD.
MOOT POINT. **NO** LADIES LIKE THE FEEL OF A ROB.
darb

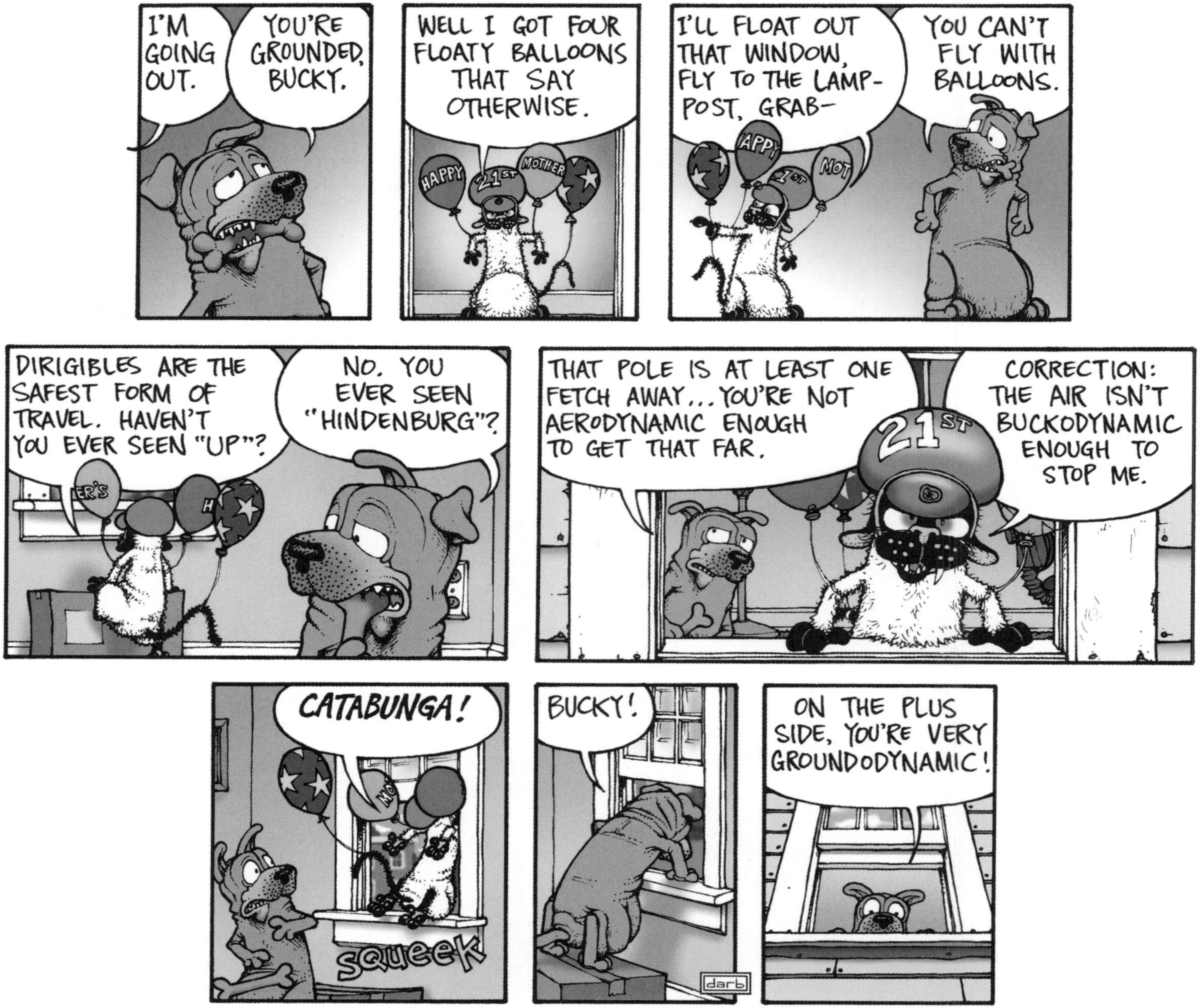
I'M GOING OUT.
YOU'RE GROUNDED, BUCKY.
WELL I GOT FOUR FLOATY BALLOONS THAT SAY OTHERWISE.
HAPPY
21ST
MOTHER
I'LL FLOAT OUT THAT WINDOW, FLY TO THE LAMP-POST, GRAB-
YOU CAN'T FLY WITH BALLOONS.
DIRIGIBLES ARE THE SAFEST FORM OF TRAVEL. HAVEN'T YOU EVER SEEN "UP"?
NO. YOU EVER SEEN "HINDENBURG"?
THAT POLE IS AT LEAST ONE FETCH AWAY... YOU'RE NOT AERODYNAMIC ENOUGH TO GET THAT FAR.
CORRECTION: THE AIR ISN'T BUCKODYNAMIC ENOUGH TO STOP ME.
CATABUNGA!
SQUEEK
BUCKY!
ON THE PLUS SIDE, YOU'RE VERY GROUNDODYNAMIC!
darb

WHAT ARE YOU DOING IN THERE?
MY NEW INVENTION IS BASED ON THE JACK-IN-THE-BOX.
IS IT A JERK-IN-A-TUBE?
CAN ALL THAT JERK STUFF.
LOOKS LIKE YOU BEAT ME TO IT!
CRUSHED CATS
ROB SAID I'M NOT ALLOWED TO **CLIMB** THE BOOKCASE, BUT HE DIDN'T SAY I'M NOT ALLOWED TO KITTYPULT DIRECTLY TO THE TOP OF—
SCIENCE of HITTING
wump!
tang!
darb
OW... NUMB... CAN'T FEEL MY BUTT...
WISH I COULDN'T!

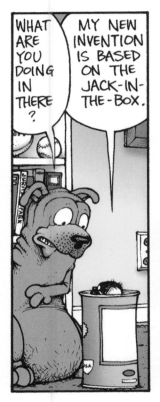

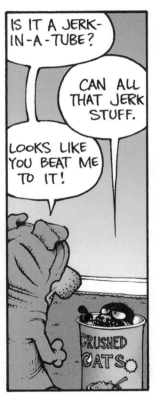

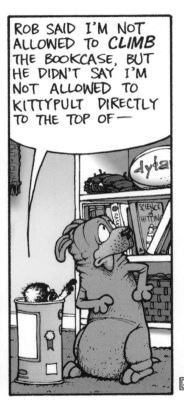

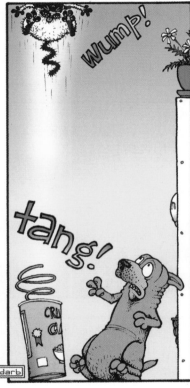

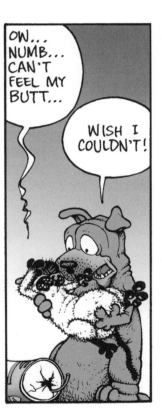

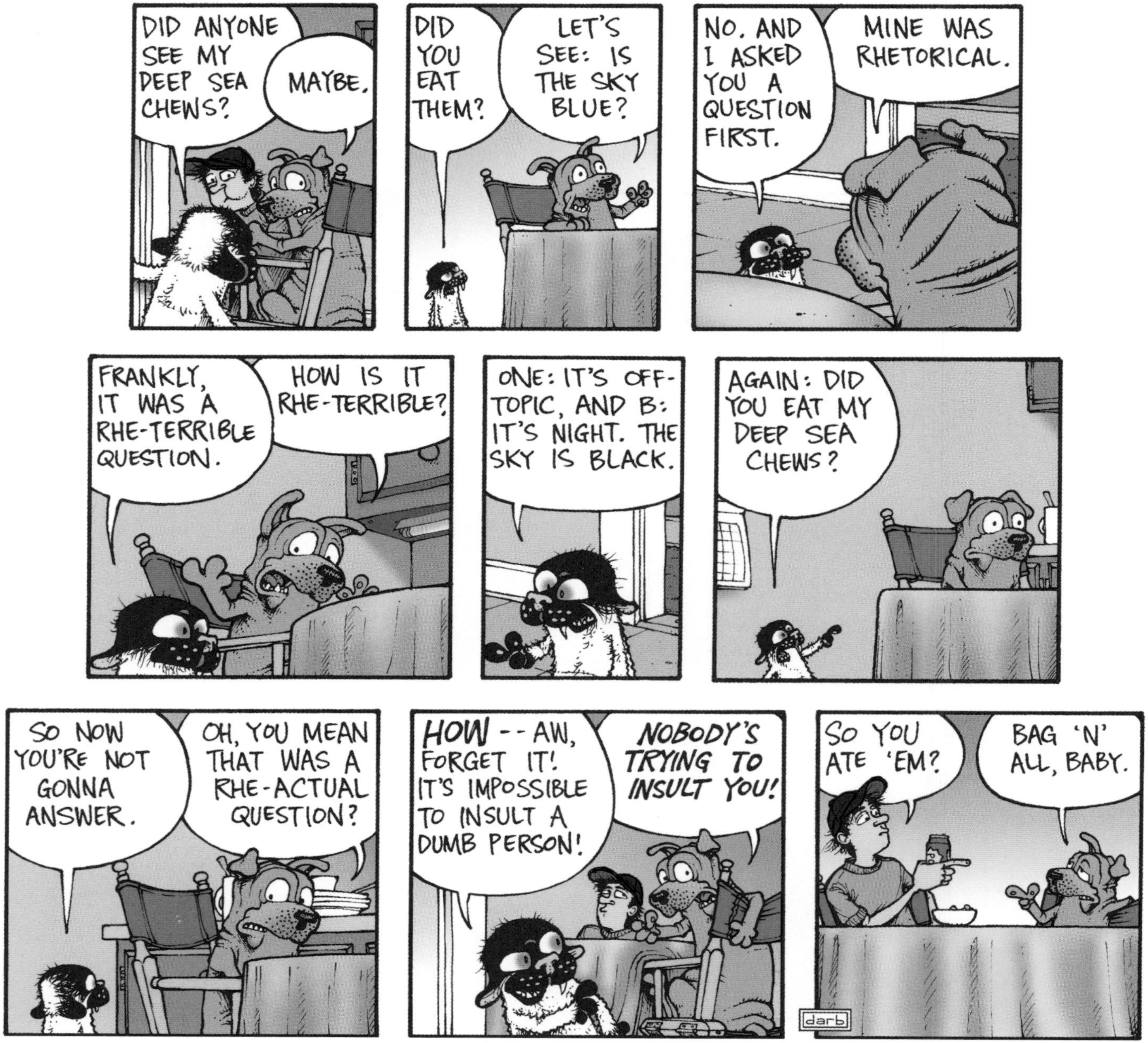
DID ANYONE SEE MY DEEP SEA CHEWS?
MAYBE.
DID YOU EAT THEM?
LET'S SEE: IS THE SKY BLUE?
NO. AND I ASKED YOU A QUESTION FIRST.
MINE WAS RHETORICAL.
FRANKLY, IT WAS A RHE-TERRIBLE QUESTION.
HOW IS IT RHE-TERRIBLE?
ONE: IT'S OFF-TOPIC, AND B: IT'S NIGHT. THE SKY IS BLACK.
AGAIN: DID YOU EAT MY DEEP SEA CHEWS?
SO NOW YOU'RE NOT GONNA ANSWER.
OH, YOU MEAN THAT WAS A RHE-ACTUAL QUESTION?
HOW -- AW, FORGET IT! IT'S IMPOSSIBLE TO INSULT A DUMB PERSON!
NOBODY'S TRYING TO INSULT YOU!
SO YOU ATE 'EM?
BAG 'N' ALL, BABY.
darb

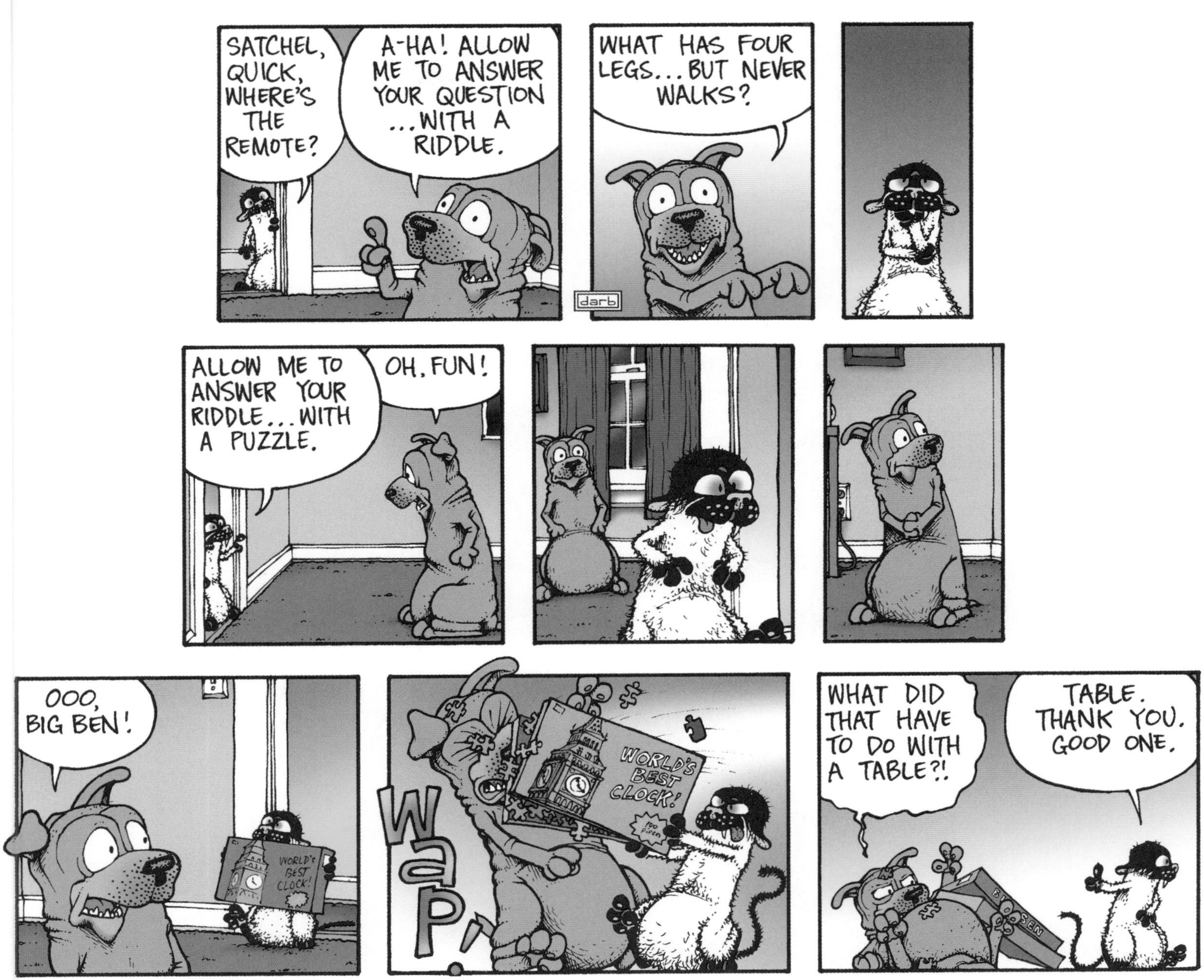
SATCHEL, QUICK, WHERE'S THE REMOTE?
A-HA! ALLOW ME TO ANSWER YOUR QUESTION ...WITH A RIDDLE.
WHAT HAS FOUR LEGS... BUT NEVER WALKS?
darb
ALLOW ME TO ANSWER YOUR RIDDLE... WITH A PUZZLE.
OH. FUN!
OOO, BIG BEN!
WORLD'S BEST CLOCK!
WORLD'S BEST CLOCK!
Wap!
WHAT DID THAT HAVE TO DO WITH A TABLE?!
TABLE. THANK YOU. GOOD ONE.

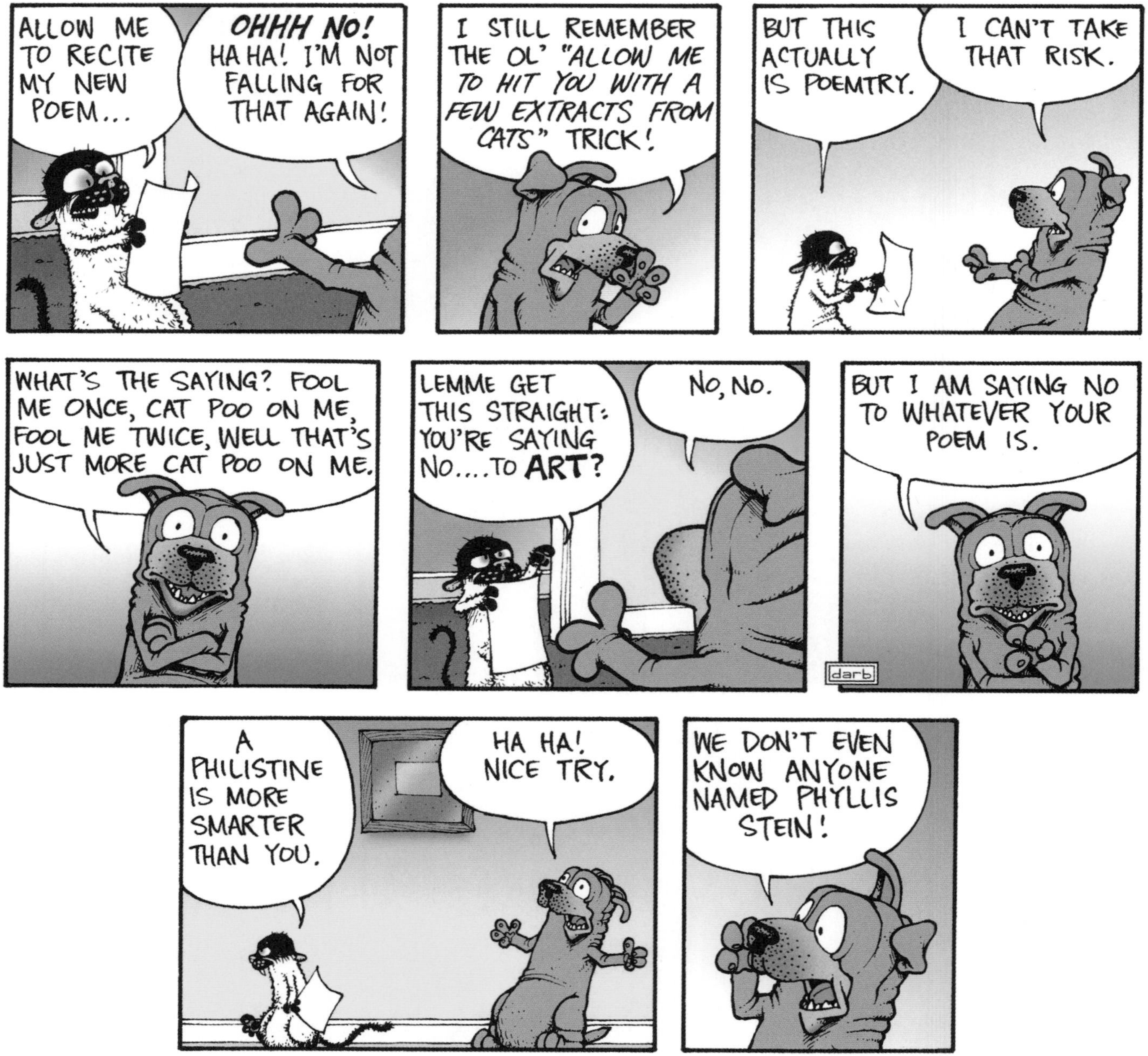
ALLOW ME TO RECITE MY NEW POEM...
OHHH NO! HA HA! I'M NOT FALLING FOR THAT AGAIN!
I STILL REMEMBER THE OL' "ALLOW ME TO HIT YOU WITH A FEW EXTRACTS FROM CATS" TRICK!
BUT THIS ACTUALLY IS POEMTRY.
I CAN'T TAKE THAT RISK.
WHAT'S THE SAYING? FOOL ME ONCE, CAT POO ON ME, FOOL ME TWICE, WELL THAT'S JUST MORE CAT POO ON ME.
LEMME GET THIS STRAIGHT: YOU'RE SAYING NO....TO ART?
NO, NO.
BUT I AM SAYING NO TO WHATEVER YOUR POEM IS.
darb
A PHILISTINE IS MORE SMARTER THAN YOU.
HA HA! NICE TRY.
WE DON'T EVEN KNOW ANYONE NAMED PHYLLIS STEIN!

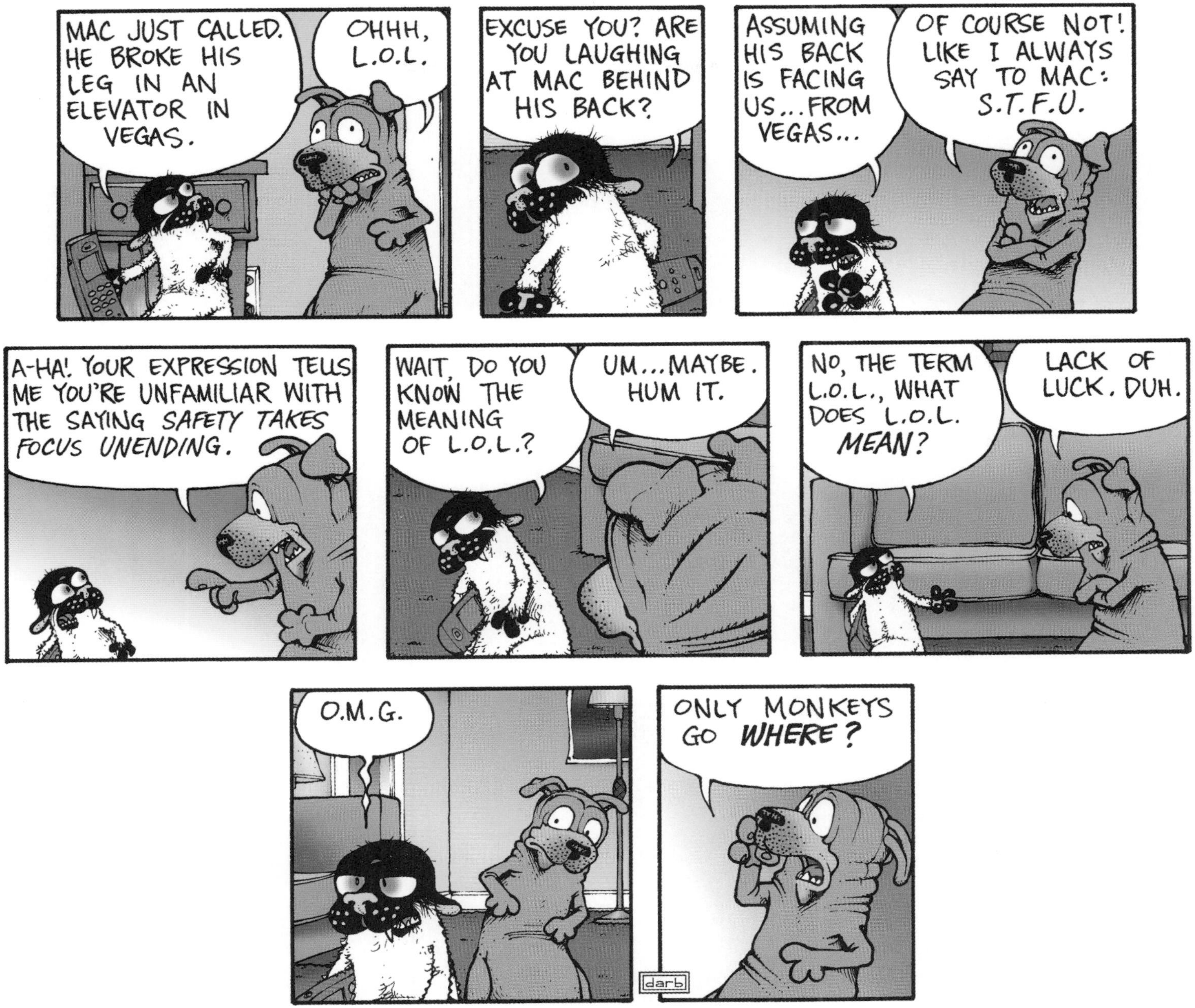
MAC JUST CALLED. HE BROKE HIS LEG IN AN ELEVATOR IN VEGAS.
OHHH, L.O.L.
EXCUSE YOU? ARE YOU LAUGHING AT MAC BEHIND HIS BACK?
ASSUMING HIS BACK IS FACING US... FROM VEGAS...
OF COURSE NOT! LIKE I ALWAYS SAY TO MAC: S.T.F.U.
A-HA! YOUR EXPRESSION TELLS ME YOU'RE UNFAMILIAR WITH THE SAYING *SAFETY TAKES FOCUS UNENDING.*
WAIT, DO YOU KNOW THE MEANING OF L.O.L.?
UM... MAYBE. HUM IT.
NO, THE TERM L.O.L., WHAT DOES L.O.L. *MEAN?*
LACK OF LUCK. DUH.
O.M.G.
darb
ONLY MONKEYS GO **WHERE?**

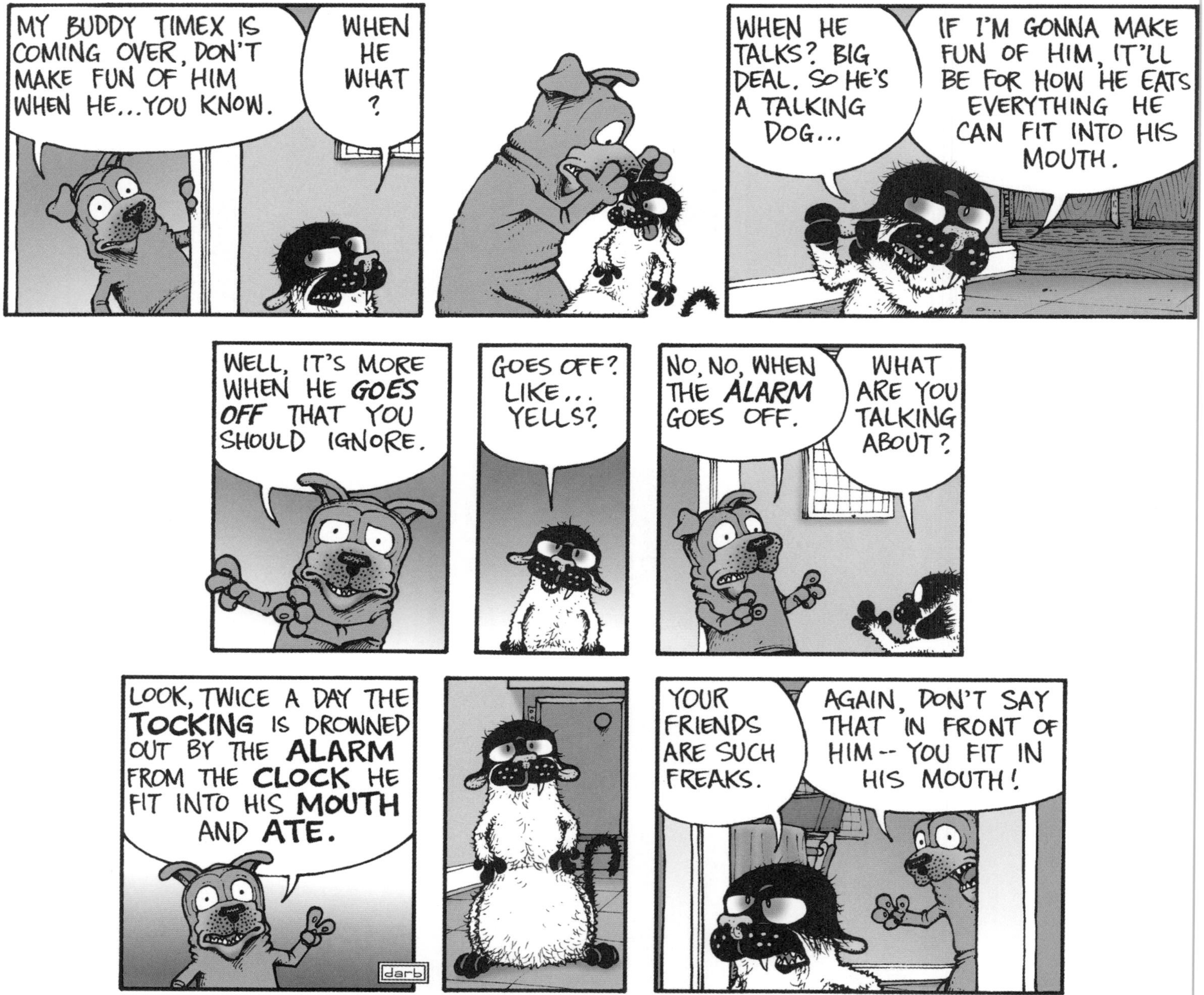
MY BUDDY TIMEX IS COMING OVER, DON'T MAKE FUN OF HIM WHEN HE...YOU KNOW.
WHEN HE WHAT?
WHEN HE TALKS? BIG DEAL. SO HE'S A TALKING DOG...
IF I'M GONNA MAKE FUN OF HIM, IT'LL BE FOR HOW HE EATS EVERYTHING HE CAN FIT INTO HIS MOUTH.
WELL, IT'S MORE WHEN HE GOES OFF THAT YOU SHOULD IGNORE.
GOES OFF? LIKE... YELLS?
NO, NO, WHEN THE ALARM GOES OFF.
WHAT ARE YOU TALKING ABOUT?
LOOK, TWICE A DAY THE TOCKING IS DROWNED OUT BY THE ALARM FROM THE CLOCK HE FIT INTO HIS MOUTH AND ATE.
darb
YOUR FRIENDS ARE SUCH FREAKS.
AGAIN, DON'T SAY THAT IN FRONT OF HIM -- YOU FIT IN HIS MOUTH!

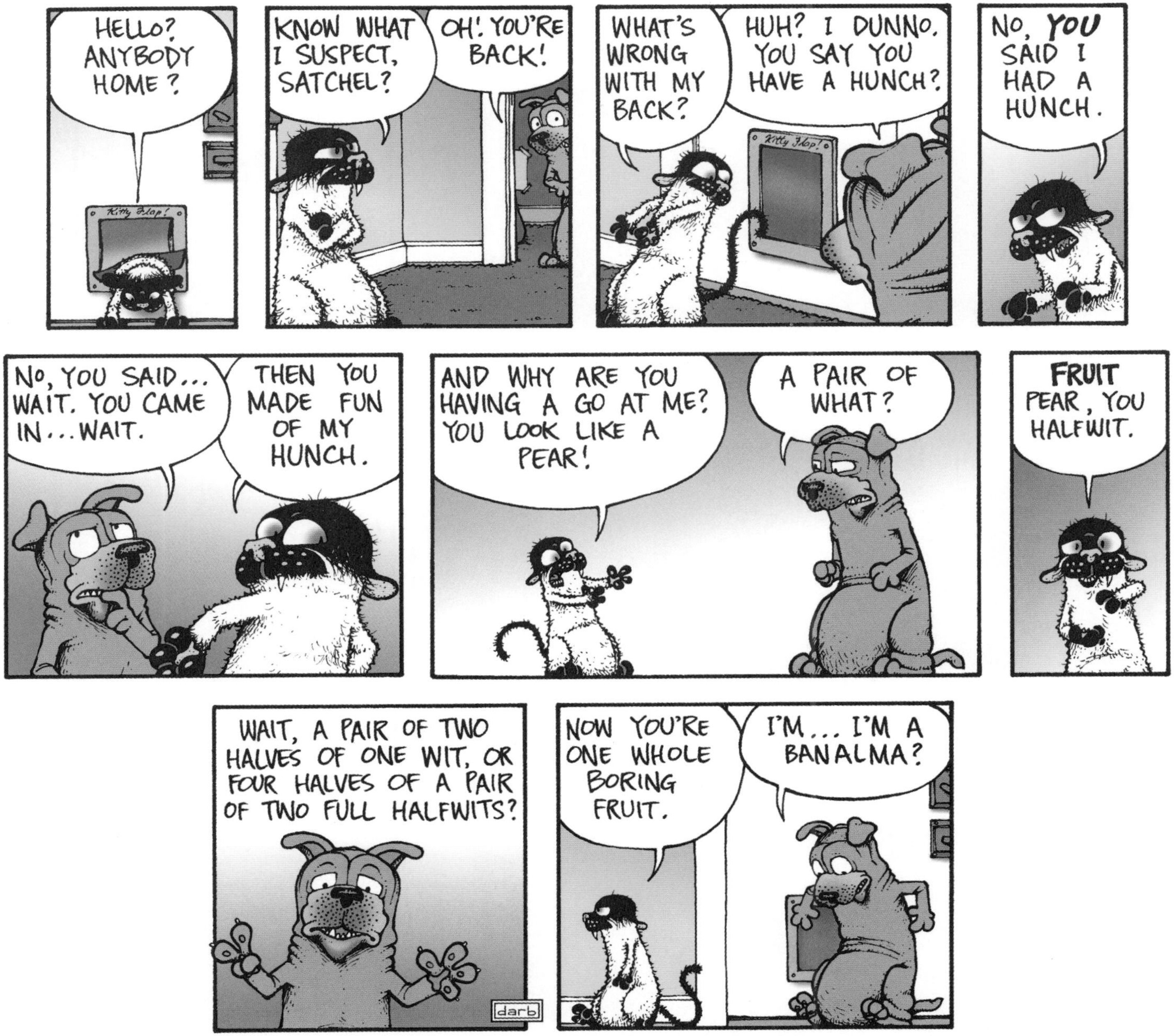

HELLO? ANYBODY HOME?
KNOW WHAT I SUSPECT, SATCHEL?
OH! YOU'RE BACK!
WHAT'S WRONG WITH MY BACK?
HUH? I DUNNO. YOU SAY YOU HAVE A HUNCH?
NO, YOU SAID I HAD A HUNCH.
NO, YOU SAID... WAIT. YOU CAME IN...WAIT.
THEN YOU MADE FUN OF MY HUNCH.
AND WHY ARE YOU HAVING A GO AT ME? YOU LOOK LIKE A PEAR!
A PAIR OF WHAT?
FRUIT PEAR, YOU HALFWIT.
WAIT, A PAIR OF TWO HALVES OF ONE WIT, OR FOUR HALVES OF A PAIR OF TWO FULL HALFWITS?
NOW YOU'RE ONE WHOLE BORING FRUIT.
I'M... I'M A BANALMA?
darb

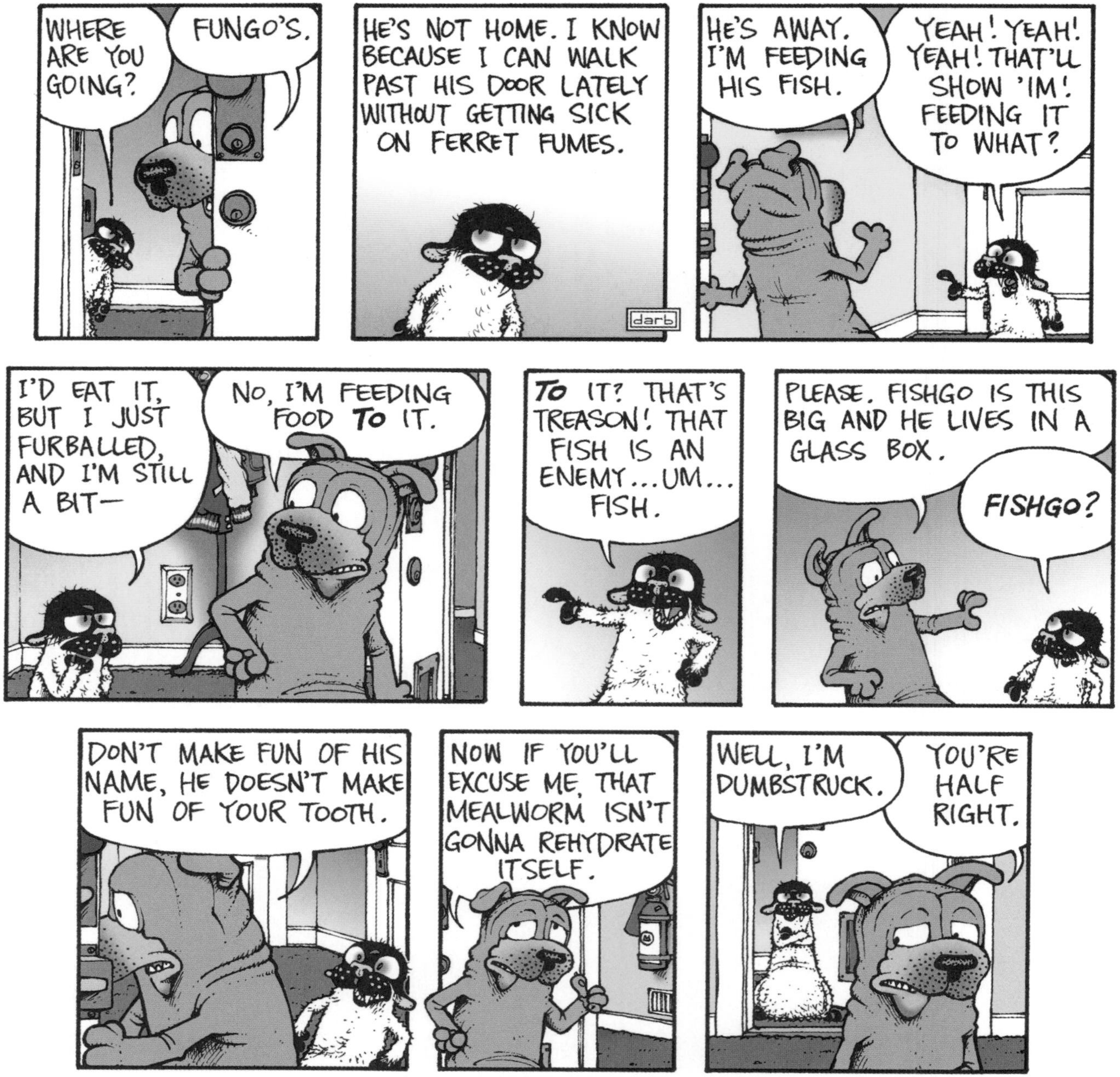
WHERE ARE YOU GOING?
FUNGO'S.
HE'S NOT HOME. I KNOW BECAUSE I CAN WALK PAST HIS DOOR LATELY WITHOUT GETTING SICK ON FERRET FUMES.
darb
HE'S AWAY. I'M FEEDING HIS FISH.
YEAH! YEAH! YEAH! THAT'LL SHOW 'IM! FEEDING IT TO WHAT?
I'D EAT IT, BUT I JUST FURBALLED, AND I'M STILL A BIT—
NO, I'M FEEDING FOOD **TO** IT.
TO IT? THAT'S TREASON! THAT FISH IS AN ENEMY...UM... FISH.
PLEASE. FISHGO IS THIS BIG AND HE LIVES IN A GLASS BOX.
FISHGO?
DON'T MAKE FUN OF HIS NAME, HE DOESN'T MAKE FUN OF YOUR TOOTH.
NOW IF YOU'LL EXCUSE ME, THAT MEALWORM ISN'T GONNA REHYDRATE ITSELF.
WELL, I'M DUMBSTRUCK.
YOU'RE HALF RIGHT.

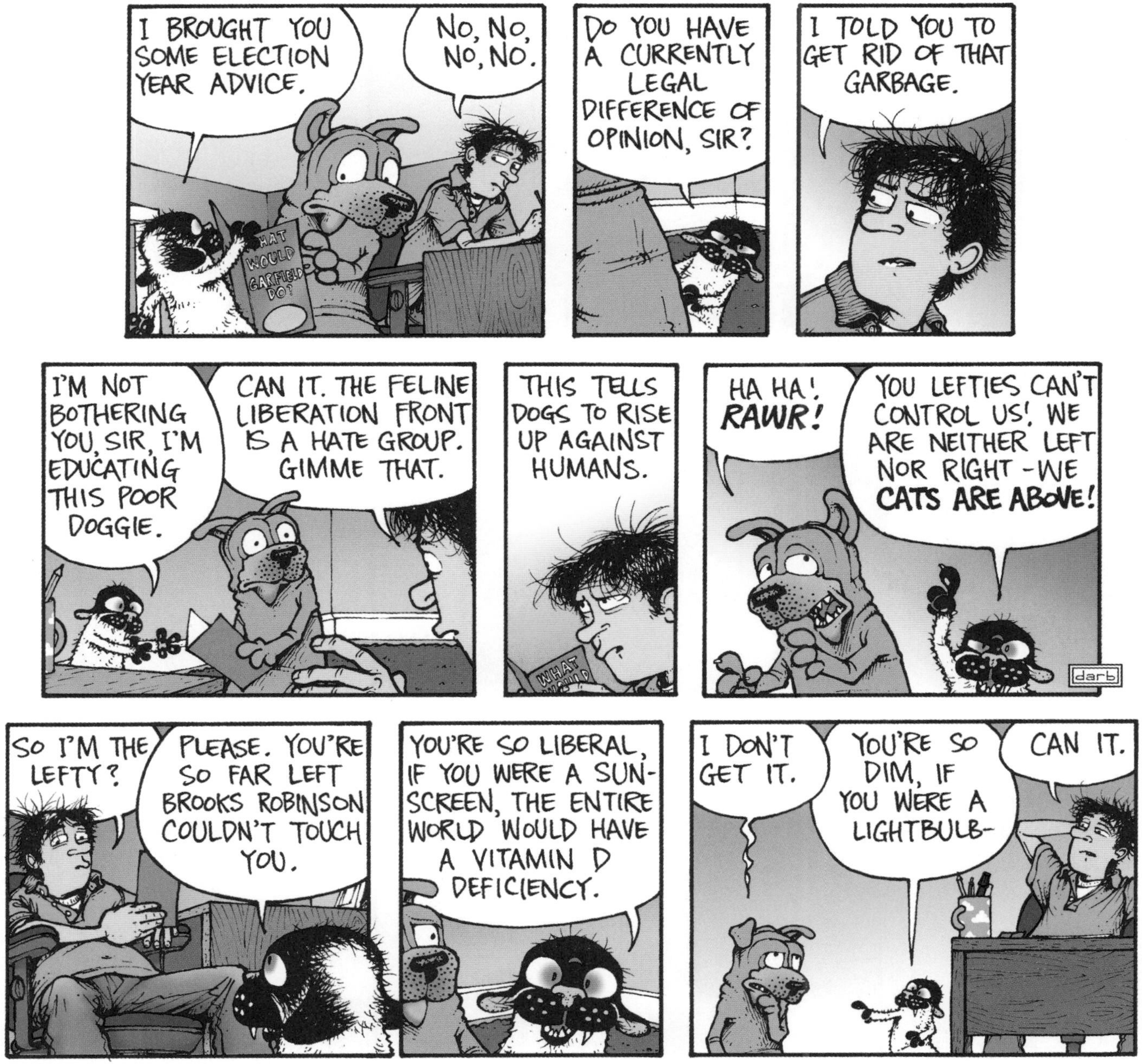
I BROUGHT YOU SOME ELECTION YEAR ADVICE.
NO, NO, NO, NO.
HAT WOULD GARFIELD DO?
DO YOU HAVE A CURRENTLY LEGAL DIFFERENCE OF OPINION, SIR?
I TOLD YOU TO GET RID OF THAT GARBAGE.
I'M NOT BOTHERING YOU, SIR, I'M EDUCATING THIS POOR DOGGIE.
CAN IT. THE FELINE LIBERATION FRONT IS A HATE GROUP. GIMME THAT.
THIS TELLS DOGS TO RISE UP AGAINST HUMANS.
HA HA! *RAWR!*
YOU LEFTIES CAN'T CONTROL US! WE ARE NEITHER LEFT NOR RIGHT - WE **CATS ARE ABOVE!**
darb
SO I'M THE LEFTY?
PLEASE. YOU'RE SO FAR LEFT BROOKS ROBINSON COULDN'T TOUCH YOU.
YOU'RE SO LIBERAL, IF YOU WERE A SUN-SCREEN, THE ENTIRE WORLD WOULD HAVE A VITAMIN D DEFICIENCY.
I DON'T GET IT.
YOU'RE SO DIM, IF YOU WERE A LIGHTBULB-
CAN IT.

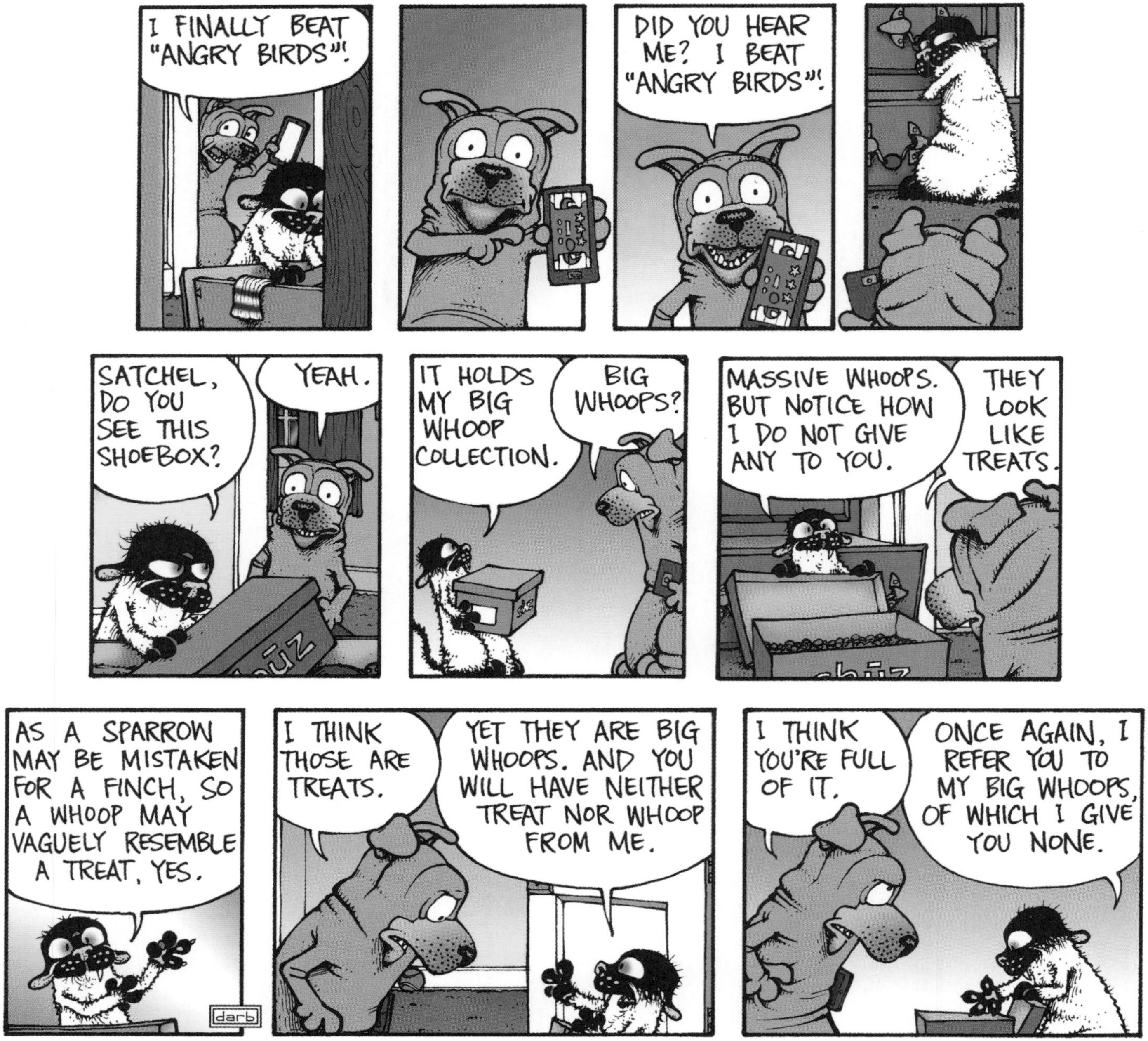
I FINALLY BEAT "ANGRY BIRDS"!
DID YOU HEAR ME? I BEAT "ANGRY BIRDS"!
SATCHEL, DO YOU SEE THIS SHOEBOX?
YEAH.
IT HOLDS MY BIG WHOOP COLLECTION.
BIG WHOOPS?
MASSIVE WHOOPS. BUT NOTICE HOW I DO NOT GIVE ANY TO YOU.
THEY LOOK LIKE TREATS.
AS A SPARROW MAY BE MISTAKEN FOR A FINCH, SO A WHOOP MAY VAGUELY RESEMBLE A TREAT, YES.
darb
I THINK THOSE ARE TREATS.
YET THEY ARE BIG WHOOPS. AND YOU WILL HAVE NEITHER TREAT NOR WHOOP FROM ME.
I THINK YOU'RE FULL OF IT.
ONCE AGAIN, I REFER YOU TO MY BIG WHOOPS, OF WHICH I GIVE YOU NONE.

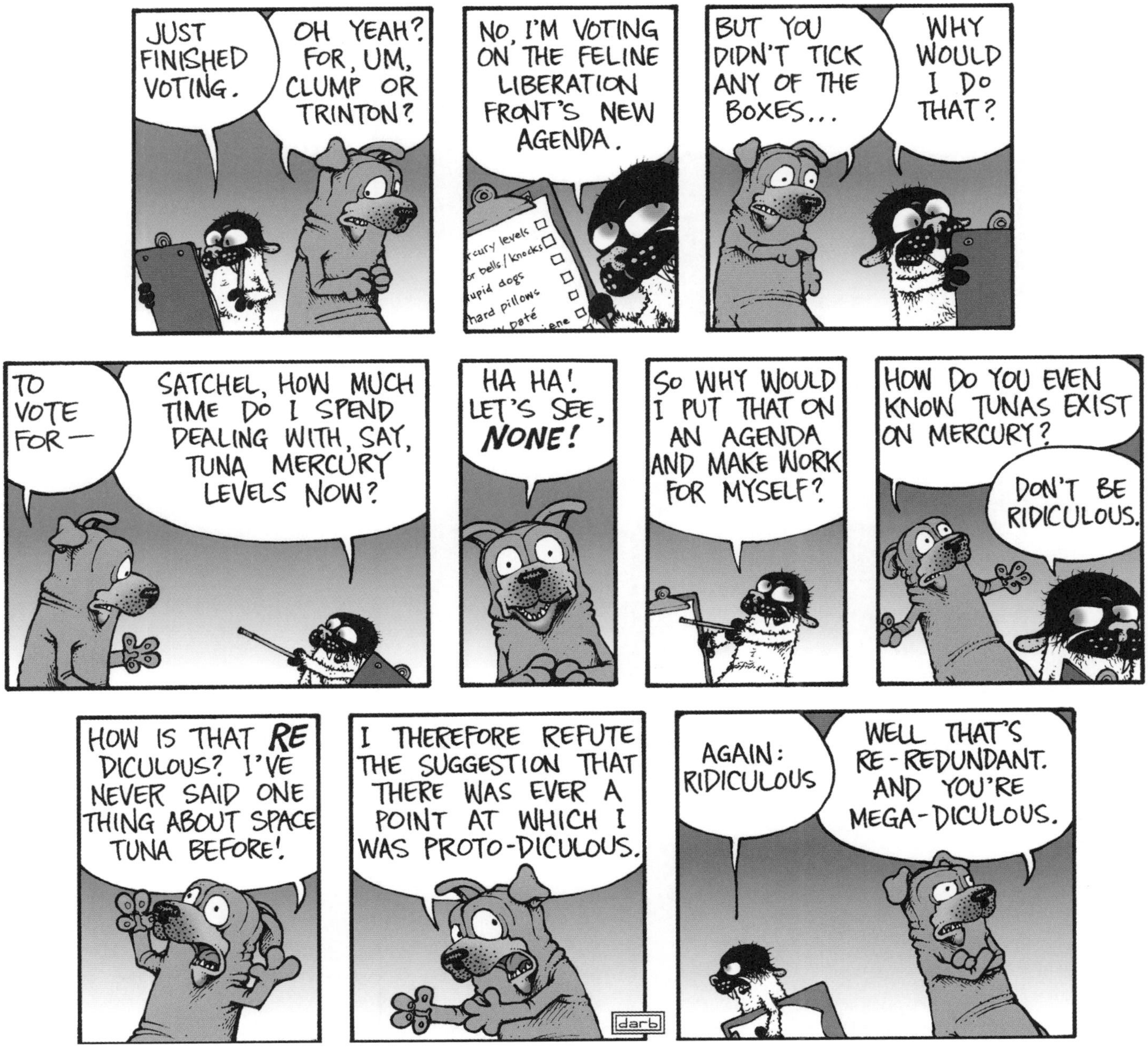
JUST FINISHED VOTING.
OH YEAH? FOR, UM, CLUMP OR TRINTON?
NO, I'M VOTING ON THE FELINE LIBERATION FRONT'S NEW AGENDA.
rcury levels
or bells / knocks
upid dogs
hard pillows
paté
BUT YOU DIDN'T TICK ANY OF THE BOXES...
WHY WOULD I DO THAT?
TO VOTE FOR—
SATCHEL, HOW MUCH TIME DO I SPEND DEALING WITH, SAY, TUNA MERCURY LEVELS NOW?
HA HA! LET'S SEE, NONE!
SO WHY WOULD I PUT THAT ON AN AGENDA AND MAKE WORK FOR MYSELF?
HOW DO YOU EVEN KNOW TUNAS EXIST ON MERCURY?
DON'T BE RIDICULOUS.
HOW IS THAT RE DICULOUS? I'VE NEVER SAID ONE THING ABOUT SPACE TUNA BEFORE!
I THEREFORE REFUTE THE SUGGESTION THAT THERE WAS EVER A POINT AT WHICH I WAS PROTO-DICULOUS.
darb
AGAIN: RIDICULOUS
WELL THAT'S RE-REDUNDANT. AND YOU'RE MEGA-DICULOUS.

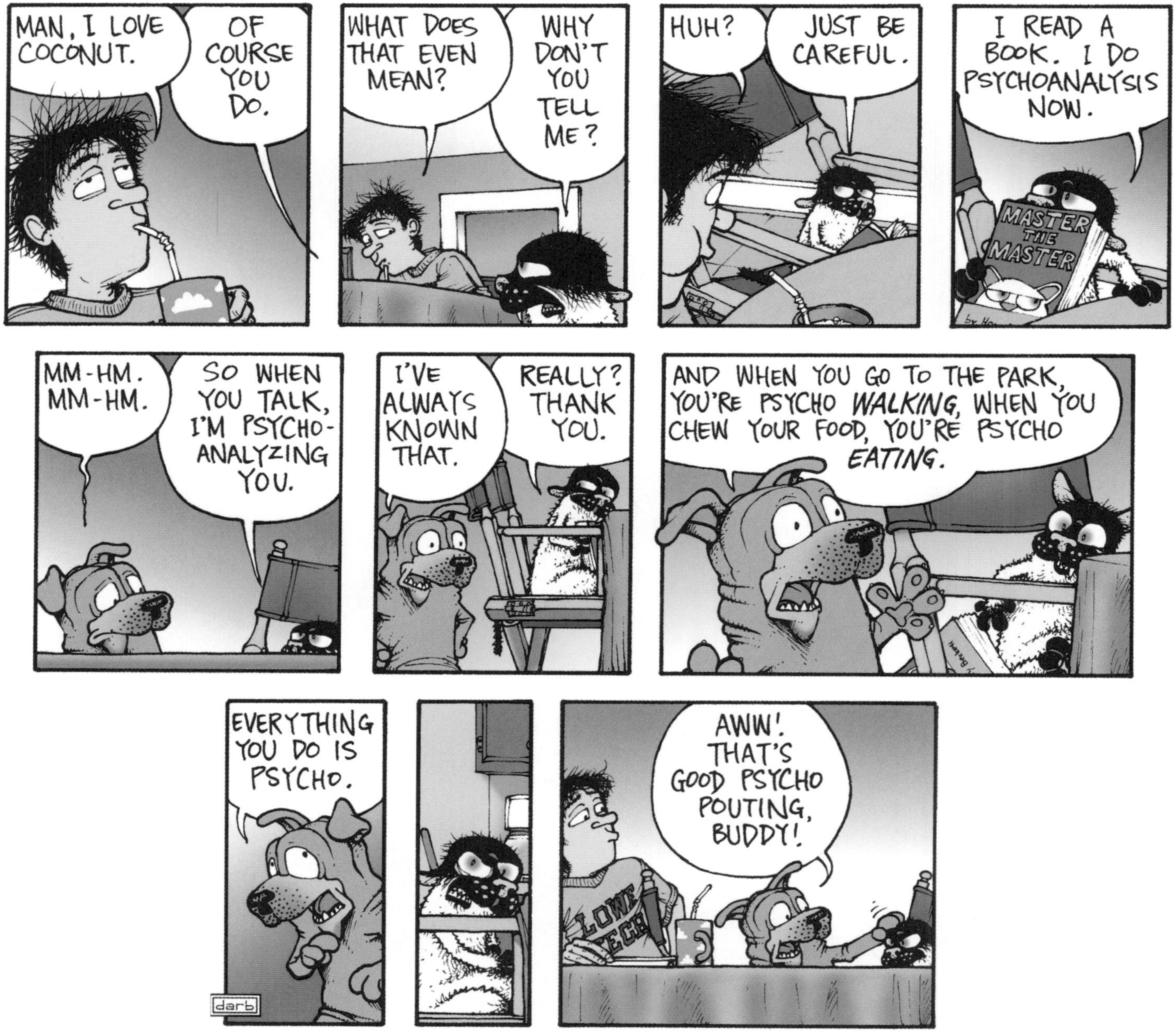
MAN, I LOVE COCONUT.
OF COURSE YOU DO.
WHAT DOES THAT EVEN MEAN?
WHY DON'T YOU TELL ME?
HUH?
JUST BE CAREFUL.
I READ A BOOK. I DO PSYCHOANALYSIS NOW.
MASTER THE MASTER
MM-HM. MM-HM.
SO WHEN YOU TALK, I'M PSYCHO-ANALYZING YOU.
I'VE ALWAYS KNOWN THAT.
REALLY? THANK YOU.
AND WHEN YOU GO TO THE PARK, YOU'RE PSYCHO *WALKING*, WHEN YOU CHEW YOUR FOOD, YOU'RE PSYCHO *EATING*.
EVERYTHING YOU DO IS PSYCHO.
darb
LOWE TECH
AWW! THAT'S GOOD PSYCHO POUTING, BUDDY!

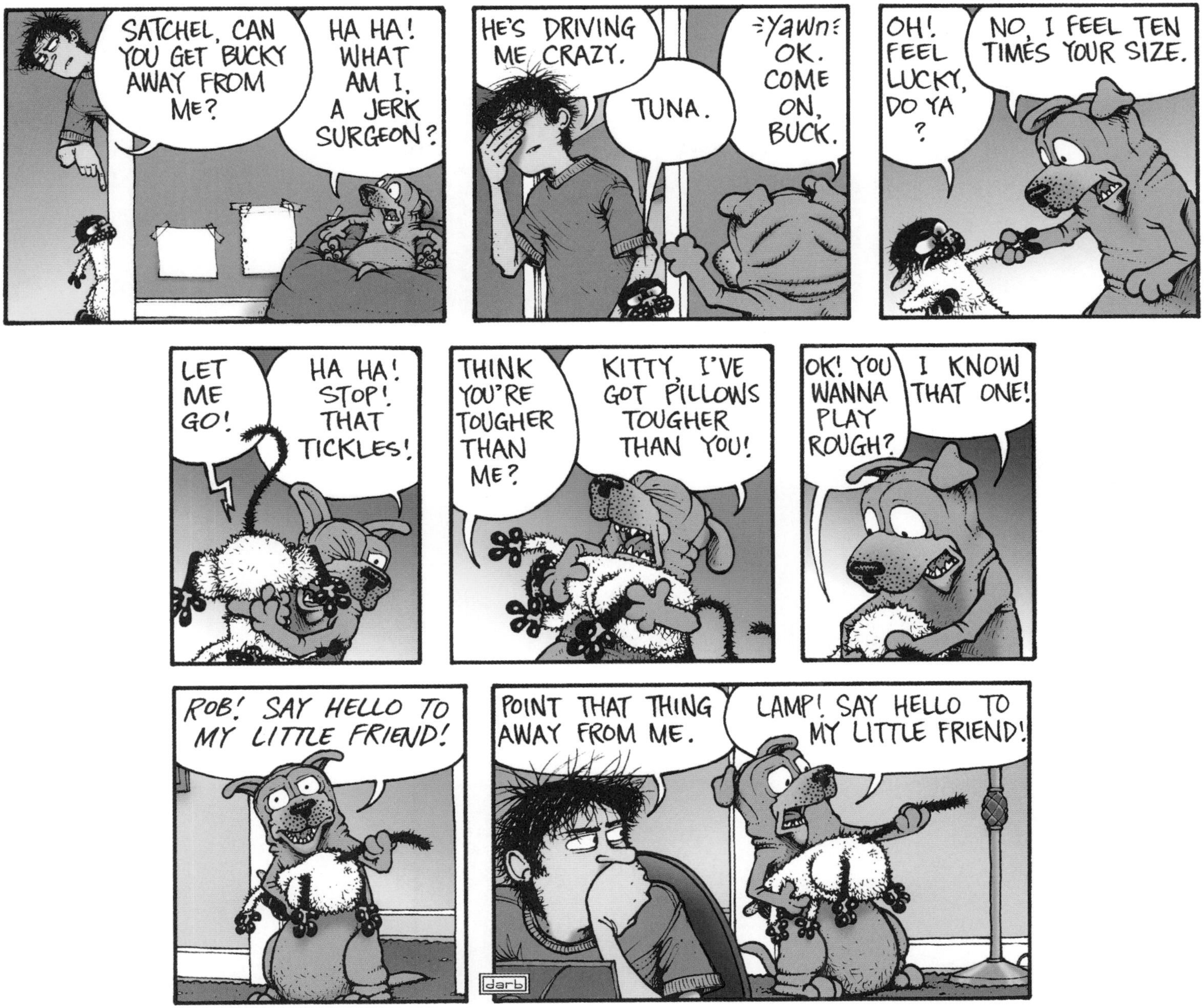
SATCHEL, CAN YOU GET BUCKY AWAY FROM ME?
HA HA! WHAT AM I, A JERK SURGEON?
HE'S DRIVING ME CRAZY.
TUNA.
≡Yawn≡ OK. COME ON, BUCK.
OH! FEEL LUCKY, DO YA?
NO, I FEEL TEN TIMES YOUR SIZE.
LET ME GO!
HA HA! STOP! THAT TICKLES!
THINK YOU'RE TOUGHER THAN ME?
KITTY, I'VE GOT PILLOWS TOUGHER THAN YOU!
OK! YOU WANNA PLAY ROUGH?
I KNOW THAT ONE!
ROB! SAY HELLO TO MY LITTLE FRIEND!
POINT THAT THING AWAY FROM ME.
LAMP! SAY HELLO TO MY LITTLE FRIEND!
darb

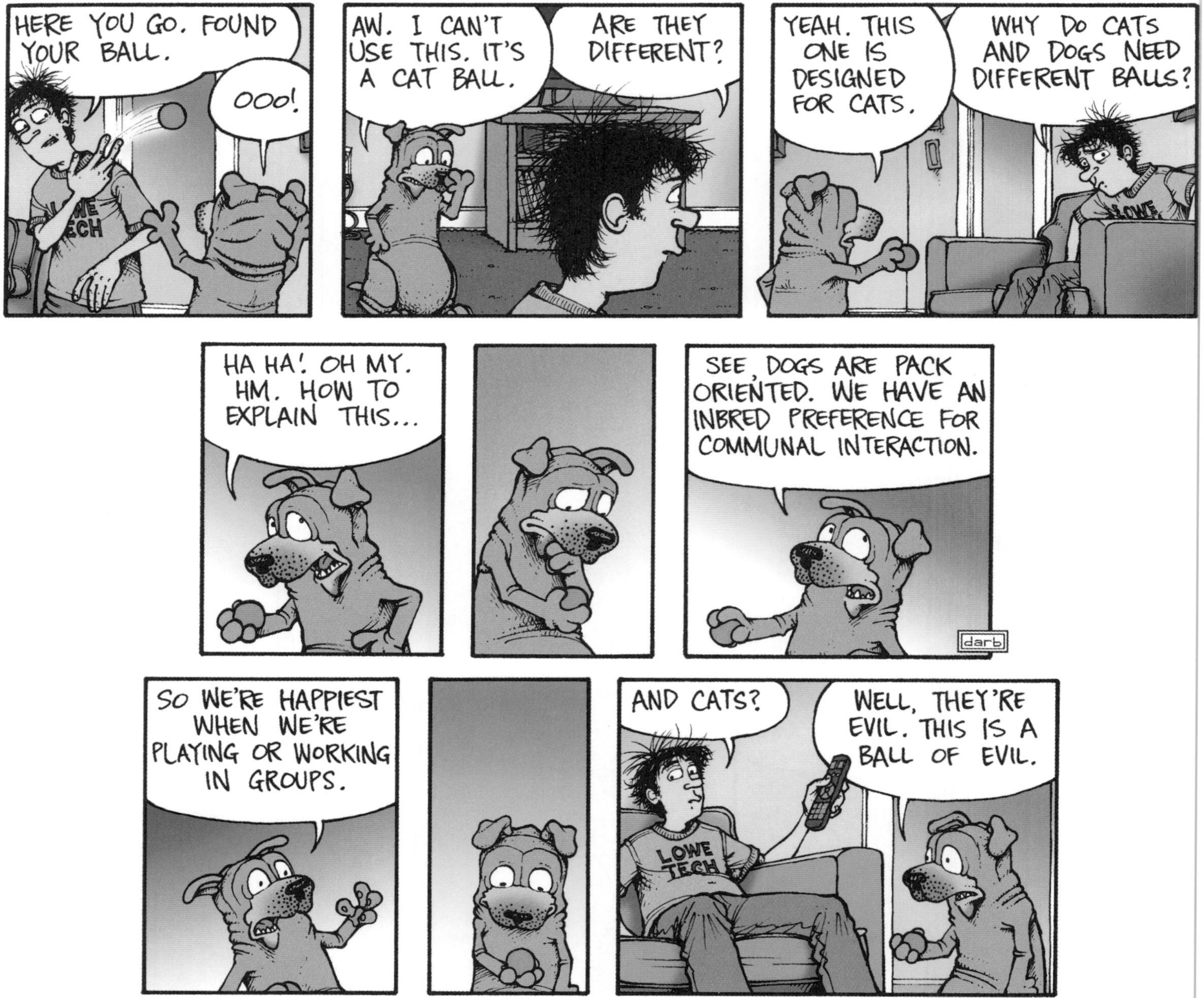
HERE YOU GO. FOUND YOUR BALL.
OOO!
AW. I CAN'T USE THIS. IT'S A CAT BALL.
ARE THEY DIFFERENT?
YEAH. THIS ONE IS DESIGNED FOR CATS.
WHY DO CATS AND DOGS NEED DIFFERENT BALLS?
HA HA! OH MY. HM. HOW TO EXPLAIN THIS...
SEE, DOGS ARE PACK ORIENTED. WE HAVE AN INBRED PREFERENCE FOR COMMUNAL INTERACTION.
darb
SO WE'RE HAPPIEST WHEN WE'RE PLAYING OR WORKING IN GROUPS.
AND CATS?
WELL, THEY'RE EVIL. THIS IS A BALL OF EVIL.

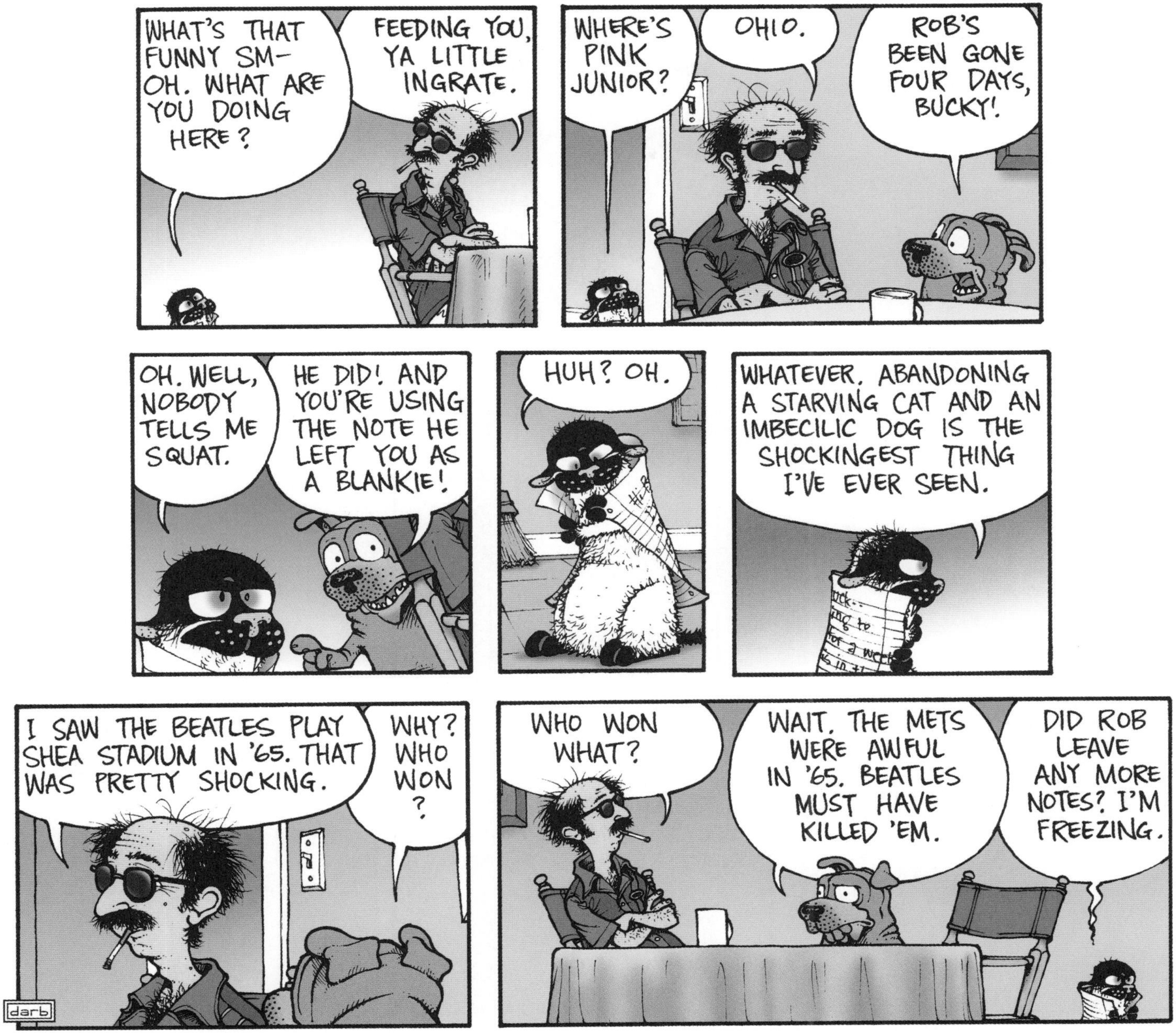
WHAT'S THAT FUNNY SM— OH. WHAT ARE YOU DOING HERE?
FEEDING YOU, YA LITTLE INGRATE.
WHERE'S PINK JUNIOR?
OHIO.
ROB'S BEEN GONE FOUR DAYS, BUCKY!
OH. WELL, NOBODY TELLS ME SQUAT.
HE DID! AND YOU'RE USING THE NOTE HE LEFT YOU AS A BLANKIE!
HUH? OH.
WHATEVER. ABANDONING A STARVING CAT AND AN IMBECILIC DOG IS THE SHOCKINGEST THING I'VE EVER SEEN.
I SAW THE BEATLES PLAY SHEA STADIUM IN '65. THAT WAS PRETTY SHOCKING.
WHY? WHO WON?
darb
WHO WON WHAT?
WAIT. THE METS WERE AWFUL IN '65. BEATLES MUST HAVE KILLED 'EM.
DID ROB LEAVE ANY MORE NOTES? I'M FREEZING.

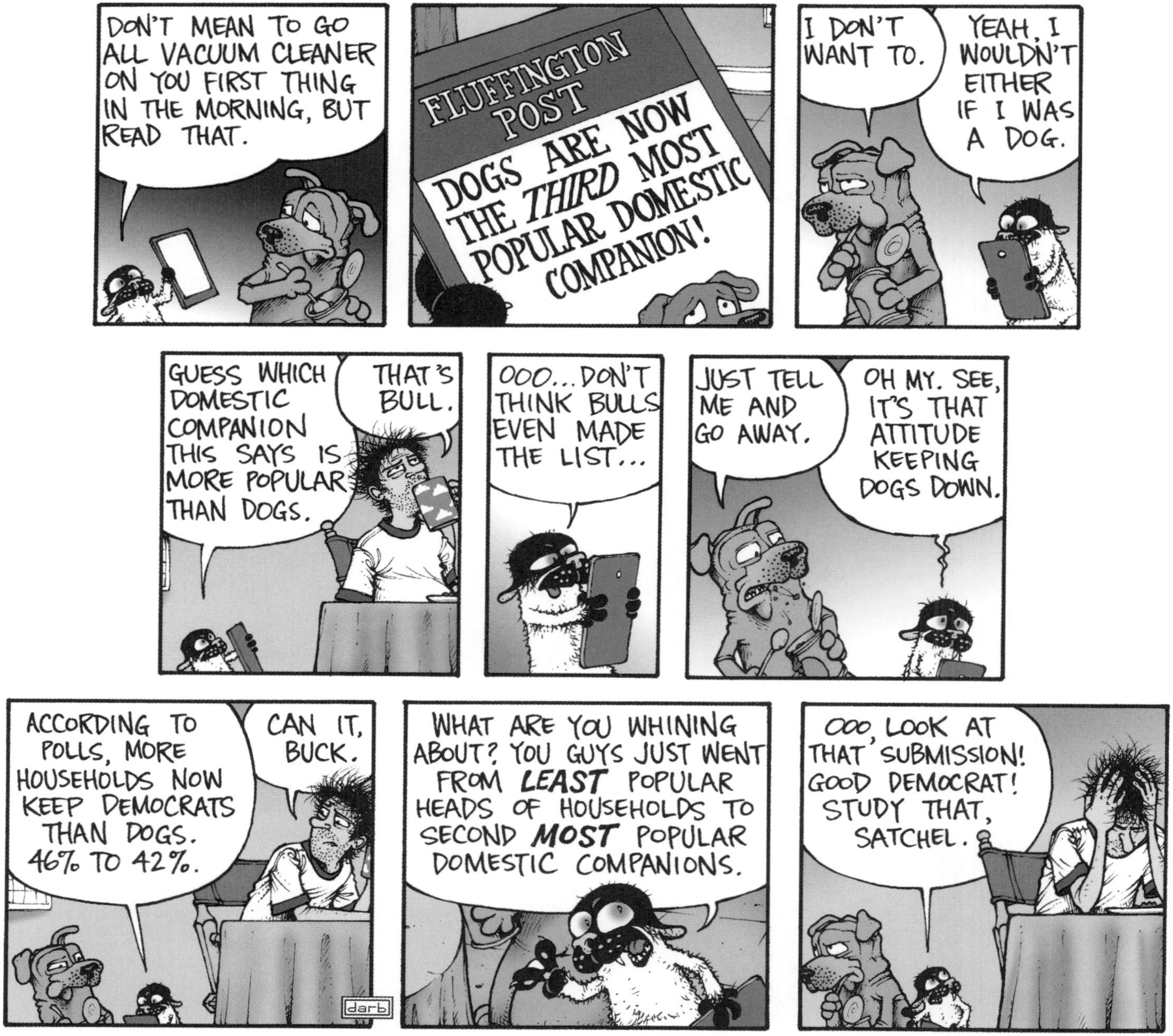

DON'T MEAN TO GO ALL VACUUM CLEANER ON YOU FIRST THING IN THE MORNING, BUT READ THAT.
FLUFFINGTON POST
DOGS ARE NOW THE THIRD MOST POPULAR DOMESTIC COMPANION!
I DON'T WANT TO.
YEAH, I WOULDN'T EITHER IF I WAS A DOG.
GUESS WHICH DOMESTIC COMPANION THIS SAYS IS MORE POPULAR THAN DOGS.
THAT'S BULL.
OOO... DON'T THINK BULLS EVEN MADE THE LIST...
JUST TELL ME AND GO AWAY.
OH MY. SEE, IT'S THAT ATTITUDE KEEPING DOGS DOWN.
ACCORDING TO POLLS, MORE HOUSEHOLDS NOW KEEP DEMOCRATS THAN DOGS. 46% TO 42%.
CAN IT, BUCK.
WHAT ARE YOU WHINING ABOUT? YOU GUYS JUST WENT FROM LEAST POPULAR HEADS OF HOUSEHOLDS TO SECOND MOST POPULAR DOMESTIC COMPANIONS.
OOO, LOOK AT THAT SUBMISSION! GOOD DEMOCRAT! STUDY THAT, SATCHEL.
darb

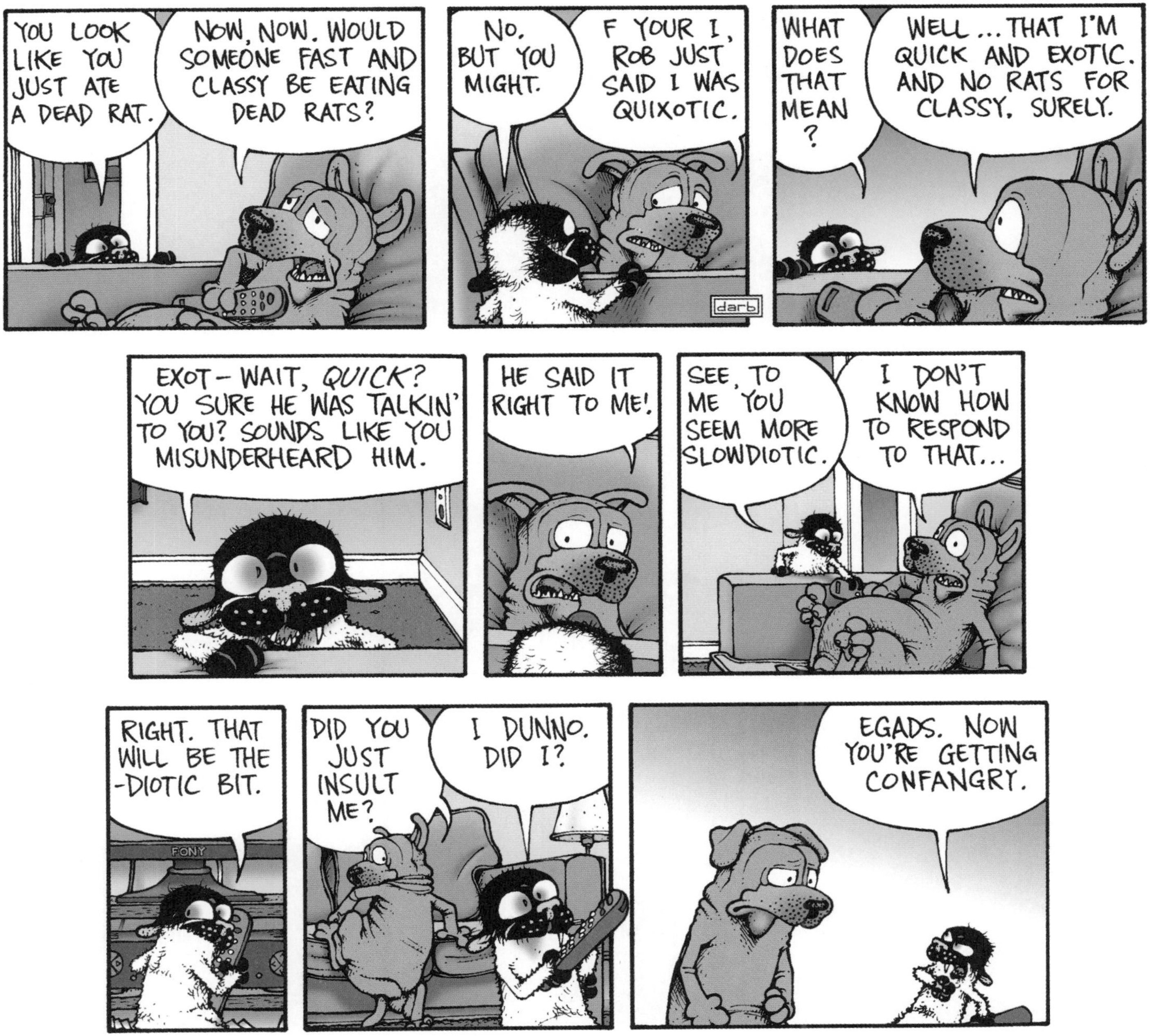
YOU LOOK LIKE YOU JUST ATE A DEAD RAT.
NOW, NOW. WOULD SOMEONE FAST AND CLASSY BE EATING DEAD RATS?
NO. BUT YOU MIGHT.
F YOUR I, ROB JUST SAID I WAS QUIXOTIC.
darb
WHAT DOES THAT MEAN ?
WELL ... THAT I'M QUICK AND EXOTIC. AND NO RATS FOR CLASSY, SURELY.
EXOT – WAIT, *QUICK*? YOU SURE HE WAS TALKIN' TO YOU? SOUNDS LIKE YOU MISUNDERHEARD HIM.
HE SAID IT RIGHT TO ME!
SEE, TO ME YOU SEEM MORE SLOWDIOTIC.
I DON'T KNOW HOW TO RESPOND TO THAT...
RIGHT. THAT WILL BE THE -DIOTIC BIT.
FONY
DID YOU JUST INSULT ME?
I DUNNO. DID I?
EGADS. NOW YOU'RE GETTING CONFANGRY.

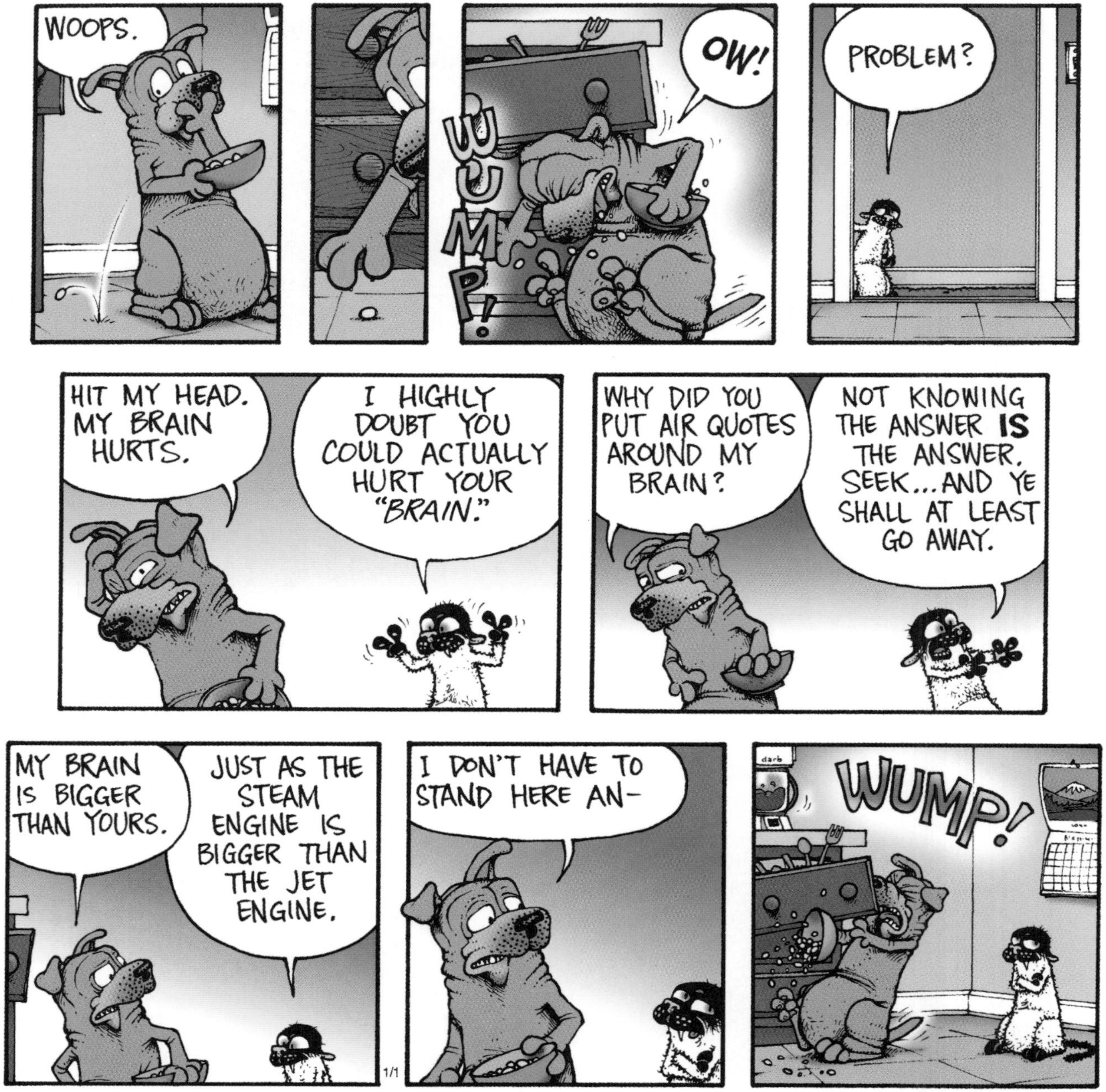
WOOPS.
WUMP!
OW!
PROBLEM?
HIT MY HEAD. MY BRAIN HURTS.
I HIGHLY DOUBT YOU COULD ACTUALLY HURT YOUR "BRAIN."
WHY DID YOU PUT AIR QUOTES AROUND MY BRAIN?
NOT KNOWING THE ANSWER **IS** THE ANSWER. SEEK... AND YE SHALL AT LEAST GO AWAY.
MY BRAIN IS BIGGER THAN YOURS.
JUST AS THE STEAM ENGINE IS BIGGER THAN THE JET ENGINE.
I DON'T HAVE TO STAND HERE AN-
WUMP!

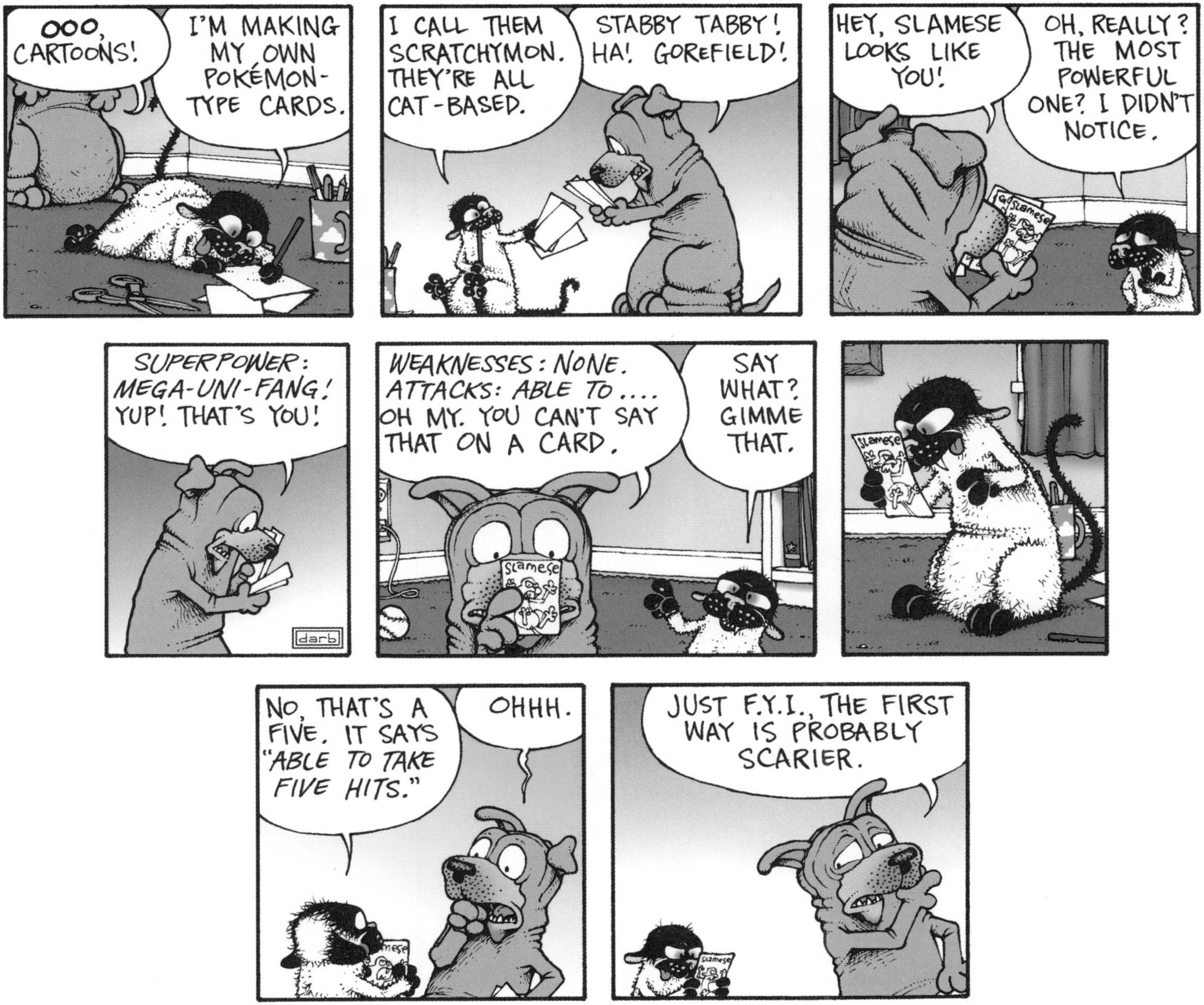
OOO, CARTOONS!
I'M MAKING MY OWN POKÉMON-TYPE CARDS.
I CALL THEM SCRATCHYMON. THEY'RE ALL CAT-BASED.
STABBY TABBY! HA! GOREFIELD!
HEY, SLAMESE LOOKS LIKE YOU!
OH, REALLY? THE MOST POWERFUL ONE? I DIDN'T NOTICE.
SUPERPOWER: MEGA-UNI-FANG! YUP! THAT'S YOU!
WEAKNESSES: NONE. ATTACKS: ABLE TO.... OH MY. YOU CAN'T SAY THAT ON A CARD.
SAY WHAT? GIMME THAT.
NO, THAT'S A FIVE. IT SAYS "ABLE TO TAKE FIVE HITS."
OHHH.
JUST F.Y.I., THE FIRST WAY IS PROBABLY SCARIER.

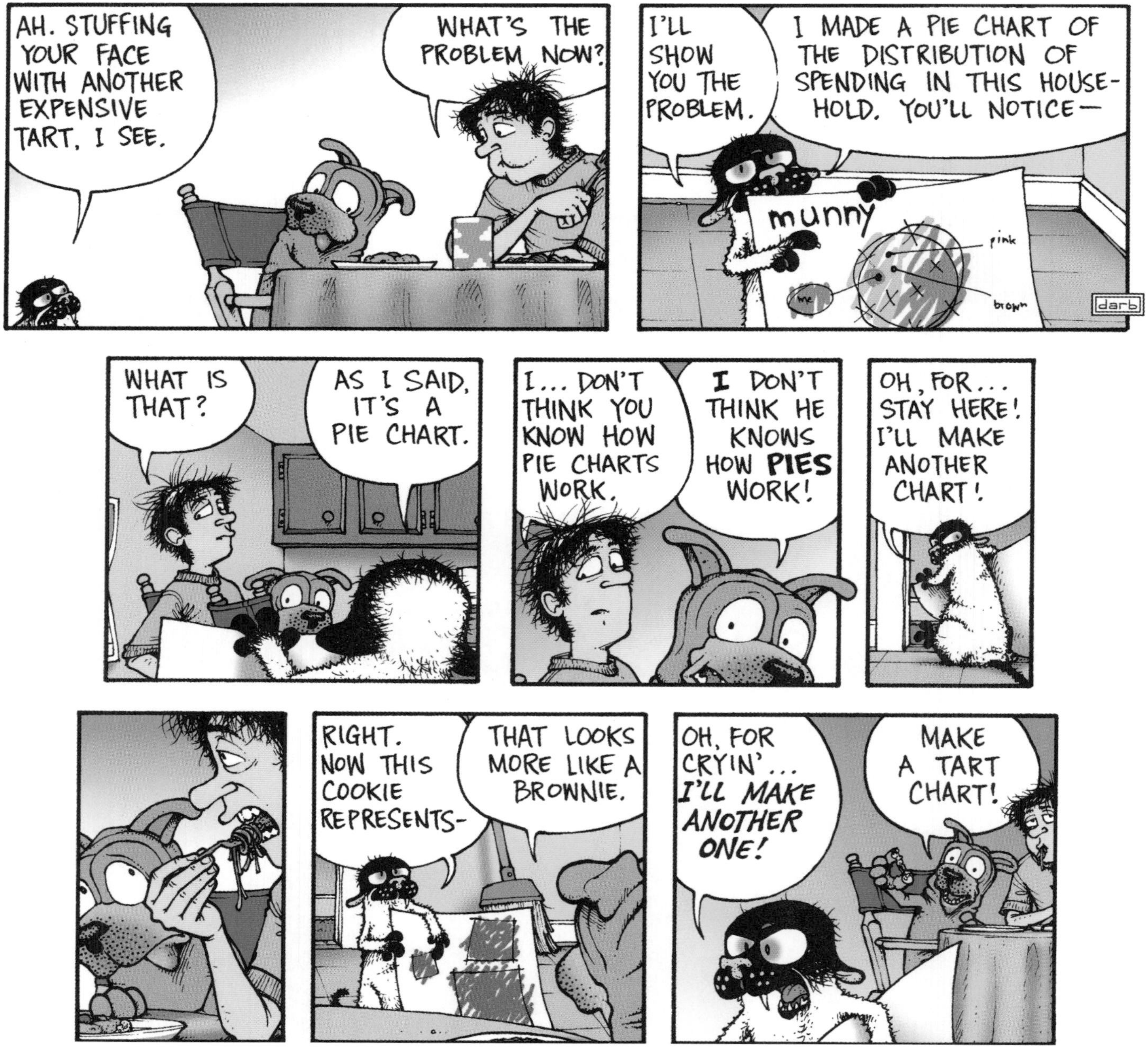
AH. STUFFING YOUR FACE WITH ANOTHER EXPENSIVE TART, I SEE.
WHAT'S THE PROBLEM NOW?
I'LL SHOW YOU THE PROBLEM.
I MADE A PIE CHART OF THE DISTRIBUTION OF SPENDING IN THIS HOUSE-HOLD. YOU'LL NOTICE—
munny
pink
me
brown
darb
WHAT IS THAT?
AS I SAID, IT'S A PIE CHART.
I... DON'T THINK YOU KNOW HOW PIE CHARTS WORK.
I DON'T THINK HE KNOWS HOW PIES WORK!
OH, FOR... STAY HERE! I'LL MAKE ANOTHER CHART!
RIGHT. NOW THIS COOKIE REPRESENTS-
THAT LOOKS MORE LIKE A BROWNIE.
OH, FOR CRYIN'... I'LL MAKE ANOTHER ONE!
MAKE A TART CHART!

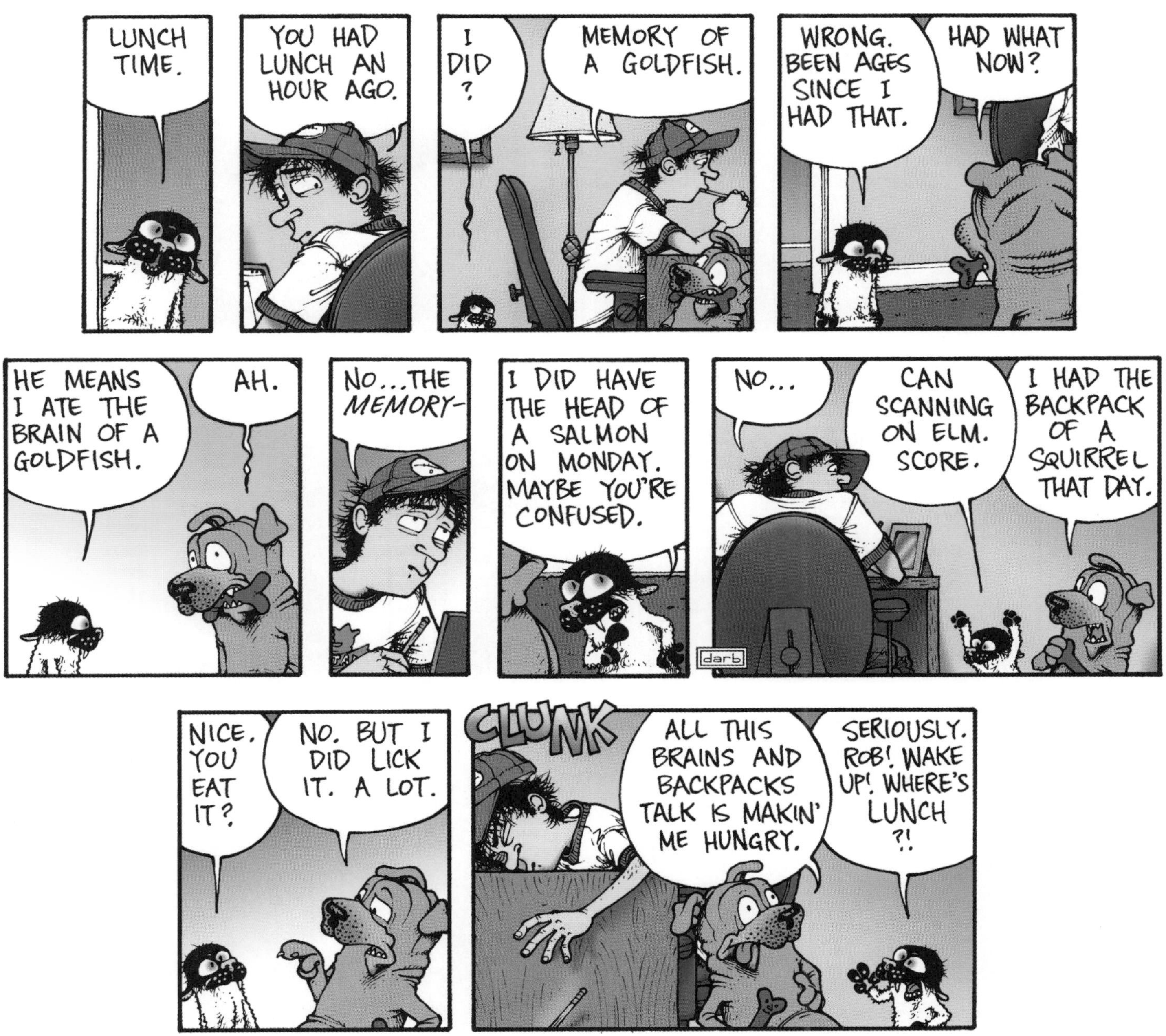
LUNCH TIME.
YOU HAD LUNCH AN HOUR AGO.
I DID ?
MEMORY OF A GOLDFISH.
WRONG. BEEN AGES SINCE I HAD THAT.
HAD WHAT NOW?
HE MEANS I ATE THE BRAIN OF A GOLDFISH.
AH.
NO...THE *MEMORY*-
I DID HAVE THE HEAD OF A SALMON ON MONDAY. MAYBE YOU'RE CONFUSED.
NO...
CAN SCANNING ON ELM. SCORE.
I HAD THE BACKPACK OF A SQUIRREL THAT DAY.
darb
NICE. YOU EAT IT?
NO. BUT I DID LICK IT. A LOT.
CLUNK
ALL THIS BRAINS AND BACKPACKS TALK IS MAKIN' ME HUNGRY.
SERIOUSLY. ROB! WAKE UP! WHERE'S LUNCH ?!

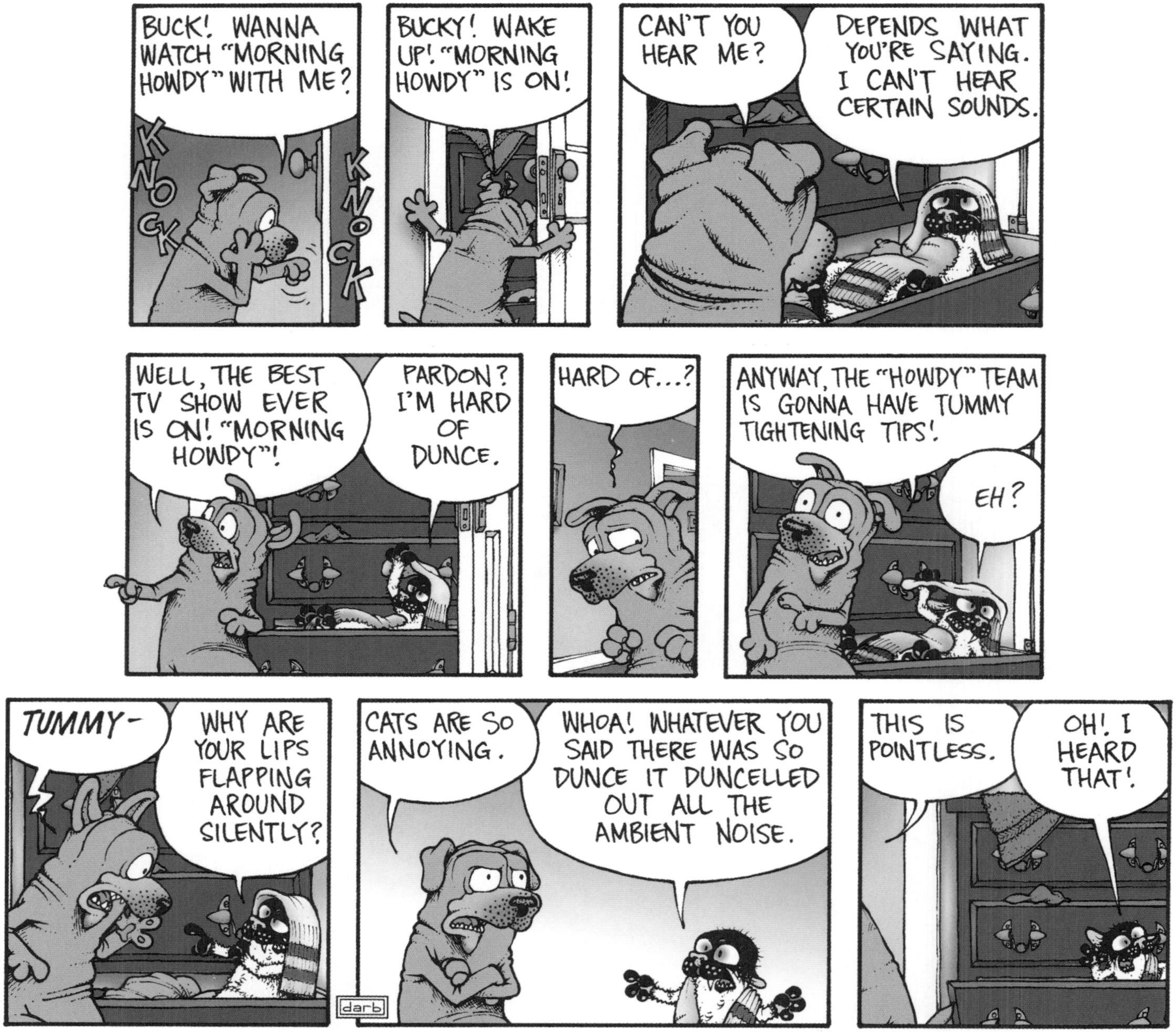
BUCK! WANNA WATCH "MORNING HOWDY" WITH ME?
KNOCK
KNOCK
BUCKY! WAKE UP! "MORNING HOWDY" IS ON!
CAN'T YOU HEAR ME?
DEPENDS WHAT YOU'RE SAYING. I CAN'T HEAR CERTAIN SOUNDS.
WELL, THE BEST TV SHOW EVER IS ON! "MORNING HOWDY"!
PARDON? I'M HARD OF DUNCE.
HARD OF...?
ANYWAY, THE "HOWDY" TEAM IS GONNA HAVE TUMMY TIGHTENING TIPS!
EH?
TUMMY-
WHY ARE YOUR LIPS FLAPPING AROUND SILENTLY?
darb
CATS ARE SO ANNOYING.
WHOA! WHATEVER YOU SAID THERE WAS SO DUNCE IT DUNCELLED OUT ALL THE AMBIENT NOISE.
THIS IS POINTLESS.
OH! I HEARD THAT!

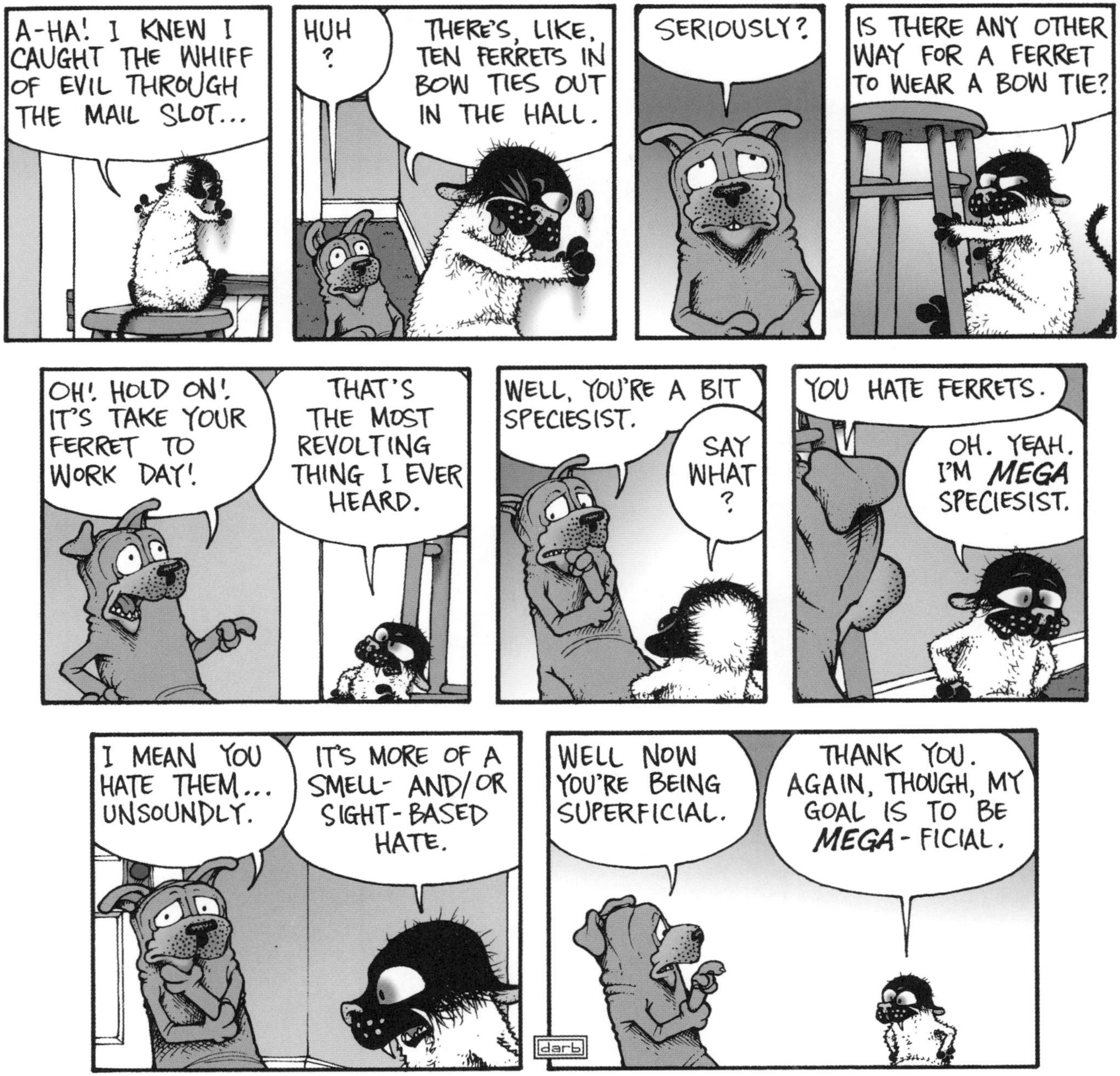
A-HA! I KNEW I CAUGHT THE WHIFF OF EVIL THROUGH THE MAIL SLOT...
HUH ?
THERE'S, LIKE, TEN FERRETS IN BOW TIES OUT IN THE HALL.
SERIOUSLY?
IS THERE ANY OTHER WAY FOR A FERRET TO WEAR A BOW TIE?
OH! HOLD ON! IT'S TAKE YOUR FERRET TO WORK DAY!
THAT'S THE MOST REVOLTING THING I EVER HEARD.
WELL, YOU'RE A BIT SPECIESIST.
SAY WHAT ?
YOU HATE FERRETS.
OH. YEAH. I'M MEGA SPECIESIST.
I MEAN YOU HATE THEM... UNSOUNDLY.
IT'S MORE OF A SMELL- AND/OR SIGHT-BASED HATE.
darb
WELL NOW YOU'RE BEING SUPERFICIAL.
THANK YOU. AGAIN, THOUGH, MY GOAL IS TO BE MEGA-FICIAL.

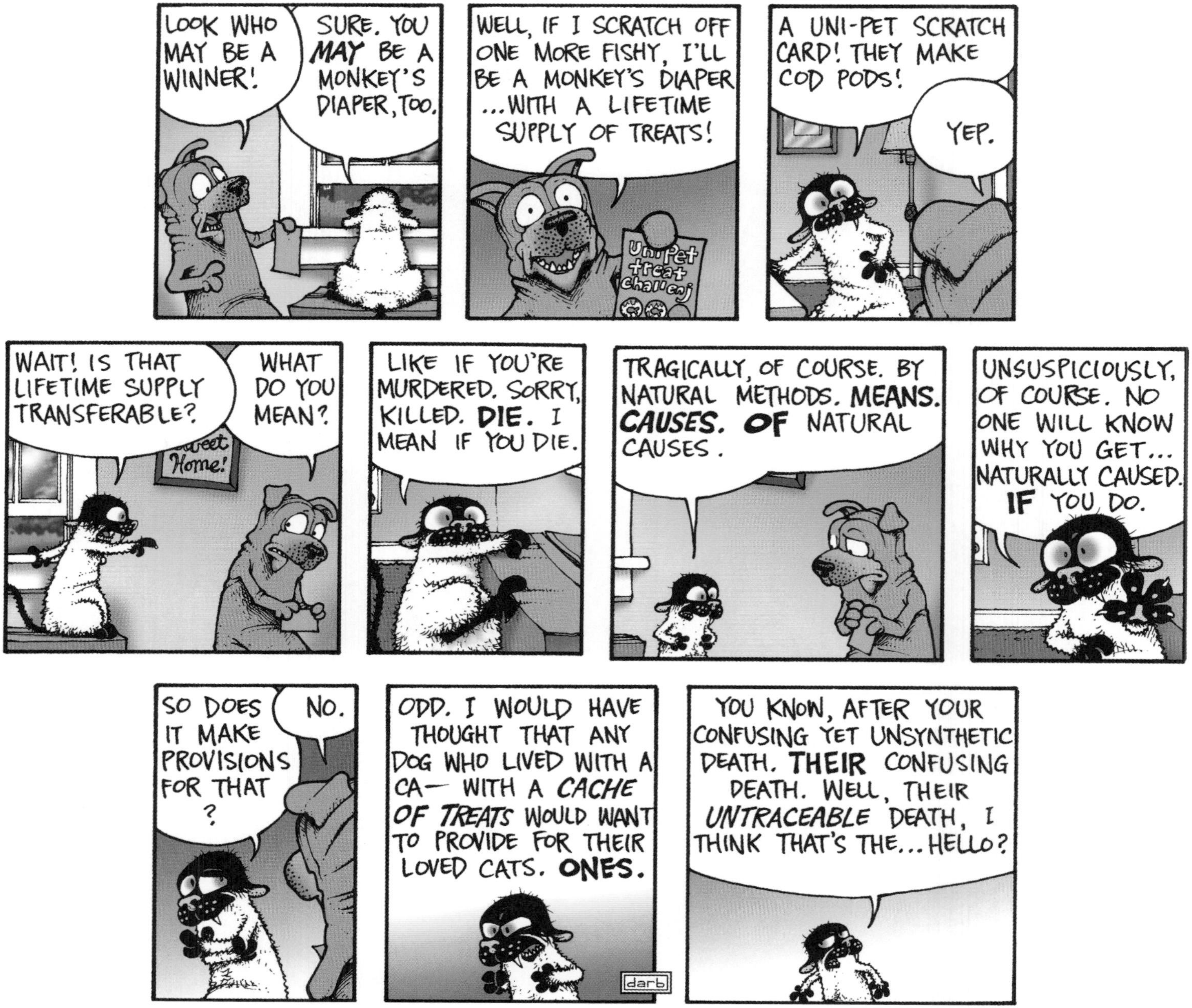
LOOK WHO MAY BE A WINNER!
SURE. YOU *MAY* BE A MONKEY'S DIAPER, TOO.
WELL, IF I SCRATCH OFF ONE MORE FISHY, I'LL BE A MONKEY'S DIAPER ...WITH A LIFETIME SUPPLY OF TREATS!
Uni-Pet treat challenj
A UNI-PET SCRATCH CARD! THEY MAKE COD PODS!
YEP.
WAIT! IS THAT LIFETIME SUPPLY TRANSFERABLE?
WHAT DO YOU MEAN?
Home!
LIKE IF YOU'RE MURDERED. SORRY, KILLED. **DIE.** I MEAN IF YOU DIE.
TRAGICALLY, OF COURSE. BY NATURAL METHODS. **MEANS.** ***CAUSES.*** **OF** NATURAL CAUSES.
UNSUSPICIOUSLY, OF COURSE. NO ONE WILL KNOW WHY YOU GET... NATURALLY CAUSED. **IF** YOU DO.
SO DOES IT MAKE PROVISIONS FOR THAT?
NO.
ODD. I WOULD HAVE THOUGHT THAT ANY DOG WHO LIVED WITH A CA— WITH A *CACHE OF TREATS* WOULD WANT TO PROVIDE FOR THEIR LOVED CATS. **ONES.**
darb
YOU KNOW, AFTER YOUR CONFUSING YET UNSYNTHETIC DEATH. **THEIR** CONFUSING DEATH. WELL, THEIR *UNTRACEABLE* DEATH, I THINK THAT'S THE... HELLO?

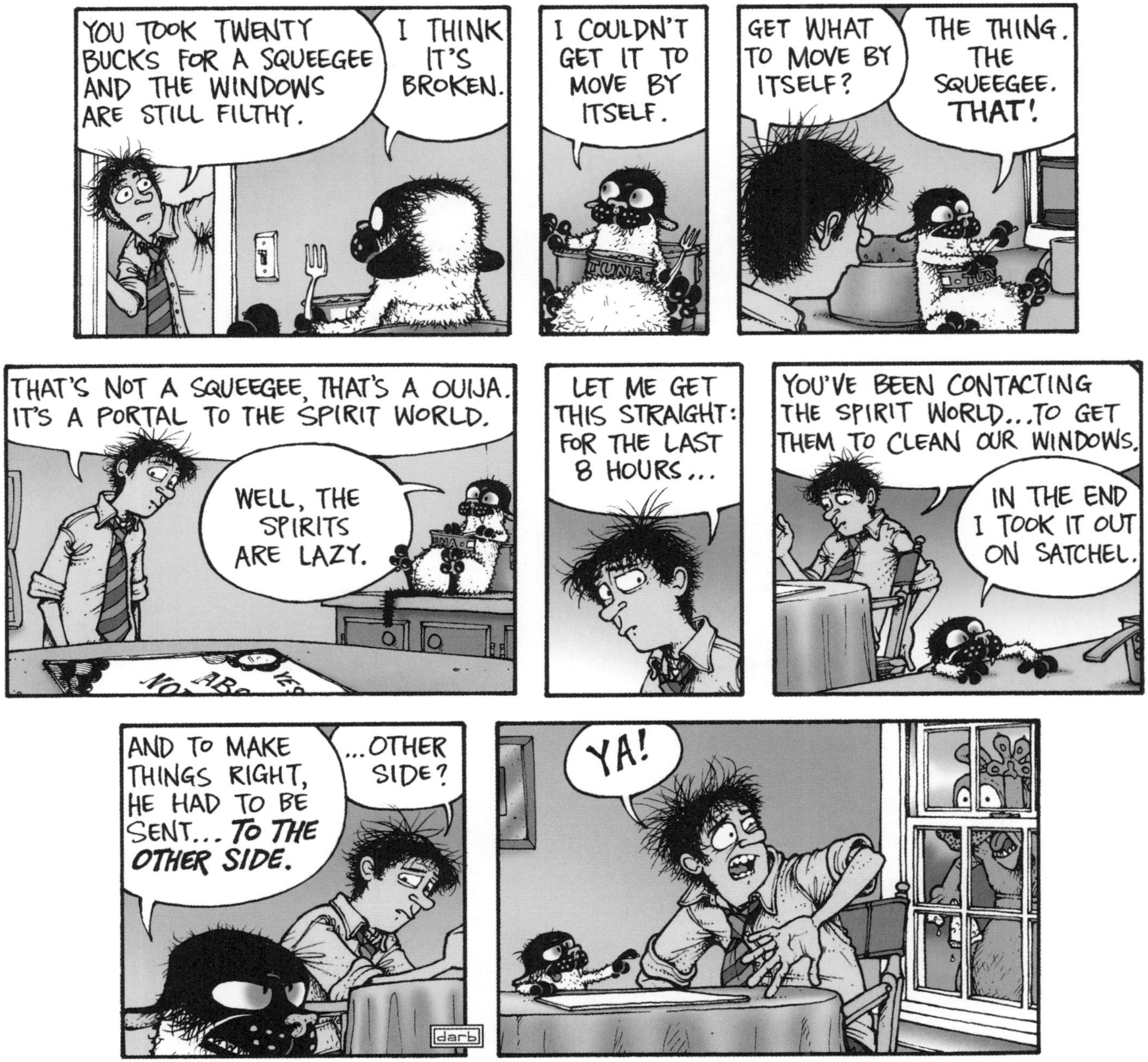
YOU TOOK TWENTY BUCKS FOR A SQUEEGEE AND THE WINDOWS ARE STILL FILTHY.
I THINK IT'S BROKEN.
I COULDN'T GET IT TO MOVE BY ITSELF.
GET WHAT TO MOVE BY ITSELF?
THE THING. THE SQUEEGEE. THAT!
TUNA
THAT'S NOT A SQUEEGEE, THAT'S A OUIJA. IT'S A PORTAL TO THE SPIRIT WORLD.
WELL, THE SPIRITS ARE LAZY.
LET ME GET THIS STRAIGHT: FOR THE LAST 8 HOURS...
YOU'VE BEEN CONTACTING THE SPIRIT WORLD...TO GET THEM TO CLEAN OUR WINDOWS.
IN THE END I TOOK IT OUT ON SATCHEL.
AND TO MAKE THINGS RIGHT, HE HAD TO BE SENT... TO THE OTHER SIDE.
...OTHER SIDE?
darb
YA!

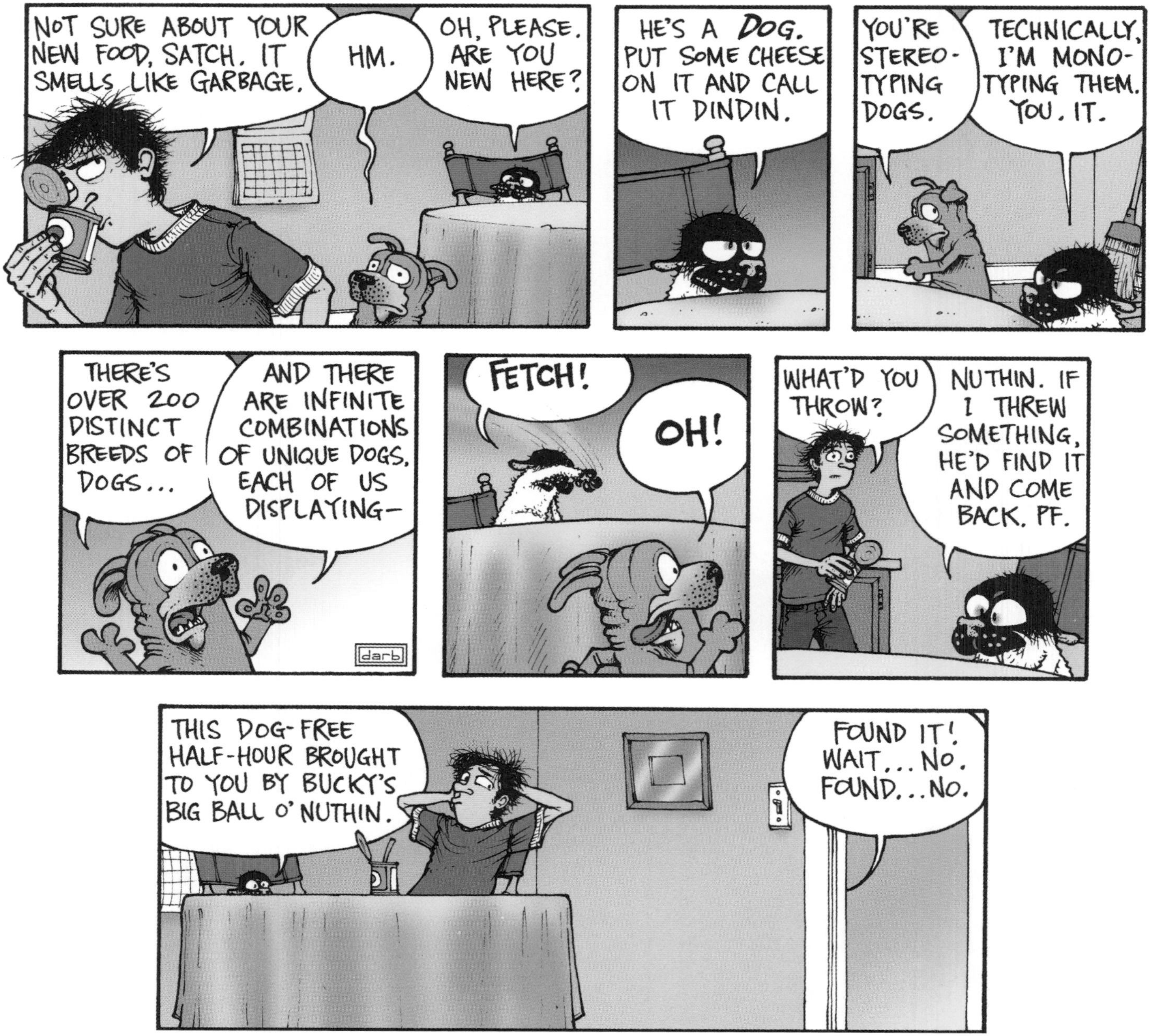

NOT SURE ABOUT YOUR NEW FOOD, SATCH. IT SMELLS LIKE GARBAGE.
HM.
OH, PLEASE. ARE YOU NEW HERE?
HE'S A DOG. PUT SOME CHEESE ON IT AND CALL IT DINDIN.
YOU'RE STEREO-TYPING DOGS.
TECHNICALLY, I'M MONO-TYPING THEM. YOU. IT.
THERE'S OVER 200 DISTINCT BREEDS OF DOGS...
AND THERE ARE INFINITE COMBINATIONS OF UNIQUE DOGS, EACH OF US DISPLAYING—
darb
FETCH!
OH!
WHAT'D YOU THROW?
NUTHIN. IF I THREW SOMETHING, HE'D FIND IT AND COME BACK. PF.
THIS DOG-FREE HALF-HOUR BROUGHT TO YOU BY BUCKY'S BIG BALL O' NUTHIN.
FOUND IT! WAIT... NO. FOUND... NO.

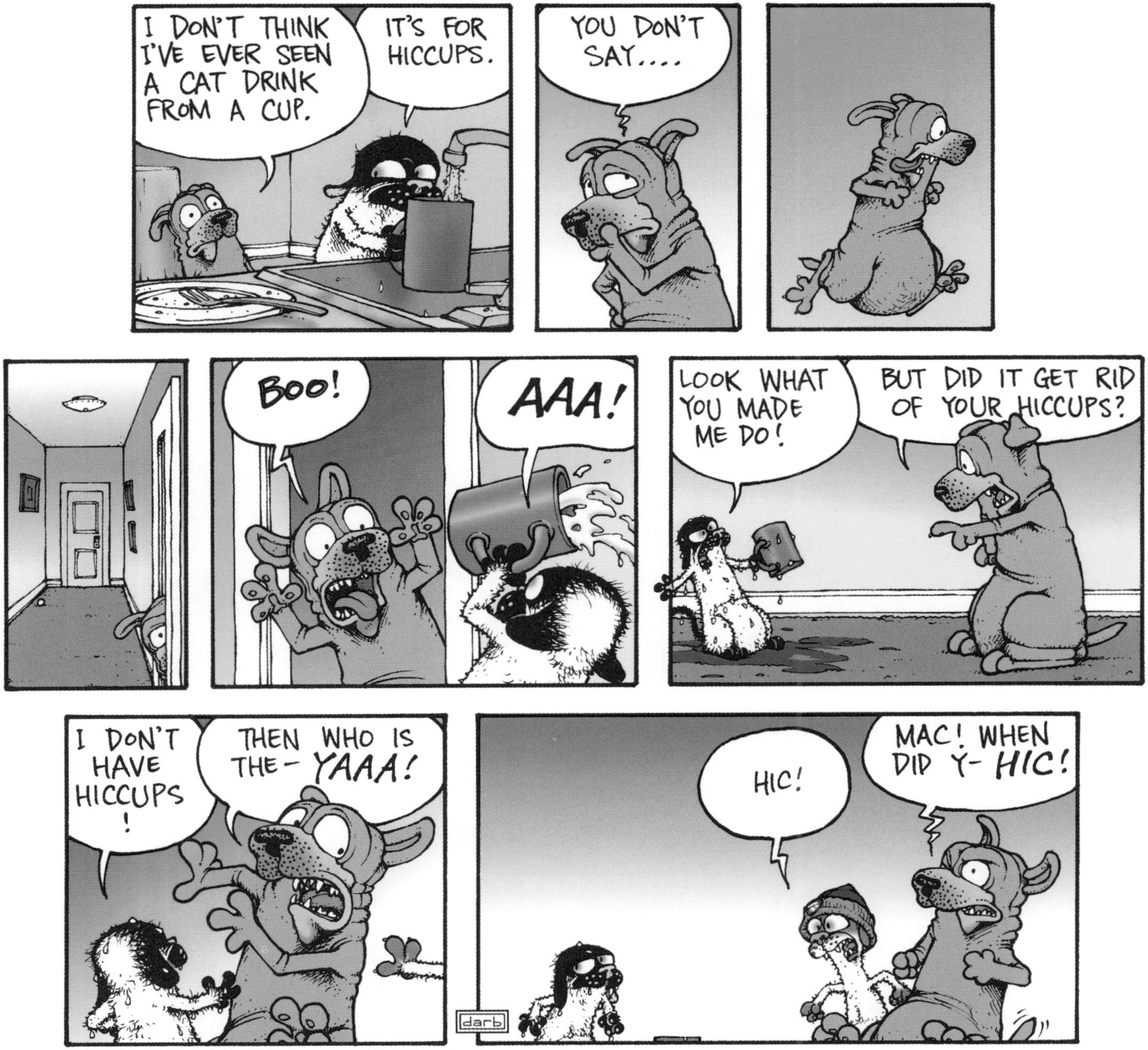
I DON'T THINK I'VE EVER SEEN A CAT DRINK FROM A CUP.
IT'S FOR HICCUPS.
YOU DON'T SAY....
BOO!
AAA!
LOOK WHAT YOU MADE ME DO!
BUT DID IT GET RID OF YOUR HICCUPS?
I DON'T HAVE HICCUPS!
THEN WHO IS THE- YAAA!
HIC!
MAC! WHEN DID Y- HIC!
darb

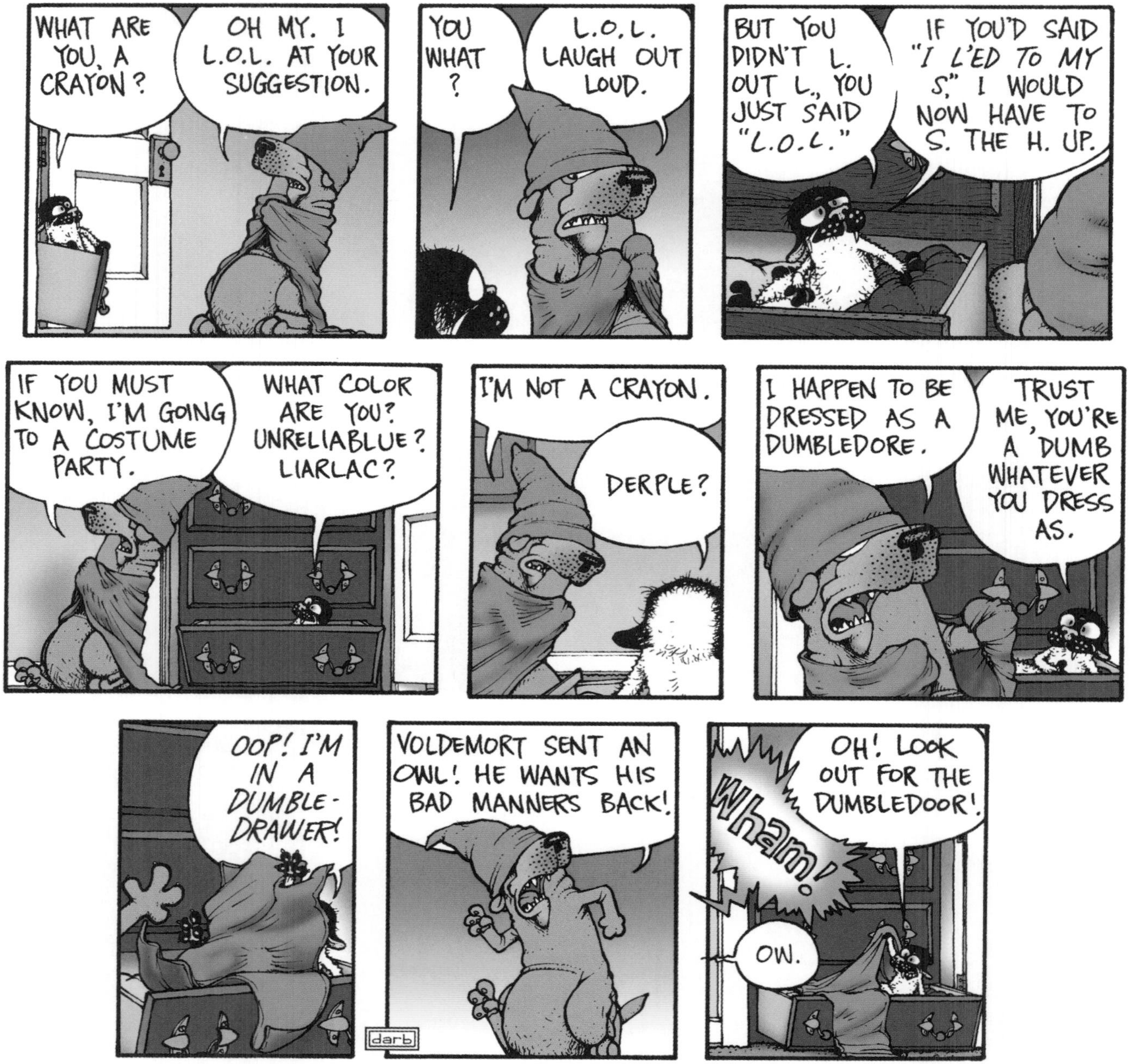
WHAT ARE YOU, A CRAYON?
OH MY. I L.O.L. AT YOUR SUGGESTION.
YOU WHAT?
L.O.L. LAUGH OUT LOUD.
BUT YOU DIDN'T L. OUT L., YOU JUST SAID "L.O.L."
IF YOU'D SAID "I L'ED TO MY S," I WOULD NOW HAVE TO S. THE H. UP.
IF YOU MUST KNOW, I'M GOING TO A COSTUME PARTY.
WHAT COLOR ARE YOU? UNRELIABLUE? LIARLAC?
I'M NOT A CRAYON.
DERPLE?
I HAPPEN TO BE DRESSED AS A DUMBLEDORE.
TRUST ME, YOU'RE A DUMB WHATEVER YOU DRESS AS.
OOP! I'M IN A DUMBLE-DRAWER!
VOLDEMORT SENT AN OWL! HE WANTS HIS BAD MANNERS BACK!
Wham!
OH! LOOK OUT FOR THE DUMBLEDOOR!
OW.
darb

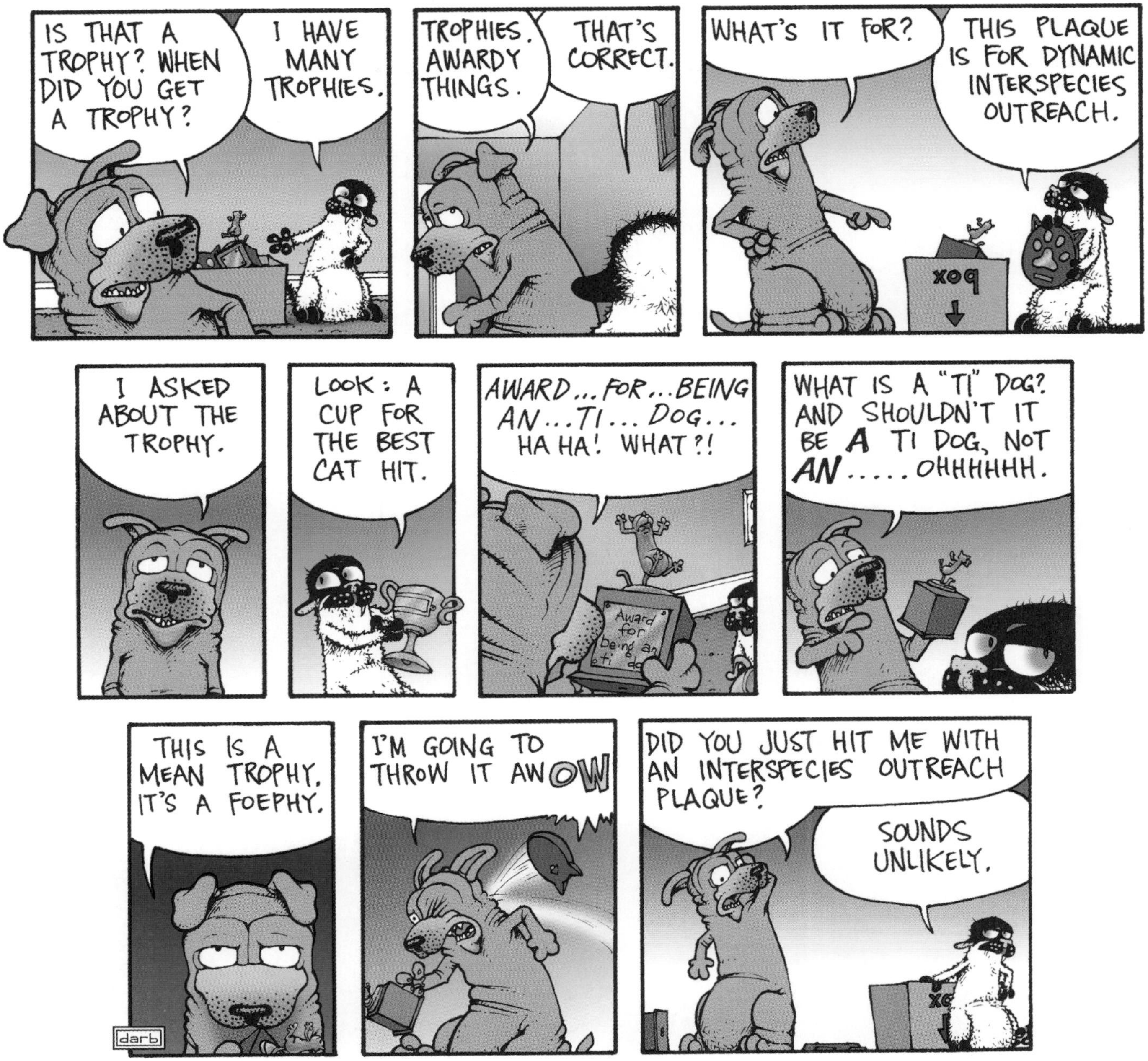
IS THAT A TROPHY? WHEN DID YOU GET A TROPHY?
I HAVE MANY TROPHIES.
TROPHIES. AWARDY THINGS.
THAT'S CORRECT.
WHAT'S IT FOR?
THIS PLAQUE IS FOR DYNAMIC INTERSPECIES OUTREACH.
box
I ASKED ABOUT THE TROPHY.
LOOK: A CUP FOR THE BEST CAT HIT.
AWARD... FOR... BEING AN... TI... DOG... HA HA! WHAT?!
Award for being an ti dog
WHAT IS A "TI" DOG? AND SHOULDN'T IT BE A TI DOG, NOT AN..... OHHHHHH.
THIS IS A MEAN TROPHY. IT'S A FOEPHY.
darb
I'M GOING TO THROW IT AWOW
DID YOU JUST HIT ME WITH AN INTERSPECIES OUTREACH PLAQUE?
SOUNDS UNLIKELY.

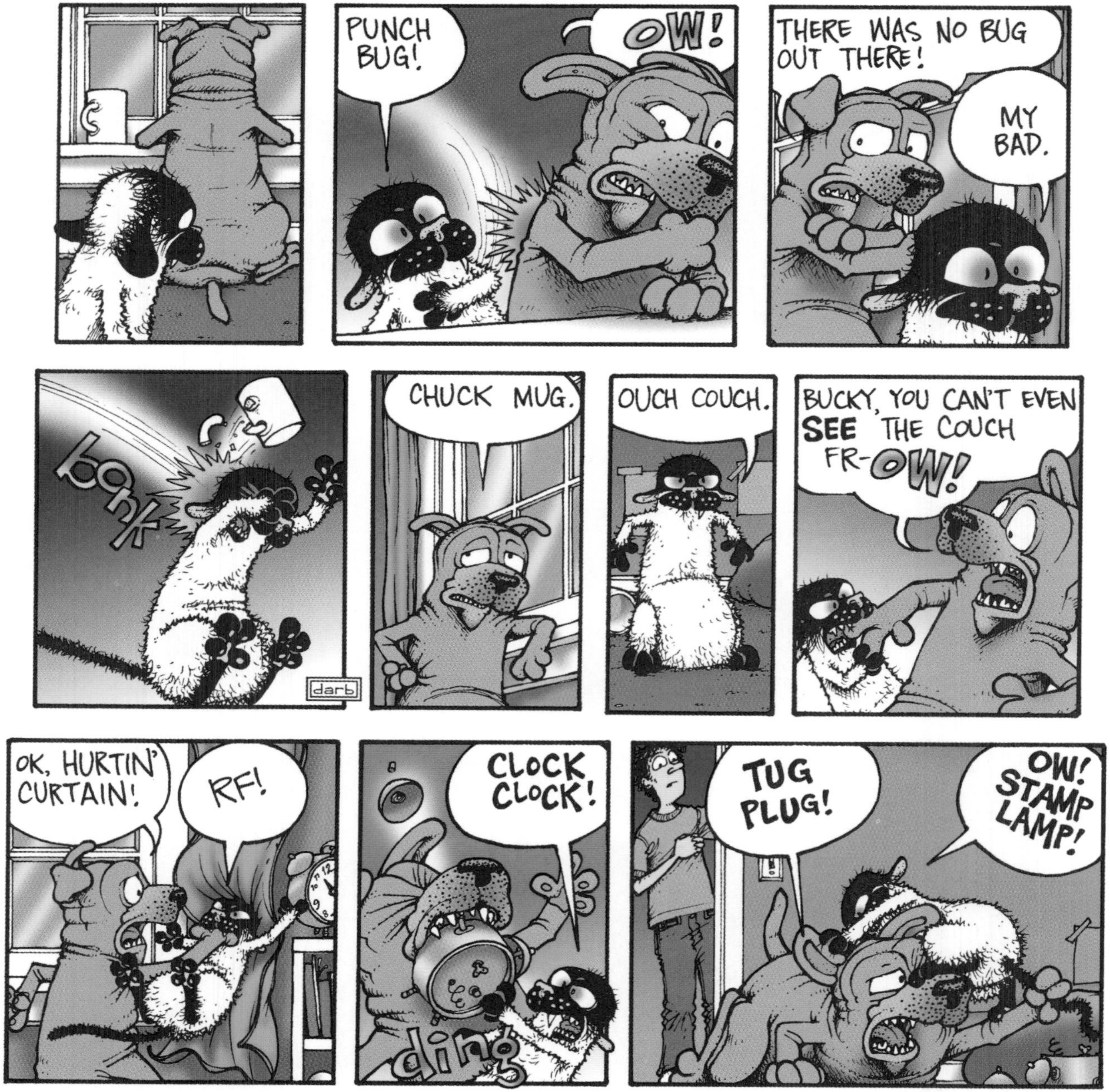
PUNCH BUG!
OW!
THERE WAS NO BUG OUT THERE!
MY BAD.
bonk
darb
CHUCK MUG.
OUCH COUCH.
BUCKY, YOU CAN'T EVEN SEE THE COUCH FR-OW!
OK, HURTIN' CURTAIN!
RF!
CLOCK CLOCK!
ding
TUG PLUG!
OW! STAMP LAMP!

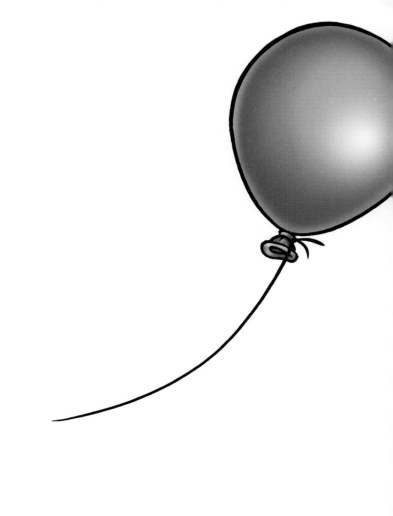

Get Fuzzy is distributed internationally by Andrews McMeel Syndication.

Andrews McMeel Publishing
a division of Andrews McMeel Universal
1130 Walnut Street
Kansas City, Missouri 64106

www.andrewsmcmeel.com

17 18 19 20 21 SDB 10 9 8 7 6 5 4 3 2 1

ISBN: 978-1-4494-8710-2

Library of Congress Control Number: 2017935891

Read **Get Fuzzy** on the Internet at
www.gocomics.com/getfuzzy

ATTENTION: SCHOOLS AND BUSINESSES

Andrews McMeel books are available at quantity discounts with bulk purchase for educational, business, or sales promotional use. For information, please e-mail the Special Sales Department: specialsales@amuniversal.com